On Educational Testing

ℜ ℜ ℜ ℜ ℜ ℜ ℜ ℜ ℜ ℜ ℜ ℜ

Intelligence,
Performance Standards,
Test Anxiety,
and Latent Traits

Scarvia B. Anderson
John S. Helmick
Editors

On Educational Testing

Jossey-Bass Publishers
San Francisco • Washington • London • 1983

ON EDUCATIONAL TESTING
Intelligence, Performance Standards,
Test Anxiety, and Latent Traits
  by Scarvia B. Anderson and John S. Helmick, Editors

Copyright © 1983 by: Jossey-Bass Inc., Publishers
                     433 California Street
                     San Francisco, California 94104
                               &
                     Jossey-Bass Limited
                     28 Banner Street
                     London EC1Y 8QE

Library of Congress Cataloging in Publication Data
Main entry under title:

On educational testing.

   Includes bibliographies and indexes.
   1. Educational tests and measurements — Addresses,
essays, lectures. I. Anderson, Scarvia B. II. Helmick,
John S.
LB3051.052   1983   371.2'6   83-48155
ISBN 0-87589-576-X

Manufactured in the United States of America

The paper in this book meets the guidelines for permanence and
durability of the Committee on Production Guidelines for Book Longevity
of the Council on Library Resources

JACKET DESIGN BY WILLI BAUM

LB
3051
.052
1983

FIRST EDITION

Code 8323

A joint publication in
The Jossey-Bass
Social and Behavioral Science Series
and
The Jossey-Bass
Higher Education Series

Preface

❦ ❦ ❦ ❦ ❦ ❦ ❦ ❦ ❦ ❦ ❦ ❦ ❦

Educational testing is a worldwide endeavor. Almost every nation finds it necessary to admit students to more advanced studies or special training, to determine students' ability to assume entry-level jobs, and to evaluate its education and training efforts. Some nations have the luxury of being able to employ measurement in the service of more sophisticated societal needs, individual fulfillment, and research on human capabilities. Although the goals, functions, and applications of measurement vary from country to country, the problems that these countries have in common are quite numerous. Thus the cause of educational testing can profit from an international sharing of concepts, formulations, and techniques. The present volume brings together the thoughts of an international group of recognized leaders in the field of educational testing on a set of interrelated issues. The variety of backgrounds and experiences provides a cumulative insight beyond that likely to emerge in any single national group.

The book begins with the measurement of intelligence, probably the oldest and most fully treated subject in mental measurement. But many problems remain unsettled here, and the topic still arouses controversy, as the chapters in Part One reveal. Although it does not settle the controversy, reviewing the concepts and even the words used to describe "intelligence" clarifies a number of the issues and minimizes the role of pseudo issues. We start with such a review and then turn to one of the issues: unwanted factors that affect the measurement of intelligence. Motivation is such a factor, and the proper treatment of it in the measurement process and in the analysis of results can alter our conclusions about individuals and groups. Traditionally we have tried to minimize unwanted influences in measuring intelligence, but in so doing we may have ended up with test behavior that is trivial and artificial. Perhaps, from a practical point of view, we might better look for performances that are more directly related to behavior of real-world concern.

Something that is of real-world concern, regardless of the content of the measurement, is how we decide how good is good enough. This, of course, is the problem of setting standards. As the chapters in Part Two clearly demonstrate, values and judgment must enter the discussion. We must be subjective, but how do we go about being objectively subjective—or should it be subjectively objective? A related question is whose values should be considered —the assessor's or the assessee's? Or, better, what relative weight should each have in the process of setting standards? The issues here extend beyond the question of assigning students to instructional sections, promoting them to the next grade or level, or admitting them to higher education. They also include granting the right to practice an occupation or profession, be it that of plumber or physician. Dealing with the problem of setting standards requires a philosophical approach but also depends on sound principles and techniques of measurement, as these chapters demonstrate.

Even a definitive resolution of the problem of standards would still leave us with the more general difficulty already touched on under the subject of intelligence. How can we be sure that any measure we obtain is an accurate representation of a person's ability or skill? Are there influences that produce a score lower than it should be or, in some cases, higher? Closely tied to the previously mentioned effects of motivation on intelligence test performance is the general problem of test anxiety. What is it? Is it an underlying characteristic of the individual or is it specific to certain situations? How much effect does it really have on test performance and how widespread are these effects in particular populations of interest? What can we do about test anxiety to ameliorate its effects or to compensate for them? Or can anxiety be helpful in some cases by leading to better preparation and hence better performance, and may it sometimes serve to reduce motivation to a level that produces more effective performance? These are among the questions explored in Part Three.

Underlying such issues as intelligence measurement, standard setting, and test anxiety is the theoretical basis for educational and psychological measurement. Advances in theory make improvements in application possible, and problems in application in turn can provide the stimulus for further theoretical development. Thus, Part Four explores latent trait theory, which has recently seemed to offer ways of dealing with a number of persistent problems of measurement. While latent trait theory may not be the magic key that some hoped would unlock all the problem boxes of measurement, an understanding of its potential is important if we are to make progress in that direction. The chapters in this section deal successively with the Rasch model, a Bayesian approach, and latent class analysis.

The Rasch model is widely used as an alternative to traditional item analysis to provide "person-free" measures of item characteristics. It can also provide a systematic approach to data analysis in general, starting from the item-person matrix. Among the analyses that can be made are those that provide estimates of the latent distribution for a group and allow comparison of groups on the basis of their latent distributions. While the Rasch approach usually provides good estimates of item characteristics from the data typically available, the estimate of one individual's ability is often not adequately achieved. Thus, a Bayesian approach is offered that can overcome some of the theoretical and practical difficulties in deriving better estimates of individual ability levels. In examining the general role of test theory, the charge is made that it has been essentially an extension of mathematics with little regard for development from a psychological base. Through the application of latent class analysis, a theoretical framework can be constructed that stems from psychological principles.

All these issues and concerns were the subject of the Fourth International Symposium on Educational Testing held in Antwerp, Belgium, in June of 1980. The chapters in this book are adaptations of the twelve invited papers presented at that symposium. They bring together current international perspectives on the four major themes described earlier: measuring intelligence, setting standards for performance, anxiety and test performance, and latent trait theories and their application to testing.

The symposium also included over fifty volunteered papers on the same general themes. We regret that space limitations precluded our publishing some of the more outstanding of those contributions here. All together, approximately 150 measurement specialists from seventeen countries attended the symposium.

Previous symposia had been sponsored by the University of Leyden, The Netherlands, through its Educational Research Center. For this fourth symposium, the University of Antwerp and the Educational Testing Service (ETS) of Princeton, N.J., joined the University of Leyden as cosponsors. These institutions were represented on the program committee by Hans Crombag (University of Leyden), George de Corte (University of Antwerp), and John Helmick and Scarvia Anderson (ETS).

Many people in addition to those on the committee and the speakers contributed to the success of the meeting and the preparation of this book. Particular thanks go to Betty Moorman of the University of Leyden, who was The Secretariat for the symposium; to Audrey Staats of ETS, who aided in preparations for both the symposium and this volume; and to William Angoff, Charles Kreitzberg, Frederic Lord, and Michael Zieky, all of ETS, who reviewed selected chapters.

Atlanta, Georgia   Scarvia B. Anderson
September 1983   John S. Helmick

Contents

꼰 꼰 꼰 꼰 꼰 꼰 꼰 꼰 꼰 꼰 꼰 꼰 꼰

Preface   ix

Tables   xv

Figures   xix

The Editors   xxiii

Contributors   xxv

Part One: Measuring Intelligence   1

1. What Do Intelligence Tests Measure?   5
    Anne Anastasi

2. Motivational Psychology and Mental Measurement   29
    John W. Atkinson

3. Is Measuring Intelligence Still Useful?   45
    Jan J. Elshout

Part Two: Setting Performance Standards   **57**

4. Standards for Placement and Certification   61
   Lorrie A. Shepard

5. Standards in Occupational Settings   91
   Albert P. Maslow

6. The Case for Compromise in Educational Selection   109
   and Grading
   Willem K. B. Hofstee

Part Three: Anxiety and Test Performance   **129**

7. Understanding and Modifying Test Anxiety   133
   Irwin G. Sarason

8. Anxiety, Coping Strategies, and Performance   150
   Heinz W. Krohne, Paul Schaffner

9. Fear of Failure and Performance on Ability Tests   175
   Willy Lens

Part Four: Latent Trait Theories and Applications   **191**

10. Analyzing Data Using the Rasch Model   193
    Erling B. Andersen

11. Bayesian Inference for Latent Abilities   224
    Charles Lewis

12. Some Theoretical Concerns About Applying Latent   252
    Trait Models in Educational Testing
    Wilhelm Kempf

Name Index   271

Subject Index   277

Tables

Chapter Two

Table 1.   Ability and Motivation as Determinants   40
           of Level of Intellective Performance
           and Cumulative Academic Achievement.

Chapter Four

Table 1.   Possible Decision Outcomes.   78

Chapter Seven

Table 1.   Selected Test Anxiety Scale (TAS)   138
           Items.
Table 2.   Cognitive Interference Questionnaire.   140
Table 3.   Mean Waiting Time and Task Times   141
           Estimates, Anagram Performance
           Scores, and Cognitive Interference
           Scores.

Chapter Eight

Table 1.   Intercorrelations Among Variables   164
            Under Good and Bad Conditions of
            Preparation.

Chapter Nine

Table 1.   The Opposite Behavioral Effects of the   183
            Tendency to Avoid Failure (*Taf*).
Table 2.   Mean Correct Arithmetic Performance   185
            According to Strength of
            Achievement-Related Motives
            Under Various Conditions.
Table 3.   Mean Intelligence Test Scores of Four   187
            Motive Groups in a Neutral and in a
            High Ego-Involvement Condition.

Chapter Ten

Table 1.   Data in Raw Form.   194
Table 2.   Number of Persons for Each Response   195
            Pattern on Four Items of the Stouffer-
            Toby Data.
Table 3.   Number of Persons for Each Response   196
            Pattern on Two Subsets of Items from
            the Law School Admission Test (LSAT).
Table 4.   Item Sums Within Score Groups for the   197
            Stouffer-Toby Data.
Table 5.   Score Group Totals and Item Totals   197
            for the Stouffer-Toby Data.
Table 6.   Score Group Totals and Item Totals   198
            for the Scholastic Aptitude Test (SAT).
Table 7.   Sufficient Statistics and Parameter   200
            Estimates for the Scholastic Aptitude
            Test (SAT).
Table 8.   Sufficient Statistics and Parameter   201
            Estimates for the Stouffer-Toby Data.

Table 9.   Item Totals and Item Parameter   202
            Estimates for the Law School Admission
            Test (LSAT), Section 6.

Table 10.   Item Totals and Item Parameter   203
            Estimates for the Law School Admission
            Test (LSAT), Section 7.

Table 11.   Score Group Item Parameter Estimates   206
            and Overall Estimates for the Scholastic
            Aptitude Test (SAT).

Table 12.   Observed and Expected Numbers in   213
            Each Score Group for the Stouffer-
            Toby Data.

Table 13.   Observed and Expected Numbers in   214
            Each Score Group for the Law School
            Admission Test (LSAT), Section 6.

Table 14.   Observed and Expected Numbers in   214
            Each Score Group for a Test on Psychic
            Vulnerability.

Table 15.   Observed and Expected Numbers in   216
            Score Groups Under the Hypotheses of
            the Same Latent Mean and Variance in
            Both Populations.

Table 16.   Summary of Test Statistics for Various   217
            Hypotheses Using the Solomon Data.

Table 17.   Observed and Expected Scores for a   217
            Test on Psychic Vulnerability.

Table 18.   Estimates for μ and σ^2 in the Four   218
            Populations Under Various Hypotheses
            — Vulnerability Data.

Table 19.   Test Statistics for the Three Hypotheses   218
            H_0, H_1, and H_2 — Vulnerability Data.

Chapter Eleven

Table 1.   Prior and Posterior Probability   232
            Distributions for Ability (Θ) of an
            Individual with All Items Correct on a
            (Hypothetical) Test of Five Items.

Table 2.   Ability Levels (Θ) Related to Estimated   234
            Difficulties of Fourteen Items on the
            Knox Cube Test.

                        Chapter Twelve

Table 1.   Type of Items and Ideal Response   268
            Patterns in a Balance Scale Test.

Figures

Chapter Two

Figure 1. Effect of Strength of Motivation on (A) Efficiency of Performance and (B) Level of Performance. 37

Figure 2. Effect of Strength of Motivation on Proportion of Time Spent in an Activity. 38

Chapter Four

Figure 1. Changes in the Contrasting-Groups Standard Caused by Differences in the Stringency of Nonmastery Classifications. 74

Figure 2. Hypothetical Relationships Between a Criterion-Referenced Test (CRT) and a Valued Outcome. 77

Chapter Six

Figure 1. Illustration of the Effects of Weighted   113
           Lottery with Overall Selection Rate of
           .45.
Figure 2. Relationship Between Scholastic   116
           Standing and Preference for Admission
           Procedures.
Figure 3. Illustration of Compromise Model for   118
           Establishing Cutoff Points.
Figure 4. Minimal Required Score on Second   125
           Testing as a Function of Score on First
           Testing.

Chapter Eight

Figure 1. Path Diagram for the Two Preparation   167
           Conditions.

Chapter Nine

Figure 1. Curvilinear Relationship Between   184
           Strength of Motivation and Level of
           Performance.

Chapter Ten

Figure 1. The ICC-Curve for a Rasch Model.   199
Figure 2. Score Group Estimates Against Overall   204
           Estimates of Item Parameters for the
           Law School Admission Test (LSAT),
           Section 6.
Figure 3. Score Group Estimates Against Overall   205
           Estimates of Item Parameters for the
           Law School Admission Test (LSAT),
           Section 7.
Figure 4. Score Group Estimates Against Overall   207
           Estimates of Item Parameters for the
           Scholastic Aptitude Test (SAT).

Figure 5. Observed Frequency Distribution of   209
Score *r* and Hypothetical Population
Density of Θ.

Figure 6. Marginal Frequency Distribution of   210
Score *r*, Population Density of Θ, and
Three Selected Conditional Frequency
Distributions $\pi(r/\Theta)$.

Figure 7. Comparison of Two Latent   215
Distributions.

Figure 8. Observed Score Distributions for the   219
Four Subpopulations — Vulnerability
Data.

Figure 9. Estimated Latent Densities for the Four   220
Subpopulations — Vulnerability Data.

Chapter Eleven

Figure 1. Prior Distribution for the Ability Θ   236
Used in Analyses of Wright and Stone's
Data.

Figure 2. Posterior Distribution for the Ability Θ   237
of an Individual with Seven out of
Fourteen Items Correct.

Figure 3. Posterior Distribution for the Ability Θ   238
of an Individual with a Perfect
Response Pattern and Six out of
Fourteen Items Correct.

Figure 4. Posterior Distribution for the Ability Θ   239
of an Individual with a Perfect
Response Pattern and Nine out of
Fourteen Items Correct.

Figure 5. Posterior Distribution for the Ability Θ   240
of an Individual with Nine out of
Fourteen Items Correct and a Pattern
with a Single Reversal.

Figure 6. Posterior Distribution for the Ability Θ   241
of an Individual with Nine out of
Fourteen Items Correct and a Pattern
with a Double Reversal.

Figure 7.   Posterior Distribution for the Ability Θ   243
            of an Individual with Seven out of
            Fourteen Items Correct and a Pattern
            with One Apparently Unusual Response.

Figure 8.   Posterior Distribution for the Ability Θ   244
            of an Individual with Seven out of
            Fourteen Items Correct and a Pattern
            with Several Apparently Unusual
            Responses.

Chapter Twelve

Figure 1.   Item Characteristic Function of the   258
            Birnbaum Model — Ability Parameter.

Figure 2.   Item Characteristic Function of the   259
            Birnbaum Model — Item Difficulty
            Parameter.

Figure 3.   The Balance Scale — "Which Side Will   263
            Go Down When the Blocks Are Moved?"

Figure 4.   Flow Diagram of Balance Scale   263
            Predictions of a Level-1 Child.

Figure 5.   Flow Diagram of Balance Scale   264
            Predictions of a Level-2 Child.

Figure 6.   Flow Diagram of Balance Scale   265
            Predictions of a Level-3 Child.

Figure 7.   Flow Diagram of Balance Scale   266
            Predictions of a Level-4 Child.

Figure 8.   Flow Diagram of Balance Scale   267
            Predictions of a Level-5 Child.

Figure 9.   Flow Diagram of Balance Scale   269
            Predictions of an Atypical Child.

The Editors

Scarvia B. Anderson is a consultant on human assessment and program evaluation, adjunct professor in the school of psychology at Georgia Institute of Technology, and a former senior vice-president of the Educational Testing Service. She received the B.S. degree in English and mathematics from Mississippi State University, the M.A. degree in psychology from George Peabody College for Teachers, and the Ph.D. degree in psychology from the University of Maryland. She was a Fulbright scholar at the Institute of Experimental Psychology, Oxford University.

Anderson's books include *Meeting the Test* (with M. Katz and B. Shimberg, 1965), *Sex Differences and Discrimination in Education* (editor, 1972), *Encyclopedia of Educational Evaluation* (with S. Ball, R. T. Murphy, and Associates, 1974), and *The Profession and Practice of Program Evaluation* (with S. Ball, 1978). She was founding editor-in-chief of the quarterly sourcebook *New Directions for Program Evaluation,* which has been adopted as the official journal of the Evaluation Research Society.

She is active in the American Educational Research Association, a fellow of the American Psychological Association, a former member of the board of directors of the National Council on Measurement in Education, and a past president of the Evaluation Research Society.

Scarvia Anderson's work has encompassed such diverse topics as early education, continuing education, problem-solving processes in children and adults, and fair assessment of the abilities of minority students. She is currently concerned with measurement of the competencies of the elderly.

John S. Helmick's expertise in measurement dates back to the Army Air Force's Aviation Psychology Program in World War II and to the Ph.D. degree in psychology, which he received from Stanford University after the war. (Earlier degrees were obtained at Northwestern and Wesleyan universities.) As vice-president and director of Educational Testing Service's western regional offices, he worked on measurement problems at every level of the educational system — with schools, colleges and universities, state departments of education, teachers' associations, educational foundations, and other agencies.

His particular interest in international testing has taken him on assignments to Brazil, Taiwan, Hong Kong, Pakistan, and Saudi Arabia, and to Europe for the United States Armed Forces Overseas Dependent Schools. Helmick was recently chosen president-elect of the International Council of Psychologists and, with Scarvia Anderson, was on the organizing committee for both the fourth and fifth International Symposia on Educational Testing.

He is a fellow of the American Psychological Association and the American Association for the Advancement of Science and a member of the American Educational Research Association and the National Council on Measurement in Education.

Contributors

Anne Anastasi, professor emeritus, Psychology, Graduate School of Arts and Sciences, Fordham University, Bronx, New York, USA

Erling B. Andersen, professor, Statistics, University of Copenhagen, Denmark

John W. Atkinson, professor, Psychology, University of Michigan, Ann Arbor, Michigan, USA

Jan J. Elshout, professor, Psychology, University of Amsterdam, The Netherlands

Willem K. B. Hofstee, professor, Psychology, University of Groningen, The Netherlands

Wilhelm Kempf, professor, Faculty of Economics and Statistics, University of Constanz, Federal Republic of Germany

Heinz W. Krohne, professor, Psychological Institute, Johannes Gutenberg–Universität Mainz, Federal Republic of Germany

xxv

Willy Lens, professor, Psychology, University of Louvain, Belgium

Charles Lewis, professor, Statistics and Measurement Theory, University of Groningen, The Netherlands

Albert P. Maslow, personnel consultant, Lauderhill, Florida, USA

Irwin G. Sarason, professor, Psychology, University of Washington, Seattle, Washington, USA

Paul Schaffner, Diplomat – Psychologe, Johannes Gutenberg – Universität Mainz, Federal Republic of Germany

Lorrie A. Shepard, associate professor and chair, Research and Evaluation Methodology, School of Education, University of Colorado, Boulder, Colorado, USA

On Educational Testing

ℜ ℜ ℜ ℜ ℜ ℜ ℜ ℜ ℜ ℜ ℜ ℜ ℜ

Intelligence,
Performance Standards,
Test Anxiety,
and Latent Traits

Part One

ℛ ℛ ℛ ℛ ℛ ℛ ℛ ℛ ℛ ℛ ℛ ℛ ℛ

Measuring Intelligence

Dear Timothy, I love and like you,
Caring little for your IQ.

That is what the American humorist Franklin P. Adams wrote
on his son's birthday. But Mr. Adams must have been about the
only parent in the last fifty years to take such a casual approach to the
matter of his child's intelligence. IQ scores have held a fascination
for the public and professionals alike ever since their conception by
Stern and their later elaboration by Terman in the early part of this
century. They have been a cornerstone in the structure of psychometrics as we know it today. They have challenged psychologists,
sociologists, physiologists, and geneticists for explanation. They
have been both a buttress and an embarrassment for educators.
They have figured in famous and infamous public policy decisions.

"The continued emphasis on the IQ can probably be attributed to several factors. It is a venerable concept in psychology and
has been comparatively well measured. Furthermore, it has a larger
collection of correlates that are predictive of success in a wide variety
of human endeavors than any other variable" (Anderson and Messick, 1974, p. 284). Unfortunately, these positive attributes have

1

been burdened with a host of misconceptions that were never intended by those who sought to measure intelligence. These misconceptions have to do with the genetic base for IQ scores, their stability and resistance to change, and the definition of intelligence implied by the questions on the tests.

Anne Anastasi reviews some of these misconceptions in Chapter One, as she seeks to bring the concept of intelligence measurement into the 1980s. Anastasi discusses both the theory and practice of intelligence testing, and along the way she makes us understand why Boring (1923) was prompted to define intelligence as "what the tests of intelligence test, until further scientific observation allows us to extend the definition" (p. 35). Unfortunately, most secondary sources leave out the last part of Boring's statement.

In Chapter Two, John W. Atkinson also acknowledges the lack of clarity that has attended the meaning of intelligence. He blames this state of affairs on the failure "to achieve the proper integration of the traditional statistical framework of mental testing and a new, advanced motivational psychology." To the argument that mental testers cannot ignore the central interests of three different fields of psychology — abilities (educational), motives (clinical), and beliefs (social) — Atkinson brings some thirty years of distinguished research in motivational psychology. And he doesn't hesitate to tell testers where they "went wrong," not only in their conceptions but also in their explanations of such newsworthy items as the decline in college aptitude test scores in the United States.

Jan J. Elshout asks us in Chapter Three if measuring intelligence is still useful and answers his own question, "Yes, but . . . ." He points out that the content of most intelligence tests was chosen "not because of its usefulness in the intellectual ecology, but because of its instrumental qualities as an indicator of [Hebb's] Intelligence A, the basic capacity for intellectual behavior." According to Elshout, this approach, confounded as it must be by concern for controlling cultural effects, has denied us insights into how individuals store and process information, fails to embrace any forms of divergent production, serves only to confuse us further in the debate about the heritability of intelligence, suggests that the distinction between intelligence and achievement tests is more important than it is, and results in trivial and uninteresting tests. Elshout would concentrate on measuring abilities that are directly useful in real-life functioning — tests of "intelligence-added."

It is obvious from all three Chapters in Part One that, in spite of the "venerability" of intelligence and the fact that it has been "comparatively well measured" in the past, our ability to understand intelligent behavior rather than just predict it (and that not too successfully) requires new thinking and new measures. It requires new thinking (1) about the relationships among intelligence, motivation, and other social and personality variables such as anxiety; (2) about biological and cultural determiners of intelligence and their interaction; and (3) about the broad range of divergent and convergent responses that constitute intelligent behavior in the popular as well as the psychological sense. It also requires new measures that will enable us to test our new thinking.

References

Anderson, S. B., and Messick, S. "Social Competency in Young Children." *Developmental Psychology,* 1974, *10*(2), 282–293.

Boring, E. G. "Intelligence as the Tests Test It." *New Republic,* 1923, *34*, 35–37.

1   Anne Anastasi

ᘓ ᘓ ᘓ ᘓ ᘓ ᘓ ᘓ ᘓ ᘓ ᘓ ᘓ ᘓ ᘓ

What Do Intelligence Tests Measure?

The term *intelligence* is used in many contexts with a diversity of meanings. Although these meanings are not irreconcilable, they certainly emphasize different aspects of intelligent behavior. For example, in their definitions of intelligence, biologists usually focus on adaptation and survival, philosophers on abstract thought, and educators on the ability to learn. The term *intelligence* is also used in a variety of meanings by psychologists who specialize in different areas or identify with different theoretical orientations. But I do not intend to dwell on these many usages of the term. It will be quite enough, within the time available, to restrict myself to the usages within psychometrics. Such a restriction is consistent with the title of Part One and with the objectives of a volume on educational *testing*.

Since the very inception of intelligence testing, psychologists and educators have been concerned about the nature of the intelligence that their tests endeavored to assess, and repeated attempts have been made to reach a consensus. As early as 1921, the editor of the *Journal of Educational Psychology* invited seventeen leading investigators to contribute their definitions and concepts of intelligence ("Intelligence and its Measurement . . . ," 1921). The resulting lack of agreement among these definitions prompted Boring

(1923) to suggest that intelligence "at the start be defined as . . . what the tests of intelligence test, until further scientific observation allows us to extend the definition" (p. 35). It is thus apparent that Boring did not offer this frequently quoted statement, either seriously or facetiously, as an acceptable definition of intelligence. He proposed it only as a starting point to delimit the problem to be investigated. If that is the particular intelligence of concern, then the obvious next question must be, "What do intelligence tests measure?" This is the question to which I shall address myself.

The Practical Context of Intelligence Tests

Historical Background. Let us begin by looking at the historical background against which the tests developed. Intelligence tests originated in the effort to meet specific practical needs. The Binet tests were constructed as a tool for coping with the problem of educational failures among French schoolchildren (Wolf, 1973). One of the earliest English translations of these tests was prepared by Goddard for identifying and classifying the mentally retarded (Tuddenham, 1962). Much later, the first Wechsler scale was developed within a clinical setting as an aid in diagnosing adult patients and in planning their treatment. Group testing was launched during World War I with the Army Alpha and Army Beta for military selection and classification. Very soon, many group intelligence tests, modeled after these prototypes, were produced to serve similar purposes in industry and in the educational system, from kindergarten to graduate and professional schools.

Because group tests were designed as mass testing instruments, they not only permitted the simultaneous examination of large groups but also simplified the instructions and administration procedures so as to demand a minimum of training on the part of the examiner. The result was overdevelopment and premature popularization of the tests. That the tests were still technically crude was often overlooked in the rush to accumulate scores and to draw practical conclusions from the results. When the tests failed to meet unwarranted expectations, skepticism and hostility toward all testing often followed. The testing boom of the twenties was a mixed blessing — if it was a blessing at all!

Among the unfortunate side effects of that early testing boom was the adoption of the term *IQ* by the general public. The misuses of this term are truly wondrous to behold. As every psychometrist knows, the intelligence quotient was introduced as a ratio between mental age and chronological age for use on age scales such as the Stanford-Binet; when derived from almost any recently developed or revised scale, however, it is actually a standard score. Nevertheless it still serves as a popular symbol, not only for a type of score — or even a type of test — but also for a basic property of the organism. Moreover, it often carries the connotation of a quality that is *hereditary, stable throughout life,* and *resistant to change.* It is largely in the effort to minimize these popular misinterpretations of test scores that many current group tests of intelligence have dropped the term *intelligence* from their titles. But the remedy was too mild to prove effective. At this point, I simply want to emphasize that, in any discussion of what intelligence tests measure, one cannot afford to ignore these pervasive and enduring popular misconceptions.

Validation Procedures. When we ask what intelligence tests measure, we are of course raising the question of their validity. In keeping with the practical, atheoretical context in which early intelligence tests developed, their validity was investigated principally by empirical methods, against concrete, everyday-life criteria. Tests were considered valid if they worked. The principal procedure employed was criterion-related validation, of either the concurrent or predictive variety. Concurrent validation can be illustrated by the comparison of two contrasted groups of persons, carefully chosen on the basis of life-history data. If the test performance of the two groups differs in the expected direction, then the test is considered a valid diagnostic indicator of the behavioral composite exemplified by these groups. Predictive validation has been employed to evaluate the effectiveness of tests to predict performance in many real-life situations, such as job assignments and achievement at various educational levels.

It should be noted that intelligence tests typically predict many different criteria with fair success, probably because of the common behavioral requirements shared by many practical activities. Thus they serve moderately well for broad, exploratory purposes. However, such tests do not predict performance in specific criterion situations as well as tests tailored to the purpose and

designed on the basis of a task analysis of the criterion to be predicted.

Practical Interpretation of Test Scores. Within the practical
contexts in which intelligence tests developed—and in which they
are currently used—what do their scores tell us about individuals?
First, like any other tests, intelligence tests yield measures of the
individual's present status. They assess what the individual has
learned to do and what he knows at the time. Tests can serve a
predictive function only insofar as they indicate to what extent the
individual has acquired the prerequisite skills and knowledge for a
designated criterion performance. Intelligence tests sample intellectual skills and knowledge that are very broadly applicable and
widely demanded within the individual's culture, whether in school,
on jobs, or in other socially valued behavior domains. Thus tests can
serve as predictors in the sense of assessing relevant prerequisites but
not in the sense of future stability. What the individual can accomplish in the future depends not only on his present intellectual status,
as assessed by the test, but also on his subsequent experiences.

Second, intelligence tests are descriptive, not explanatory.
The intelligence assessed by the test score is an attribute of behavior,
not of the person. This view was expressed by Binet himself and has
been reiterated by several writers from time to time, but it seems to
have had little effect in stemming prevalent misconceptions (See
Anastasi, 1976, Ch. 12; Chein, 1945; Matarazzo, 1972, Ch. 3;
Tuddenham, 1962). The score provides an evaluation of the quality of a behavior sample, not of an entity within the person. No
intelligence test can indicate the reason for one's performance. To
attribute inadequate performance on a test or in everyday activities
to "inadequate intelligence" is a tautology and in no way advances
our understanding of the individual's handicap. In fact, it may halt
efforts to explore the causes of the handicap in the individual's
experiential history. Intelligence tests should be used, not to label
individuals, but to assess their current status. To bring persons to
their maximum functioning level, we need to start where they are at
the time; we need to identify their strengths and weaknesses and plan
accordingly. An important goal of testing, moreover, is to contribute to self-understanding and personal development. The information provided by tests is being used more and more to assist individ-

uals in educational and vocational planning and in making decisions about their own lives.

The Search for a Theoretical Framework

With regard to our basic question — "What do intelligence tests measure?" — we have thus far examined the sort of answers given within practical contexts. Since the middle of this century, however, there has been a growing interest in exploring this question within a theoretical orientation. This shift in viewpoint reflects in part the movement away from blind empiricism and toward the development of theory in American psychology as a whole. In this context, we shall consider in turn the contributions of construct validation, factor analysis, developmental psychology, and cognitive psychology.

Construct Validity. Construct validity was first formally recognized in the "Technical Recommendations for Psychological Tests and Diagnostic Techniques" issued by the American Psychological Association (1954), which was the precursor of the current *Standards for Educational and Psychological Tests* (1974). The concept was more fully explicated in a 1955 article by Cronbach and Meehl. Essentially, the construct validity of a test represents a statement of what the test measures in terms of theoretical constructs or traits. In actual practice, test makers usually begin with some construct that they want to measure, however vaguely conceived. The construct is generally defined in terms of a culturally significant behavior domain, such as academic aptitude, verbal ability, or quantitative reasoning. Test items are assembled that seem to fit the chosen construct, and then the validity of the test is investigated. Much of the research on the construct validity of intelligence tests has been conducted a posteriori. The investigator begins with an existing test and asks what constructs it measures. This sequence is partly the result of historical accident, since most intelligence tests were developed to meet practical needs, during a predominantly atheoretical period. The focus on theoretical interpretations came later.

Construct validation is a comprehensive validation procedure, requiring the gradual accumulation of data from various sources. The results of criterion-related validation studies may be utilized along with other data in building a picture of what the test measures. Among the many special methods available for construct validation, a few are of particular interest. One method is concerned with the specific procedures respondents use in solving test problems. For instance, individual examinees may be directed to "think aloud" while they formulate or choose each response; or, after completing a problem, they may be asked how they arrived at the answer. The test may also be modified in some way in order to observe the effect of the modification on the score. Thus the questions from a reading comprehension test may be administered *before* subjects have read the passage, to see how many items they can answer correctly simply from prior information.

Much can be learned from an analysis of errors in test responses. It should be noted that this method has been advocated and pursued by investigators representing different orientations and working in different time periods. The analysis of errors was a major technique used by Piaget in his early explorations of the development of children's thinking. It was recommended by Brigham in *A Study of Error* (1932; see also Donlon, 1979), in which he proposed systematic analyses of the incorrect options chosen in multiple-choice items from the College Board Scholastic Aptitude Test. And it has been employed in the development of training programs for improving the intellectual ability of academically retarded persons (Feuerstein, 1979; Whimbey, 1975, 1977), as well as in research on the teaching of arithmetic, writing, and scientific concepts (Glaser, 1981). But the procedure is only now being recognized as a promising source of leads for construct validation.

A major quantitative method for construct validation is the analysis of correlations between the test and other tests or performance indicators. These analyses permit the formulation of a network of relationships between the test and other variables—a network that is basic to the idea of construct validity. One systematic pattern for analyzing such correlations involves convergent and discriminant validation, first described by Campbell and Fiske (1959). To demonstrate construct validity, according to Campbell (1960), one must show not only that a test correlates highly with those variables with which it should theoretically correlate (convergent validity) but also that it does not correlate significantly with variables from which it should differ (discriminant validity). The correlation of a quantitative reasoning test with subsequent grades in a mathematics course would be an example of convergent validation. For the same test, discriminant validity would be illustrated by a low, insignificant correlation with scores on a reading comprehension test, since reading ability is an irrelevant variable in a test designed to measure quantitative reasoning.

Factor Analysis. Factor analysis represents a further refinement of the application of correlational procedures in construct validation (Anastasi, 1982, Ch. 13; Horn, 1976; Tuddenham, 1962). However, because of its highly specialized techniques and its extensive use in theoretically oriented research on the nature of intelligence, factor analysis merits separate consideration in its own right, on a par with construct validation. The principal object of factor analysis is to simplify the description of data by reducing the number of necessary variables or dimensions. For example, beginning with the intercorrelations among twenty tests, we may be able to show that two or three factors are sufficient to account for nearly all the common variance in the set. These are the types of factors identified in such factor-analytic systems as Thurstone's primary mental abilities and Guilford's structure-of-intellect model. If we obtain our data from a sufficiently heterogeneous population, Spearman's g factor may emerge as a second-order factor to account for correlations found among the factors themselves.

By whatever statistical procedures such factors are found — and however elaborate these procedures may be — we must bear in mind that the factors, like the test scores from which they were derived, are descriptive and not explanatory. To say that a child obtains a low score on a vocabulary test because he or she is deficient in the verbal comprehension factor is no more enlightening than to attribute poor scholastic performance to a low Stanford-Binet IQ. The abilities identified through factor analysis do not represent underlying entities, causal factors, or fixed personal characteristics. The very composition of intelligence may alter as a result of the individual's experiences. The pattern of abilities tends to change with age, as one's environment fosters and encourages the development of some aptitudes and deemphasizes other aptitudes. Factor-analytic research has demonstrated that experiential differences may influence not only the level of performance reached in different abilities but also the way in which intelligence becomes differentiated into identifiable traits. There is empirical evidence that the number and nature of traits or abilities may change over time and may differ among cultures or subcultures, socioeconomic levels, and school curricula (Anastasi, 1983; Fleishman, 1972).

A mechanism for the emergence of factors is provided by the familiar concepts of learning set and transfer (Carroll, 1966; Ferguson, 1954, 1956; Whiteman, 1964). The establishment of learning sets enables one to learn more efficiently when presented with a new problem of the same kind. The individual has thus "learned how to learn" this type of problem. Similarly, many of the skills developed through formal schooling, such as reading and arithmetical computation, are applicable to a wide variety of subsequent learning situations. Efficient and systematic problem-solving techniques can likewise be applied to the solution of new problems. Individual differences in the extent to which these skills have been acquired will thus be reflected in the performance of a large number of different tasks; and in a factor analysis of these tasks, these widely applicable skills will emerge as broad group factors. The breadth of the transfer effect, or the variety of tasks to which the skill is applicable, will thus determine the breadth of the resulting group factor.

Contributions of Developmental Psychology. As we turn from the contributions to the assessment of intelligence made by factor analysts to those made by developmental psychologists, we find many contrasts between the two approaches. Since the 1960s, there has been a revival of interest in the work of Piaget on the development of children's thinking (Flavell, 1963; Ginsburg and Opper, 1969; Green, Ford, and Flamer, 1971; J. McV. Hunt, 1961). Piaget's approach focuses on stages of cognitive development from infancy to the midteens. The emphasis is on qualitative description of thought processes. Piaget's *méthode clinique* is best adapted to individual examination and is as much concerned with the reasons for wrong answers as with the frequency of correct responses. Piagetian tasks assess the development of specific concepts, or cognitive schemata, rather than broad abilities. Well-known examples of such schemata include object constancy and conservation of quantity. Some Piagetian tasks have been organized into standardized scales, although all such scales are still in experimental form. In accordance with Piaget's approach, these instruments are ordinal Guttman-type scales, in which the attainment of each stage is contingent upon completion of the earlier stages in the development of the child's thinking processes.

A major obstacle encountered in all these ordinal scales is what Piagetian researchers call *décalage*, or inconsistencies in the anticipated sequences. There is a growing body of data that casts doubt on the implied continuities and regularities of intellectual development. Too often the stage corresponding to a given individual's performance varies with the task, not only when different processes are required for its solution but also when the same process is applied to different contents (Goodnow, 1976; Horn, 1976; Tuddenham, 1971; Ward, 1972). It might also be noted that Piagetian scales have been found to correlate substantially with standardized intelligence tests (Gottfried and Brody, 1975; Kaufman, 1971) and to correlate about as high with school achievement of first-grade children as did a group intelligence test (Kaufman and Kaufman, 1972). What these findings suggest is that, despite pronounced differences in methodology, Piagetian scales, standardized intelligence tests, and school achievement have much in common in the overall assessment of children that they provide. The Piagetian scales are more difficult to administer and much more time-consuming, but they yield a much richer picture of what the child can do and how he or she does it.

Apart from its specialized methodologies for assessing intelligence, however, the Piagetian approach has made significant contributions to our understanding of the nature of intelligence across the life span. Essentially, Piaget's observations suggest that intelligence may be qualitatively different at different life periods. This conclusion has found considerable support in the work of other investigators, especially those studying the behavior of infants and young children (Bayley, 1968, 1970; Lewis, 1973; Lewis and McGurk, 1972; McCall, Hogarty, and Hurlburt, 1972). Such findings are also consistent with the concept of developmental tasks proposed by several psychologists in a variety of contexts (Erikson, 1950; Havig-

hurst, 1953; Super and others, 1957).   Educationally and vocation-
ally, as well as in other aspects of daily life, the individual encounters
typical behavioral demands and problems at different life stages,
from infancy to senescence.   Although both the problems and the
appropriate reactions vary somewhat among cultures and subcultures, modal requirements can be specified within a particular cultural setting.   Each life stage makes characteristic demands on the
individual.   Mastery of the developmental tasks of earlier stages
influences the person's handling of the behavioral demands of the
next.

In summary, developmental psychology provides evidence
from several sources that the definition of intelligence may vary
across the life span.   What intelligence tests measure—and what
they ought to measure—may differ qualitatively at different life
stages from infancy through adulthood.

Contributions of Cognitive Psychology.   An outstanding example
of the growing rapprochement between psychometrics and experimental psychology is to be found in the current contributions of
cognitive psychology to an understanding of what intelligence tests
measure.   Some of the investigations in this area represent the work
of psychologists trained in both disciplines; others result from the
auspicious collaboration of specialists in the two fields.

Since the 1950s cognitive psychologists have been applying
the concepts of information processing to describe what occurs in
human problem solving.   Some have designed computer programs
that carry out these processes and thereby simulate human thought.
Programs can be written to simulate the performance of persons at
different levels of skill, and with such programs it should be possible
to predict the number and kinds of errors made and the time
required for different responses.   In designing a program, the investigator usually begins with a task analysis that may include intro-
specting about his or her own method of solving the problem, having
subjects think aloud, or using more refined observational procedures.   By comparing the performance of the computer with that of
children and adults in solving the same problems, investigators can
test their hypotheses about what persons do in carrying out the tasks
and, if necessary, modify and refine the program.   Examples of the
tasks investigated by these methods include conventional puzzles,

problems in logic, the game of chess, algebra word problems, and spelling English words (Simon, 1976).

The "basic abilities" identified by these procedures consist of processes and knowledge. The cognitive models specify the intellectual processes used to perform the task, the way the processes are organized, the relevant knowledge store, and how this knowledge is represented in memory and retrieved when needed. A distinction is usually made between short-term, intermediate-term, and long-term memory. Increasing attention is also being given to what has been called an *executive process.* This term refers to the control the individual exerts over his own choice of processes, representations, and strategies for carrying out the task.

In the 1970s, a few psychologists began to apply these information-processing and computer-simulation techniques to an exploration of what intelligence tests measure (Resnick, 1976). Individual investigators approached this goal from different angles. Let me cite a few examples. Carroll (1976) offered a provisional scheme for classifying the cognitive tasks appearing in psychometric tests in terms of information-processing parameters. Beginning with the abilities most commonly identified through factor analysis (factors and tests from French, Ekstrom, and Price, 1963), he relied on his acquaintance with the available literature on cognitive information processing to code the tests and thence locate the cognitive processes and memory stores associated with the corresponding factors. For instance, Carroll (1976) writes: "*Factor N (Number Facility)* involves (1) retrieving appropriate number associations and algorithms from [long-term memory] and (2) performing serial operations on the stimulus materials using these associations and algorithms. Individual differences could appear in both content and temporal aspects of these retrieval and manipulative operations. Special strategies possibly contributing to individual differences might be special ways of "chunking" numerical materials (e.g., mentally adding two-digit numbers both digits at a time rather than by the more "elementary" one-digit-and-carrying methods)" (p. 50).

Other investigators have used empirical methods to test their hypotheses about psychometric tests. Earl Hunt and his associates (E. Hunt, 1976; E. Hunt, Frost, and Lunneborg, 1973) correlated subjects' performance on information-processing parameters from laboratory tasks with their scores from psychometric tests, and then factor-analyzed all these variables together. They also selected individuals who differed in conventional psychometric test scores and compared them on more basic memory tasks. Some suggestive relations were found between performance on verbal intelligence tests and speed of processing information in short-term, intermediate-term, and long-term memory; but the relations were not high, and the results are still quite tentative.

Simon (1976) and his associates have conducted many studies with computer programs written to simulate human problem solving. Although this research was not directed specifically to the understanding of intelligence, some of the tasks investigated play an important part in common intelligence tests. A major example is provided by sequential pattern tasks, which are involved in such tests as number series completion and Raven Progressive Matrices. Klahr (1976) has been exploring simulation models that may help to explain intellectual development, including the transitions from one Piagetian stage to another. He describes a preliminary model for a self-modifying system, which includes both performance and learning mechanisms.

One of the most ambitious and systematic efforts to relate intelligence test performance to cognitive psychology is to be found in the research of Sternberg (1979) on componential analysis. This analysis has been applied to tasks that resemble complex intelligence test materials more closely than do the usual simplified and artificial laboratory tasks. Sternberg organizes mental abilities into four levels:

1. Composite tasks, which correspond to the tasks usually encountered in intelligence tests, such as analogies, classification, and series completion.
2. Subtasks, into which the composite task can be decomposed. This step facilitates the identification of information-processing components.
3. Information-processing components, which constitute the level of primary interest. These include general components required by all tasks in a given task universe, more restricted class components, and specific components limited to a single task.

4.   Information-processing metacomponents, representing the control individuals exert over their own cognitive processes.

The experimental procedure for developing a componential task specification includes the manipulation, or systematic alteration, of both task variables and subject variables. The effects of such manipulations on the corresponding response time, response choice, and error data are then compared with the effects predicted from the model.

What can we conclude about the contributions that cognitive psychology has made thus far to a clarification of intelligence test performance? It must be recognized at the outset that efforts to bridge the gap between psychometrics and cognitive psychology are still in an early exploratory stage. Information-processing approaches have contributed heuristic concepts to guide further research and have clearly focused attention on processes rather than end products in problem solving. Analyzing intelligence test performance in terms of basic cognitive processes should certainly strengthen and enrich our understanding of what the tests measure. Moreover, analyzing individuals' performance at the level of component processes should eventually make it possible to pinpoint each person's sources of weakness and strength and thus enhance the diagnostic use of tests (Estes, 1974; Sternberg, 1979). This in turn should facilitate the tailoring of training programs to the individual's needs.

At the same time, we should not be carried away by the heady promise of these new vistas. It is unlikely that intelligence tests will change drastically in content as a result of information-processing analyses. We started by defining intelligence as what the intelligence tests measure. As one astute observer put it, let us not now proceed to define it as "what the models model" (Neisser, 1979). If our tests are to continue to serve practical ends, they must maintain a firm hold on the intellectual demands of real life. We should also guard against attaching excess meanings to the emerging terms. Basic cognitive skills do not represent fixed or innate properties of the organism any more than do IQs or primary mental abilities. Let me emphasize that these words of caution are not intended to diminish the contributions of cognitive psychologists or to imply that they have succumbed to any of these pitfalls. On the contrary, some investigators have themselves called attention to these potential hazards. Once the new concepts become widely publicized, however, popular misinterpretations are all too likely to follow.

Cultural Frames of Reference

For a full understanding of what intelligence tests measure, we must consider the cultural frame of reference within which they were developed. No intelligence test can be culture free, because human intelligence is not culture free. If we look at some traditional attempts to define intelligence, we find that they come up against the environmental context of all behavior. For instance, if intelligence is regarded as adaptability, the next question is, Adaptability to what? Persons who adapt successfully to their own culture may be totally unable to survive in another. Similarly, if intelligence is regarded as learning ability, we must then ask, Ability to learn what? Learning does not emerge as a common factor in factor-analytic research. To be sure, there is ample evidence that, biologically, human behavior is more highly modifiable than is the behavior of other species. But *what* the human is able to learn depends on the individual's prior learning history. The same person may be an excellent learner of one type of content and a poor learner of other types.

It is apparent that there are, not one, but many kinds of intelligence. Each culture demands, fosters, and rewards a somewhat different set of abilities. Research in cross-cultural psychology provides a rich store of examples to illustrate this fact (Berry, 1972; Goodnow, 1976; Neisser, 1976, 1979). Cultures differ in the value they place on generalization and on the search for common features in disparate experiences. In some cultures, behavior is more specifically linked to contexts and situations than is implied by typical intelligence tests. The response depends on who asks a question and on what type of content is involved. The individual may have learned to apply a particular operation, such as grouping or counting, to one type of content but not to another. Cultural differences in task interpretation may also influence what individuals select from their available response repertoire. For instance, functional classification in terms of use (such as placing knife with orange) may be chosen because it is considered more appropriate and sensible than classification into superordinate abstract classes, such as fruit and tools (Glick, 1975).

Viewing the diverse concepts of intelligence from a different angle, Neisser (1976, 1979) proposes that intelligence is not a quality of a person but a resemblance to a prototype. And he proceeds to demonstrate that there are multiple prototypes of the "intelligent person." Even within our own culture, he differentiates between academic intelligence and natural, "real-life" intelligence. The former is measured by traditional intelligence tests and is important in school achievement and in many other activities that depend on formal schooling. The latter is more diversified; it is more closely adapted to specific situations; and it is influenced by the individual's own interests and goals. In other cultures, the prototype of an intelligent person may differ even more conspicuously from that implied by academic intelligence, as suggested by data on the conceptions of intelligence in preliterate, nonindustrial cultures. For example, one investigator reported that "various groups of Ugandans tend to associate their concept of intelligence with slowness, but not with quickness" (Wober, 1972, p. 327). The same study found that, following prolonged attendance at Western-type schools, this association tended to diminish and to be replaced by its opposite.

Some sociologists have coined the term *modern consciousness* to describe the psychological effects of being reared and educated in advanced industrial societies (Berger, Berger, and Kellner, 1973). Subsequently, one of the coauthors, Brigitte Berger, applied this concept to an examination of what intelligence tests measure. She concluded that IQs assess the extent to which the individual has internalized "the cognitive requirements of the modern technological-rationalistic world" (B. Berger, 1978, p. 35). An example of such cognitive requirements is a high level of abstraction, whereby each element of knowledge can be viewed apart from its immediate context. Another is "componentiality," whereby the components of reality can be isolated, disassembled, and reassembled in new combinations.

A similar view has been expressed by Olson (1976), who observes that intelligence tests measure how well the individual has mastered the techniques of abstraction and rationality, which "are to a large extent the necessary but unintended consequences of technological developments" (pp. 200–201). Olson argues that the invention of a particular technology may alter the cognitive activities that constitute intelligence, and he illustrates this point with the invention of phonetic writing systems. He contrasts oral tradition with written language as a means of codifying and preserving the knowledge of a culture. Oral transmission concentrates on persons, events, aphorisms, and commandments; it is not well adapted to the formulation of principles, laws, and formulas. With the introduction of written language, meaning became less dependent on context or on shared prior knowledge.

If we wish to understand and describe the intelligence of different cultures, we need naturalistic observations to identify the cognitive demands of particular environments (Charlesworth, 1976). A task analysis of the behavioral requirements of a given culture (or subculture) represents an appropriate first step in constructing an intelligence test to assess how well individuals have acquired the skills and knowledge valued in that culture. If, however, we want an intelligence test to facilitate mobility into another environment, it is the cognitive demands of *that* environment that are relevant. The test should then be constructed from a task analysis of the new environment into which the individual wishes to move — whether it be an educational institution, an academic program, a vocational career, a country to which one is immigrating, or an emerging technology in a developing nation. One approach helps us to understand how individuals arrived where they are in intellectual development; the other tells us what they need in order to go where they want to be.

Modifiability of Intelligence

In sketching this picture of what intelligence tests measure, I must call attention to one more feature, namely, the modifiability of intelligence. Contrary to the still-prevalent popular notion regarding the fixity of the IQ, there is a rapidly growing body of evidence that the behavior domain sampled by intelligence tests is responsive to training. It is interesting to note that, despite subsequent misinterpretations of the Binet scales, Binet himself rejected the view that intelligence is unchangeable. He and his associates developed procedures, which they called *mental orthopedics*, for raising the intellectual level of mental retardates. As early as 1911, Binet wrote that for "children who did not know how to listen, to pay attention, to keep quiet, we pictured our first duty as being . . . to teach them how to learn" (p. 150).

The decades of the 1960s and 1970s witnessed a strong upsurge of interest in programs for improving academic intelligence. These programs were developed largely in the United States and in Israel, where there were large minority populations that were having difficulty in adapting to the majority culture. By far the largest number of these programs were directed to the infant and preschool levels (Brown, 1978; Consortium, 1978; Day and Parker, 1977; J. McV. Hunt, 1975; Peleg and Adler, 1977; Zigler and Valentine, 1980). These educational programs varied widely in content and quality. A few were well designed and are relevant to the present topic insofar as they endeavored to develop cognitive skills judged to be prerequisite for subsequent schooling. It is these programs that yielded the most promising results. The more successful programs also included parental involvement as a means of supplementing the preschool experiences and ensuring their continuation after the program terminates.

Other programs, on a smaller scale, have been designed for school-age children (Bloom, 1976; Jacobs and Vandeventer, 1971; Olton and Crutchfield, 1969; Resnick and Glaser, 1976). While these programs are still at a research stage, their preliminary findings are encouraging. Some investigators have focused on still older age levels, working with college and professional school students (Bloom and Broder, 1950; Whimbey, 1975, 1977). It is noteworthy that they, too, report significant improvement in academic achievement and in performance on scholastic aptitude tests. Still other investigators have concentrated on educable mentally retarded children and adolescents, again with significant intellectual improvements (Babad and Budoff, 1974; Budoff and Corman, 1974; Feuerstein, 1979, 1980).

At all age levels, these programs have been directed primarily at persons from educationally disadvantaged backgrounds. In connection with his work with mental retardates in Israel, Feuerstein (1980) offers a provocative definition of cultural deprivation. He identifies the culturally deprived as persons who have become alienated from their own culture through a disruption of intergenerational cultural transmission and a paucity of mediated learning experience. As a result, they have failed to acquire certain learning skills and habits that are required for high-level cognitive functioning. Culturally different persons, by contrast, having learned to adapt to their own culture, have developed the prerequisite skills and habits for continued modifiability and can adapt to the demands of the new culture after a relatively brief transition period. The same concept underlies the work of Whimbey (1975) with college students. Designating his approach as "cognitive therapy," Whimbey observed that it resembles "the type of parent-child verbal dialogue in problem solving that researchers believe constitutes the academic advantage middle-class children have over lower-class children" (p. 68).

Another important concept that emerges from this training research is that of self-monitoring. This is reminiscent of Binet's inclusion of self-criticism as a component of intelligent behavior (Binet, 1911, p. 122). Whimbey (1975, pp. 137–138) also emphasizes the need for training in self-monitoring, in view of the high frequency of shoddy, careless, and impulsive responses among poor test performers. Flavell (1979) has devoted special attention to cognitive monitoring under the broader heading of metacognition, which includes the individual's knowledge about himself and others as cognitive processors.

In summary, the training research on intelligence has yielded some provocative concepts and some promising procedures for developing the academic intelligence measured by traditional tests. Improvement can occur at considerably later ages than heretofore anticipated. But the later the training is begun, the more limited will be its effectiveness. Through special training programs, one can learn widely applicable cognitive skills, problem-solving strategies, efficient study habits, and other useful behavioral processes. It takes a long time, however, to accumulate the relevant content store in long-term memory, and this content store is also a part of intelligence and contributes to the person's readiness to learn more advanced material. Although the older person, armed with efficient learning techniques, can build up this content store more quickly than he or she could have as a child, it is nevertheless unrealistic to expect this to occur after short training periods distributed over a few months. There are no shortcuts to intellectual development — at least not *that* short! It is well to bear this limitation in mind. Otherwise, if unrealistic expectations remain unfulfilled, there is danger that disillusionment will weaken confidence in the entire training approach. Intelligence *can* be improved at any age; the earlier one begins, however, the greater will be the returns from one's efforts.

References

American Psychological Association. "Technical Recommendations for Psychological Tests and Diagnostic Techniques." *Psychological Bulletin*, 1954, *51* (2), part 2, 201–238.

Anastasi, A. *Psychological Testing.* (5th ed.) New York: Macmillan, 1982.

Anastasi, A. "Evolving Trait Concepts." *American Psychologist*, 1983, *38*, 175–184.

Babad, E. Y., and Budoff, M. "Sensitivity and Validity of Learning Potential Measurement in Three Levels of Ability." *Journal of Educational Psychology*, 1974, *66*, 439–447.

Bayley, N. "Behavioral Correlates of Mental Growth: Birth to Thirty-Six Years." *American Psychologist*, 1968, *23*, 1–17.

Bayley, N. "Development of Mental Abilities." In P. Mussen (Ed.), *Carmichael's Manual of Child Psychology.* Vol. 1. New York: Wiley, 1970.

Berger, B. "A New Interpretation of the IQ Controversy." *The Public Interest*, Winter 1978, pp. 29–44.

Berger, P. L., Berger, B., and Kellner, H. *The Homeless Mind: Modernization and Consciousness.* New York: Random House, 1973.

Berry, J. W. "Radical Cultural Relativism and the Concept of

Intelligence." In L. J. Cronbach and P. J. D. Drenth (Eds.), *Mental Tests and Cultural Adaptations.* The Hague: Mouton, 1972.

Binet, A. *Les Idées Modernes sur les Enfants.* Paris: Flammarion, 1911.

Bloom, B. S. *Human Characteristics and School Learning.* New York: McGraw-Hill, 1976.

Bloom, B. S., and Broder, L. *Problem-Solving Processes of College Students.* Chicago: University of Chicago Press, 1950.

Boring, E. G. "Intelligence as the Tests Test It." *New Republic,* 1923, *34,* 35–37.

Brigham, C. C. *A Study of Error.* New York: College Entrance Examination Board, 1932.

Brown, B. (Ed.). *Found: Long-Term Gains from Early Intervention.* Boulder, Colo.: Westview Press, 1978.

Budoff, M., and Corman, L. "Demographic and Psychometric Factors Related to Improved Performance on the Kohs Learning Potential Procedure." *American Journal of Mental Deficiency,* 1974, *78,* 578–585.

Campbell, D. T. "Recommendations for APA Test Standards Regarding Construct, Trait, and Discriminant Validity." *American Psychologist,* 1960, *15,* 546–553.

Campbell, D. T., and Fiske, D. W. "Convergent and Discriminant Validation by the Multitrait-Multimethod Matrix." *Psychological Bulletin,* 1959, *56,* 81–105.

Carroll, J. B. "Factors of Verbal Achievement." In A. Anastasi (Ed.), *Testing Problems in Perspective.* Washington, D.C.: American Council on Education, 1966.

Carroll, J. B. "Psychometric Tests as Cognitive Tasks: A New 'Structure of Intellect'". In L. B. Resnick (Ed.), *The Nature of Intelligence.* Hillsdale, N.J.: Erlbaum, 1976.

Charlesworth, W. R. "Human Intelligence as Adaptation: An Ethological Approach." In L. B. Resnick (Ed.), *The Nature of Intelligence.* Hillsdale, N.J.: Erlbaum, 1976.

Chein, I. "On the Nature of Intelligence." *Journal of General Psychology,* 1945, *32,* 111–126.

Consortium for Longitudinal Studies. *Lasting Effects After Pre-*

school. DHEW Publication No. (OHDS) 79-30178. Washington, D.C.: U.S. Government Printing Office, 1978.

Cronbach, L. J., and Meehl, P. E. "Construct Validity in Psychological Tests." *Psychological Bulletin,* 1955, *52,* 281–302.

Day, M. C., and Parker, R. K. (Eds.). *The Preschool in Action: Exploring Early Childhood Programs.* Boston: Allyn & Bacon, 1977.

Donlon, T. F. "Brigham's Book." *College Board Review,* Fall 1979, pp. 24–30.

Erikson, E. H. *Childhood and Society.* New York: Norton, 1950.

Estes, W. K. "Learning Theory and Intelligence." *American Psychologist,* 1974, *29,* 740–749.

Ferguson, G. A. "On Learning and Human Ability." *Canadian Journal of Psychology,* 1954, *8,* 95–112.

Ferguson, G. A. "On Transfer and the Abilities of Man." *Canadian Journal of Psychology,* 1956, *10,* 121–131.

Feuerstein, R. *The Dynamic Assessment of Retarded Performers.* Baltimore, Md.: University Park Press, 1979.

Feuerstein, R. *Instrumental Enrichment: An Intervention Program for Cognitive Modifiability.* Baltimore, Md.: University Park Press, 1980.

Flavell, J. H. *The Developmental Psychology of Jean Piaget.* New York: D. Van Nostrand, 1963.

Flavell, J. H. *"Metacognition and Cognitive Monitoring: A New Area of Cognitive-Developmental Inquiry."* American Psychologist, 1979, *34,* 906–911.

Fleishman, E. A. "On the Relation Between Abilities, Learning, and Human Performance." *American Psychologist,* 1972, *27,* 1017–1032.

French, J. W., Ekstrom, R. B., and Price, L. A. *Kit of Reference Tests for Cognitive Factors.* Princeton, N.J.: Educational Testing Service, 1963.

Ginsburg, H., and Opper, S. *Piaget's Theory of Intellectual Development: An Introduction.* Englewood Cliffs, N.J.: Prentice-Hall, 1969.

Glaser, R. "The Future of Testing: A Research Agenda for Cognitive Psychology and Psychometrics." *American Psychologist,* 1981, *36,* 923–936.

Glick, J. "Cognitive Development in Cross-Cultural Perspective." In F. D. Horowitz (Ed.), *Review of Child Development Research.* Vol. 4. Chicago: University of Chicago Press, 1975.

Goodnow, J. J. "The Nature of Intelligent Behavior: Questions Raised by Cross-Cultural Studies." In L. B. Resnick (Ed.), *The Nature of Intelligence.* Hillsdale, N.J.: Erlbaum, 1976.

Gottfried, A. W., and Brody, N. "Interrelationships Between and Correlates of Psychometric and Piagetian Scales of Sensorimotor Intelligence." *Developmental Psychology,* 1975, *11,* 379–387.

Green, D. R., Ford, M. P., and Flamer, G. B. (Eds.). *Measurement and Piaget.* New York: McGraw-Hill, 1971.

Havighurst, R. J. *Human Development and Education.* New York: Longmans, Green, 1953.

Horn, J. L. "Human Abilities: A Review of Research and Theory in the Early 1970s." *Annual Review of Psychology,* 1976, *27,* 437–485.

Hunt, E. "Varieties of Cognitive Power." In L. B. Resnick (Ed.), *The Nature of Intelligence.* Hillsdale, N.J.: Erlbaum, 1976.

Hunt, E., Frost, N., and Lunneborg, C. "Individual Differences in Cognition." In G. Bower (Ed.), *The Psychology of Learning and Motivation: Advances in Research and Theory.* Vol. 7. New York: Academic Press, 1973.

Hunt, J.McV. *Intelligence and Experience.* New York: Dutton, 1961.

Hunt, J.McV. "Reflections on a Decade of Early Education." *Journal of Abnormal Child Psychology,* 1975, *3,* 275–330.

"Intelligence and its Measurement: A Symposium." *Journal of Educational Psychology,* 1921, *12,* 123–147, 195–216.

Jacobs, P. I., and Vandeventer, M. "The Learning and Transfer of Double-Classification Skills: A Replication and Extension." *Journal of Experimental Child Psychology,* 1971, *12,* 140–157.

Kaufman, A. S. "Piaget and Gesell: A Psychometric Analysis of Tests Built from Their Tasks." *Child Development,* 1971, *42,* 1341–1360.

Kaufman, A. S., and Kaufman, N. L. "Tests Built from Piaget's and Gesell's Tasks as Predictors of First-Grade Achievement." *Child Development,* 1972, *43,* 521–535.

Klahr, D. "Steps Toward the Simulation of Intellectual Development." In L. B. Resnick (Ed.), *The Nature of Intelligence.* Hillsdale, N.J.: Erlbaum, 1976.

Lewis, M. "Infant Intelligence Tests: Their Use and Misuse." *Human Development,* 1973, *16,* 108–118.

Lewis, M., and McGurk, H. "Evaluation of Infant Intelligence: Infant Intelligence Scores—True or False?" *Science,* 1972, *178*(4066), 1174–1177.

Matarazzo, J. D. *Wechsler's Measurement and Appraisal of Adult Intelligence.* (5th ed.) Baltimore, Md.: Williams & Wilkins, 1972.

McCall, R. B., Hogarty, P. S., and Hurlburt, N. "Transitions in Infant Sensorimotor Development and the Prediction of Childhood IQ." *American Psychologist,* 1972, 27, 728–748.

Neisser, U. "General, Academic, and Artificial Intelligence." In L. B. Resnick (Ed.), *The Nature of Intelligence.* Hillsdale, N.J.: Erlbaum, 1976.

Neisser, U. "The Concept of Intelligence." *Intelligence,* 1979, *3,* 217–227.

Olson, D. R. "Culture, Technology, and Intellect." In L. B. Resnick (Ed.), *The Nature of Intelligence.* Hillsdale, N. J.: Erlbaum, 1976.

Olton, R. M., and Crutchfield, R. S. "Developing the Skills of Productive Thinking." In P. H. Mussen, J. Langer, and M. Covington (Eds.), *Trends and Issues in Developmental Psychology.* New York: Holt, Rinehart and Winston, 1969.

Peleg, R., and Adler, C. "Compensatory Education in Israel: Conceptions, Attitudes, and Trends." *American Psychologist,* 1977, *32,* 945–958.

Resnick, L. B. (Ed.). *The Nature of Intelligence.* Hillsdale, N.J.: Erlbaum, 1976.

Resnick, L. B., and Glaser, R. "Problem Solving and Intelligence." In L. B. Resnick (Ed.), *The Nature of Intelligence.* Hillsdale, N.J.: Erlbaum, 1976.

Simon, H. A. "Identifying Basic Abilities Underlying Intelligent Performance of Complex Tasks." In L. B. Resnick (Ed.), *The Nature of Intelligence.* Hillsdale, N.J.: Erlbaum, 1976.

Standards for Educational and Psychological Tests. Washington, D.C.: American Psychological Association, 1974.

Sternberg, R. J. "The Nature of Mental Abilities." *American Psychologist,* 1979, *34,* 214–230.

Super, D. E., and others. *Vocational Development: A Framework for Research.* New York: Teachers College Press, 1957.

Tuddenham, R. D. "The Nature and Measurement of Intelligence." In L. Postman (Ed.), *Psychology in the Making.* New York: Knopf, 1962.

Tuddenham, R. D. "Theoretical Regularities and Individual Idiosyncrasies." In D. R. Green, M. P. Ford, and G. B. Flamer (Eds.), *Measurement and Piaget.* New York: McGraw-Hill, 1971.

Ward, J. "The Saga of Butch and Slim." *British Journal of Educational Psychology,* 1972, *42,* 267–289.

Whimbey, A. *Intelligence Can Be Taught.* New York: Dutton, 1975.

Whimbey, A. "Teaching Sequential Thought: The Cognitive-Skills Approach." *Phi Delta Kappan,* 1977, *59,* 255–259.

Whiteman, M. "Intelligence and Learning." *Merrill-Palmer Quarterly,* 1964, *10,* 297–309.

Wober, M. "Culture and the Concept of Intelligence: A Case in Uganda." *Journal of Cross-Cultural Psychology,* 1972, *3,* 327–328.

Wolf, T. H. *Alfred Binet.* Chicago: University of Chicago Press, 1973.

Zigler, E., and Valentine, J. (Eds.). *Project Head Start: A Legacy of the War on Poverty.* New York: Free Press, 1980.

2   John W. Atkinson

ℜ ℜ ℜ ℜ ℜ ℜ ℜ ℜ ℜ ℜ ℜ ℜ ℜ

Motivational Psychology and Mental Measurement

The term *intelligence* has always escaped clear definition because mental testing is founded on a statistical conceptual framework and nothing more. It has always been isolated from the important advances in basic motivational psychology that could enlighten the interpretation of individual differences in test scores. Although Cronbach (1957) deplored the isolation of what he referred to as "the two scientific disciplines of psychology" and thus raised general awareness of the chronic fragmentation of the field more than twenty-five years ago, he may — without intending to — have provided justification for the continued isolation of "correlational" and "experimental" approaches to behavior by dignifying each as a discipline. It might have hastened their integration to have identified them in more demeaning terms, that is, as two very limited techniques of investigation. This would have emphasized their fundamental inadequacies in isolation from one another.

No one has ever stated the objective of scientific psychology and the relatedness of differential psychology to the search for the basic laws of behavioral processes better than Lewin. I never tire of repeating what I believe should be the common creed of psychologists: "A law is expressed in an equation which relates certain variables: Individual differences have to be conceived as various specific values which these variables have in a particular case. In other words, general laws and individual differences are merely two aspects of one problem; they are virtually dependent on each other, and the study of the one cannot proceed without the study of the other" (Lewin, 1946, p. 794).

When Sears (1950) composed the article on Personality for the first volume of the *Annual Review of Psychology*, he also provided some justification for separating the statistical or correlational analysis of behavior from the experimental one. I now believe he was mistaken in identifying the problem of dynamics (motivational psychology), the problem of development (developmental psychology), and the problem of structure (correlational analysis) as essentially different and, by implication, equally justifiable paradigms for the study of individual differences in personality.

Motivational and Developmental Psychology

Contrary to Sears's view, there are not three paradigms, only two. The consensus achieved in the 1940s in experimental and theoretical analysis of animal behavior concerning the distinction between the problems and principles of learning, on the one hand, and of performance, on the other, provided the model for the more general distinction between the motivational and developmental paradigms of contemporary psychology.

Intelligence refers to one of the ways in which people differ in personality. But they differ in other ways as well. They differ in their motives and in their beliefs and conceptions. These three categories correspond to the central interests of three different fields of psychology: educational psychology (abilities), clinical psychology (motives), and social psychology (beliefs and conceptions). It is the business of motivational psychology to explain how these various differences in personality are expressed in behavior. It is the business of developmental psychology to explain how these various differences in personality have come about.

In the motivational paradigm, such dimensions of personality as abilities, motives, and beliefs are among the causes of differential behavior. In the developmental paradigm, these same dimensions of personality are among the dependent variables; that is, they are the effects of differences in historical antecedents, heredity, and formative environment. The last embraces the whole process of socialization and formal educational training.

Those interested in contemporaneous determinants of behavior are guided by Lewin's famous equation, $B = f(P,E)$. This defines the general problem of motivational psychology. Notice that it includes interest in expressions of individual differences in personality (traditional differential psychology), the effect of variations in the immediate environment (traditional experimental psychology), and, more important, the interaction of personal and situational determinants of behavior (contemporary motivational psychology).

Those who are interested in the historical determinants of personality and changes in it work in the developmental paradigm of psychology. They are guided by a comparable programmatic equation that defines their problem: $P = f(H,E_f)$. Here again we have the possibility of one-sided interest and argument, and we have witnessed both in the long debate about the role of nature (heredity) and nurture (formative environment) in the genesis of intelligence. In fact, here again we confront an important interaction that must always be taken into account, as well as the need for principles of learning and maturation that specify the nature of the interaction with reference to how essential attributes of personality develop.

When we put the two paradigms of contemporary psychology in logical order — that is, $B = f(P,E)$ and $P = f(H,E_f)$ — something else becomes vividly clear. Since individual differences in personality (P) lie under the skin, these latent behavioral dispositions can be seen and measured only when they are manifested in observable behavior (B). At this moment, for example, I am not doing anything that would enable you to assess my ability to play the saxophone. I am doing something that expresses more or less ability to do theoretical psychology. Quite obviously, then, those working within the motivational paradigm — that is, those primarily concerned with identifying the immediate determinants of actions or performances — are the ones who have the responsibility for identifying the essential dimensions of individual differences in personality. The question they must ask is this: What characteristics of people need to be taken into account in order to explain what they do, when they do it, and how well they do it?   Motivational psychology has the tough job of specifying *when* a given activity will occur and for how long. The new theory of dynamics of action (Atkinson and Birch, 1970, 1974, 1978) does this—with elegant precision.

Ability, Motivation, and Performance

Without question, the effort to identify basic dimensions of individual differences in personality has always been an explicit central interest within the statistical correlational analysis of behavior, which is the traditional conceptual home of "intelligence." But this has been my central interest, as well, in my effort to apply the most recent theoretical developments in motivational psychology to important educational problems.   One problem is to understand what happens when ability and motivation are confounded as determinants of individual differences in the level of intellective *performance*, so long taken for granted as merely an expression of individual differences in ability.   Another problem is to understand why the correlation of intelligence test scores and educational achievement as measured by grade averages in American colleges should be only modest (Atkinson and Raynor, 1974, 1978; Atkinson, Lens, and O'Malley, 1976; Atkinson and Birch, 1978; Atkinson and Lens, 1980).

Before discussing the new perspective on the meaning of *intelligence* provided by this work, I would like to argue that traditional test theory, standing alone, is itself a theory of motivation (Atkinson and Birch, 1978).   The logic of its basic equation—obtained score equals true score *plus* error (see de Groot, 1969, p. 267)—is essentially the same as the logic expressed in the two traditional conceptions of motivation that were the product of a half century of experimental-conceptual analysis of animal behavior, beginning with Thorndike's *Law of Effect* (1911).   Test theory says that the observed and measured behavior (the obtained score) is almost never exactly what it is expected to be (the true score) because of random variation (error of measurement) from one occasion to the next.   The theories of motivation that were developed to explain particular reactions of animals to a stimulus situation (as measured by latency of response, its probability within a fixed interval, its magnitude, or choice) said essentially the same thing. For example, for those in the tradition of stimulus-response behavior theory (Hull, 1943; Spence, 1956), the proposal that the momentary effective reaction potential ($_sE_r$) expressed in behavior is a function of the product of Drive times Habit (analogous to the true score) and a random oscillation process has guided thinking about motivation of behavior for forty years. And among those in the tradition of Tolman and Lewin, who opted for a cognitive theory (as we also did in constructing the theory of achievement motivation), the resultant tendency expressed in behavior is attributable to the product of Expectancy of the consequence times Valence of the consequence and a similar random moment-to-moment oscillation that is attributable to momentary variations in the strength of Expectancy, or degree of certainty, according to Cartwright and Festinger's (1943) formal statement.

To see the similarity to which I am calling attention, one must think of individual differences in level of intellective performance on a so-called intelligence, ability, or aptitude test as analogous to individual differences in the level of maze performance (as measured by time and errors) in a sample of animals. The consensus of theoretical opinion in scientific psychology is that the mental tester's interpretation of the meaning of test scores has never expressed a deep understanding of the distinction between the effect of *learning* (whether conceived as a habit, a cognitive expectancy, or an ability) and *performance*. The latter refers to behavior that is observed and measured and that is always influenced by individual differences in other variables that affect the immediate motivational state. In animal research, it has long been known that one can study the effects of learning experience on ability to solve the puzzle of the maze only by holding constant the motivational state, the other determinant of performance. One cannot identify what one is *able* to do by what one *does* unless there is a motive and an incentive to express the ability in overt action. That was the dramatic and significant point of the latent learning research of the 1920s and 1930s (Tolman, 1951). And the famous Hullian equation, $_sE_r = (f)D x_sH_r$, specifically states what the experimental evidence then required. Variations in either the motivational state (then conceived as drive) or in the ability (then conceived as habit strength) are completely confounded determinants of performance unless one has experimentally controlled one or the other variable.

If mental testers had this distinction between learning and performance clearly in mind (something I doubt), they could not jump so easily from observed variance among people in intellective performance in a stressful social situation to the inference of directly corresponding variance in ability (that correspondence blurred only by random error of measurement). To make this leap, given the generally accepted distinction between what has been learned and what is done, requires one or more of the following assumptions: (1) Individuals do not differ in the strength of motivation to perform well when taking a test; (2) they do differ in motivation, but conditions have somehow been arranged to remove the behavioral effects of those differences; (3) they do differ in motivation, but motivation has no important influence on their behavior. None of these assumptions can be justified.

Recent statements about the meaning of declining college aptitude test scores in America by spokesmen for testing (College Board, 1977) suggest that the learning-performance distinction may be appreciated but that it is not given any special emphasis because it is presumed that both high ability and strong motivation will always tend to enhance both intellective performance and academic achievement. So even if the two determinants are utterly confounded, both horses should at least be pulling in the same direction. Since there is more interest in the predictive validity of tests than in understanding what is going on, the importance of the disturbing matter is minimized.

In fact, however, the problem of confounding individual differences in ability and in strength of motivation has come to assume increasing importance not only to theoreticians but also to various segments of society who see tests as a barrier to achieving their desired goals. They do not understand why the tests are required or why they do not do better on them, but they want to improve. They do not necessarily use the words *motivation* and *ability*, but these concepts are crucial to dealing with their concerns.

The relationship between strength of motivation and efficiency of performance (that is, how adequately one expresses one's true ability in performance) is curvilinear and best described by an

inverted U-shaped curve (Atkinson, 1974b). The level of performance increases as strength of motivation at the time of performance
increases up to a certain point; beyond the point of optimal motivation there is a performance decrement. This is not a new idea. I
come to it as the most tenable generalization about how strength of
motivation influences the level of performance much later than
others (Yerkes and Dodson, 1908; McClelland, 1951; Eysenck,
1966b; Hebb, 1972; Broadhurst, 1959; Birch, 1945; Vroom, 1964;
Duffy, 1962).

Eysenck (1966a) quite correctly called attention to my having
ignored the Yerkes-Dodson law completely in the first edition of my
text on motivation (Atkinson, 1964). At that point, however, the
problem had simply not come up in the mainstream of the conceptual analysis of motivation that finally produced the mechanistic and
cognitive alternatives of Hull on the one side and Tolman and Lewin
on the other. And our own research on behavioral effects of
individual differences in achievement motivation had not yet
reached the point of being able to arouse such strong motivation in
some people experimentally as to make the idea of an overmotivation decrement in level of performance obvious or credible. Since
then we have improved the sensitivity of our experiments. And we
have sufficient reason to be confident of our conception of the
determinants of the strength of motivation to take seriously our own
cumulative evidence that finally catches up with the earlier proposal
of others who have worked with lower animals, analyzed the function of the brain, and studied the efficiency of human behavior
(Atkinson, 1974b; Atkinson and Birch, 1978). All these approaches
have found that the relationship between strength of motivation and
efficiency of performance is curvilinear.

Ability and Efficiency

Recall my earlier quotation of Lewin's statement concerning
general laws and individual differences as I now state a provisional
law about the relationship between intellective ability in a person and
the level of intellective performance that we observe, measure, and
so often mistakenly refer to as intelligence, ability, or aptitude: Level
of Performance equals Ability times Efficiency.

Here is another provisional law, shown graphically on the left side of Figure 1, concerning how intensity of motivation in an individual at the time of performance influences the efficiency of performance (for whatever reason). And on the right side of the figure we see the implications of the utter confounding of individual differences in ability and immediate motivational effects on level of intellective performance — a confounding that has existed since Binet's great innovation, the so-called intelligence test.

When we bring the measurement of intelligence into the orbit of the more general explanatory theories of psychology, as I am now doing, we do not change the predictive utility of our present tests. Rather, we change our understanding of what intelligence tests measure. And, most important, we enhance the sophistication of our discussion with the general public about what differences in test scores may mean.

So far, for example, the debate about racial differences in average intelligence test scores has belabored the issue of nature versus nurture, the problem of developmental psychology as it is summarized in the equation $P = f(H,E_f)$. It is appalling that the issue of whether differences in ability are genetically determined should take center stage since, prior to wondering about the antecedents of ability, we must address the question of whether the observed difference in performance is attributable to a difference in ability or to a difference in strength of motivation (and therefore in efficiency) at the time of the intellective performance.

It is a humbling experience to confront the general public and to say we don't know if this is a difference in ability (however determined) or in motivation (however determined). It is even conceivable, and consistent with experimental evidence, that a particular social group scoring lower on an intelligence test than another group is both superior in ability to and much more highly motivated than the other group. The group may be so highly motivated to perform well that its intellective performance is very inefficient. If this seems incredible, I ask you to recall the last time your favorite Olympic skater fell in the final competition, or the expert skier tumbled and broke a leg. It is also a humbling experience not to know how to interpret a difference in intelligence test scores, more so when we recognize that the real cause of our failure

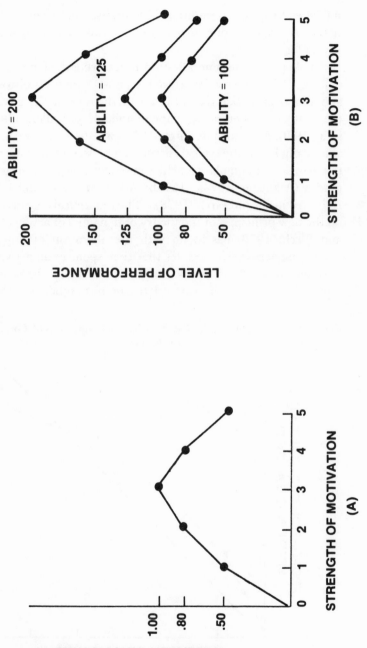

Figure 1. Effect of Strength of Motivation on (A) Efficiency of Performance and (B) Level of Performance.

must be attributed to traditional blindness, indifference, or unjusti-
fiable arrogance in one or both of "the two scientific disciplines of
psychology."

Applying the generalization about strength of motivation and
efficiency of performance, as well as another theoretical conclusion
about motivation that is consistent with the *matching law* advanced in
the context of operant behavior in animals (deVilliers and Herrnstein, 1976; Atkinson and Birch, 1978, pp. 364–366), we have been
able to dig below the typical correlation between scholastic aptitude
test scores and cumulative achievement in college as measured by
grades (Atkinson, 1974a, 1974b; Atkinson, Lens, and O'Malley,
1976; Atkinson and Birch, 1978). The theoretical conclusion based
on the new principles of the theory of dynamics of action (Atkinson
and Birch, 1970) has to do with the allocation of time among
competing activities. It states that time spent in an activity — for
example, in academic work — will depend upon the strength of
motivation for academic work relative to the number and strength of

**Figure 2. Effect of Strength of Motivation on Proportion of Time Spent in
an Activity.**

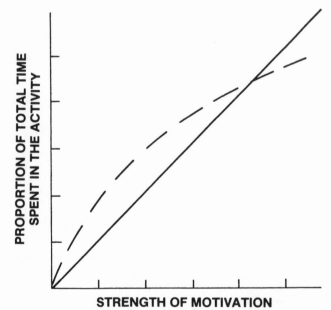

PROPORTION OF TOTAL TIME
SPENT IN THE ACTIVITY

STRENGTH OF MOTIVATION

motivational tendencies for other competing, time-consuming activities. The relationship is shown in Figure 2. Computer simulations based on current theory show this to be a negatively accelerated function (dashed line). Linearity is assumed for the sake of simplicity.

Motivation and Test Scores

Armed with these two generalizations about how motivation influences behavior, one may construct a simple arithmetical model of what is going on to determine both test scores (that is, intellective performance in a situation providing the strongest incentives) and achievement in the long run at college. Table 1 is a brief version of the analysis I accomplished while a participant in the American College Test Research Institute a few years ago. It is presented in more detail elsewhere (Atkinson, 1974a, 1974b; Atkinson, Lens, and O'Malley, 1976; Atkinson and Birch, 1978). The individuals in the table, who are all hypothetical, were created so as to differ in ability and independently in motivation (and therefore in efficiency) at the time of the important diagnostic test. Notice how the level of test performance departs from the true level of ability when inefficiency attributable to undermotivation or overmotivation at the time of performance is taken into account. On the right side of Table 1 it is assumed that the arousal of motivation in everyone is one unit less during normal college work than at the time of the critically important test. The individuals differ in motivation, as before, but the average level of motivation is weaker. Note how the change in motivation produces a change in efficiency. Subject A4, who suffered from inefficiency while taking a scholastic aptitude test, is now optimally motivated and perfectly efficient at college, so the level of intellective performance is higher than when he was taking the test. There are other changes; A3, the test-taking star, is now less motivated and less efficient and so performs less well.

Finally, in the last three columns of Table 1 there is another provisional law: *Cumulative achievement is the product of level of performance (while engaged in academic work) and the time spent in academic work.* Time spent is here represented as linearly related to the strength of motivation. The cumulative achievement (the simple

Table 1. Ability and Motivation as Determinants of Level of Intellective Performance and Cumulative Academic Achievement.

Name of subject[a]	Ability Test Situation				Normal Everyday Conditions				
	True ability	Motivation	Efficiency	Level of test performance	Motivation	Efficiency	Level of performance	× Time spent in work	= Cumulative achievement
A3	100	3	1.00	100	2	.80	80	2	160
B3	90	3	1.00	90	2	.80	72	2	144
A2	100	2	.80	80	1	.50	50	1	50
A4	100	4	.80	80	3	1.00	100	3	300
C3	80	3	1.00	80	2	.80	64	2	128
B2	90	2	.80	72	1	.50	45	1	45
B4	90	4	.80	72	3	1.00	90	3	270
C2	80	2	.80	64	1	.50	40	1	40
C4	80	4	.80	64	3	1.00	80	3	240

Note: In this hypothetical numerical illustration, it is assumed that all students are more strongly motivated (+1) when taking a test than under normal everyday conditions.

[a] Subjects are named according to their true level of ability (A = 100, B = 90, C = 80) and their strength of motivation in the ability test situation.

Based on Atkinson, 1974a.

product of level of performance and time spent) represents the cumulative achievement, which is the basis for the college grade average of each student.

This simple table is a model of more complete analyses with larger hypothetical samples and various assumptions about the initial correlation between ability and strength of motivation in the subjects (Sawusch, 1974; Atkinson, 1974b; Atkinson, Lens, and O'Malley, 1976). According to this type of analysis, the *expected* linear correlation between intellective test and cumulative achievement should fall somewhere in the range of .33 to .45. This corresponds so closely to the range of approximately .30 to .50 reported by the testing agencies (Angoff, 1971, p. 129; American College Testing Program, 1973, Vol. 1, p. 178) that we have the satisfying sense of having brought an important new perspective to mental testing.

Table 1, however, also says something new and different about the disturbing decline in the scholastic aptitude test scores of American college entrants since the mid 1960s. Acknowledge the utter confounding of ability and motivational determinants in intellective performance. Then assume that there has been no change in ability since the mid 1960s but rather an intensification of motivation during the period of the declining trend in test scores. Let subject B3 represent the average student of a decade ago and B4 the average student of today. Quite obviously, there has been a decline in test scores. But now look at the cumulative college achievement of B3 and B4 that would be recorded in the grade average in the extreme right column. Grades go up as the test scores decline! It is a powerful deduction, one that handles two facts — the correspondence of declining test scores and so-called grade inflation — in a single breath.

This kind of argument is the product of thirty fruitful years of research on human motivation. Yet, so far it has failed to raise a spark of interest in the mental test establishment. But it must, for society demands a more enlightened discussion of what mental testing is all about. It is time for us to achieve the proper integration of the traditional statistical framework of mental testing with a new, advanced motivational psychology. To dig below a correlation and to explain what is going on to produce the correlation is equivalent to spelling out why lightning always produces thunder.

The habitual toleration of the simplicity of the traditional account of the meaning of test scores must be challenged. As I have noted elsewhere: "The stakes have become too high. It is apparent that we now have more and better theory of motivation than we have ever had of intelligence. Today any measured difference in what has been called general intelligence, scholastic aptitude, or ability, which is always obtained from performance under highly achievement-oriented conditions, can be given a motivational interpretation with no less scientific justification than the traditional aptitudinal interpretation" (Atkinson, 1974b, p. 395).

The time for conceptual unification of our discipline is now. It requires a complete and coherent social psychology to explain thoroughly what happens during mental measurement. Motivational and developmental psychology are its major paradigms; statistical analysis alone is not enough.

References

American College Testing Program. *Assessing Students on the Way to College: Technical Report for the ACT Assessment Program.* Vol. 1. Iowa City, Iowa: American College Testing Program, 1973.

Angoff, W. H. (Ed.). *The College Board Admissions Testing Program: A Technical Report on Research and Development Activities Relating to the Scholastic Aptitude Test and Achievement Tests.* New York: College Board, 1971.

Atkinson, J. W. *An Introduction to Motivation.* New York: D. Van Nostrand, 1964.

Atkinson, J. W. "Motivational Determinants of Intellective Performance and Cumulative Achievement." In J. W. Atkinson and J. O. Raynor (Eds.), *Motivation and Achievement.* New York: Halsted, 1974a.

Atkinson, J. W. "Strength of Motivation and Efficiency of Performance." In J. W. Atkinson and J. O. Raynor (Eds.), *Motivation and Achievement.* New York: Halsted, 1974b.

Atkinson, J. W., and Birch, D. *The Dynamics of Action.* New York: Wiley, 1970.

Atkinson, J. W., and Birch, D. "The Dynamics of Achievement-Oriented Activity." In J. W. Atkinson and J. W. Raynor (Eds.), *Motivation and Achievement.* New York: Halsted, 1974.

Atkinson, J. W., and Birch, D. *An Introduction to Motivation.* (Rev. ed.) New York: D. Van Nostrand, 1978.

Atkinson, J. W., and Feather, N. T. (Eds.). *A Theory of Achievement Motivation.* New York: Wiley, 1966.

Atkinson, J. W., and Lens, W. "Fähigkeit und Motivation als Determinanten Momentaner und Kumulativer Leistung." In H. Heckhausen (Ed.), *Fähigkeit und Motivation in Erwartungswidriger Schulleistung.* Göttingen: Hogrefe, 1980.

Atkinson, J. W., Lens, W., and O'Malley, P. M. "Motivation and Ability: Interactive Psychological Determinants of Intellective Performance, Educational Achievement, and Each Other." In W. H. Sewell, R. M. Hauser, and D. L. Featherman (Eds.), *Schooling and Achievement in American Society.* New York: Academic Press, 1976.

Atkinson, J. W., and Raynor, J. O. (Eds.). *Motivation and Achievement.* New York: Halsted, 1974.

Atkinson, J. W., and Raynor, J. O. *Personality, Motivation, and Achievement.* New York: Halsted, 1978.

Barker, R. G. *The Stream of Behavior.* New York: Appleton-Century-Crofts, 1963.

Birch, H. G. "The Role of Motivational Factors in Insightful Problem Solving." *Journal of Comparative Psychology,* 1945, *38,* 295–317.

Broadhurst, P. L. "The Interaction of Task Difficulty and Motivation: The Yerkes-Dodson Law Revived." *Acta Psychologica,* 1959, *16,* 321–338.

Cartwright, D., and Festinger, L. "A Quantitative Theory of Decision." *Psychological Review,* 1943, *50,* 595–621.

College Board. *On Further Examination: Report of the Advisory Panel on the Scholastic Aptitude Test Score Decline.* New York: College Board, 1977.

Cronbach, L. J. "The Two Disciplines of Scientific Psychology." *American Psychologist,* 1957, *12,* 671–684.

de Groot, A. D. *Methodology: Foundations of Inference and Research in the Behavioral Sciences.* The Hague: Mouton, 1969.

deVilliers, P. A., and Herrnstein, R. J. "Toward a Law of Response Strength." *Psychological Bulletin,* 1976, *83,* 1131–1153.

Duffy, E. *Activation and Behavior.* New York: Wiley, 1962.

Eysenck, H. J. "Historical and Integrative: A Review of *An Intro-*

duction to Motivation by J. W. Atkinson." *Contemporary Psychology,* 1966a, *11,* 122–126.

Eysenck, H. J. "Personality and Experimental Psychology." *British Psychological Society Bulletin,* 1966b, *19*(62), 1–28.

Hebb, D. O. *Textbook of Psychology.* (3rd ed.) Philadelphia: Saunders, 1972.

Hull, C. L. *Principles of Behavior.* New York: Appleton-Century-Crofts, 1943.

Lewin, K. "Behavior and Development as a Function of the Total Situation." In L. Carmichael (Ed.), *Manual of Child Psychology.* New York: Wiley, 1946.

McClelland, D. C. *Personality.* New York: William Sloane, 1951.

Sawusch, J. R. "Computer Simulation of the Influence of Ability and Motivation on Test Performance and Cumulative Achievement and the Relation Between Them." In J. W. Atkinson and J. O. Raynor (Eds.), *Motivation and Achievement.* New York: Halsted, 1974.

Sears, R. R. "Personality." In P. R. Farnsworth and Q. McNemar (Eds.), *Annual Review of Psychology.* Vol. 1. Stanford: California Annual Reviews, 1950.

Spence, K. W. *Behavior Theory and Conditioning.* New Haven, Conn.: Yale University Press, 1956.

Thorndike, E. L. *Animal Intelligence.* New York: Macmillan, 1911.

Tolman, E. C. *Collected Papers in Psychology.* Berkeley: University of California Press, 1951.

Vroom, V. H. *Work and Motivation.* New York: Wiley, 1964.

Yerkes, R. M., and Dodson, J. D. "The Relation of Strength of Stimulus to Rapidity of Habit Formation." *Journal of Comparative and Neurological Psychology,* 1908, *18,* 459–482.

3   Jan J. Elshout

જી જી જી જી જી જી જી જી જી જી જી જી જી

Is Measuring Intelligence Still Useful?

The question I want to raise here is whether the various abilities measured by our tests of intelligence are useful in and of themselves. For example, an acceptable test item for four- and five-year-old children would require them to name the fingers of one hand in an arbitrary order indicated by the examiner. Is this a useful ability in itself (or a part of such an ability)? From the literature on early reading we know that the level on which the child performs this simple task is the single most valid predictor of progress in learning to read. Does this mean that finger-naming ability functions as an *aid* or *tool* (Cattell, 1972) in learning to read? Or, as a general alternative hypothesis, have we here just a *correlational indicator*? In operational terms, would it *help* for the teacher to bring all children to the same acceptable level on this finger-naming skill before starting formal reading instruction?

Many enrichment programs intended to better the educational potential of small children from economically depressed families have been designed with the conviction that interventions like this do help. In many of them, a direct attempt is made to enlarge the vocabulary of the children and thus to take advantage of the well-known high positive relationship between verbal comprehension and school achievement. These attempts generally succeed in the short term and fail in the longer term; after the children have gone for some years without special instruction, both their verbal comprehension and educational achievement are back to control-group levels. Somehow the predicted sequence—better word knowledge leading to better verbal comprehension leading to better reading and understanding generally—fails to occur.

From this unhappy fact some would draw the conclusion that the question we started out with has already been answered—in the negative: The skills and knowledge typically measured by intelligence tests do not in themselves have value as tools for further development. However, I do not think the facts are sufficient to close the matter at this point. For one thing, the generally very low correlations between test scores of young children in successive years do not support the optimistic causal reasoning that launched this type of intervention. At the ages of two to five, present capabilities, whether enlarged by manipulation or not, have little influence on *future* abilities compared to other influences.

Classical Conceptions of Intelligence

Originally, intelligence was never meant to be equated with the skills and knowledge that a test in fact measures. Had writers such as Galton, Spearman, and Burt been familiar with contemporary jargon, they presumably would have agreed with the position that the construct of intelligence pertains to the characteristics of our human hardware that together form the necessary condition for all intelligent—correct, adaptable, and efficient—information processing. Intelligence in this classical sense is thus a matter of potential, not a tool or an instrument. As a concept it is comparable, say, to maximal aerobic capacity, that is, to our body's capacity to use oxygen. Hebb (1950) coined the term *Intelligence A* for this construct. However, holding this basic classical view does not preclude our examining what tests of intelligence do in fact directly measure; for instance, word knowledge *may* be useful to the individual. Indeed it was R. B. Cattell, whom we may consider a neoclassicist on this subject, who introduced the terms *tool* and *aid* for the subject-matter-bound capabilities that tests measure. Together these capabilities make up what Hebb called *Intelligence B*.

In the classical view, what we may term the subject matter of an intelligence test was chosen primarily not because of its usefulness in the intellectual ecology but because of its instrumental qualities as an indicator of Intelligence A, the basic capacity for intellectual behavior. Intelligence in this sense cannot be measured directly and independently from performance (for example, by chemical analysis). To measure it, we must elicit some kind of performance from the human information-processing system (IPS). And in order to perform, an IPS needs software, that is, knowledge of various kinds, ranging from data structures to complex programs for handling these structures in various ways. Next, an IPS needs to be motivated, and it requires a task to perform.

From the outset it was recognized that the *indirect* measurement of intelligence is open to all kinds of obscuring influences. The "fathers" of the intelligence movement were not rationalists in the philosophical sense. They would never have subscribed to the notion that the major constructs and cognitive programs of our culture somehow are given in our genetic code. They were empiricists. To them intelligence was a broad capacity for intelligent information processing, and it played king to a number of other talents of a more specialized nature, such as musical ability, mathematical ability, a talent for poetry, and ability to handle people. On our way to adulthood, according to this view, our intelligence does not develop in the way a tulip bulb develops into a tulip. The capacity surely gets larger, but the more important thing is that it is *used* in the development of the knowledge and cognitive skills that make intelligent performance possible. R. B. Cattell says that intelligence is invested, and it is clear that for a profitable investment we need opportunity.

Modern versions of the classical view on the interplay of capacity and opportunity have been provided independently by Cattell (1972), Hunt (1976), and Simon (1976). Their accounts are strikingly similar. The level of intellectual performance *now* is seen as a joint function of qualities of the hardware and of the software (for example, knowledge and strategies) and of some other factors (for example, luck and motivation). Furthermore, the quality of the software that is used is a function of the quality of the hardware and the software at some earlier date, as well as of the opportunities afforded in the present.

Because it is clear that the opportunities to experience and to learn are not equal for all individuals and all intellectual subject matters, this historical view of the interplay between biologically given hardware and opportunity leads directly to the following principle of measurement: To measure capacity (Intelligence A), we should see to it that the conditions of equal opportunity are met. First, the testing situation should be arranged in a standard way so that all those being tested have an equal opportunity for reaching their levels of optimal performance.   Among other things, this means not testing subjects who are ill or who are not able to understand the instructions; it also means trying to keep test anxiety and test motivation within reasonably narrow bounds.   Second, in measuring intelligence, we should occupy ourselves exclusively with intellectual skills and knowledge that all persons in the relevant culture or age group have had an equal opportunity to acquire. Subjects who do not speak the language should be excluded; test items that ask for specialized knowledge should be avoided; and so on.

Constructing tests in accordance with these two selection rules drastically narrows the range of acceptable content or subject matter for tests of intelligence.   Psychology, subscribing to the principles of equal opportunity, had to turn to item types that measure invariants of our intellectual culture at each age level — invariants that may or may not be psychologically interesting in themselves (for example, naming fingers).   These merit the name of basic abilities.   I will argue later on that this drastic restriction, forced upon us by the aim of obtaining pure measures of a hypothetical capacity, was too high a price to pay, both in terms of practical validity and in terms of the scope and nature of the Intelligence B abilities that are in fact called upon by the tests.   In addition, the resulting total conceptual structure, combining a hypothetical explanatory biological construct with very restrictive selection rules (that are in essence sociological and not psychological), is very complex and abstract.   In my opinion, it is this very complexity that has been the prime source of the many problems and difficulties that have plagued the intelligence movement since its inception eighty years ago.   Intelligence, defined in the classical way, may be too difficult a concept for most of us.   Most of us indeed think of intelligence as being the ability to learn, solve problems, and handle language—a quality that differentiates the bright from the dull and is generally predictive of intellectual excellence. Most of us are wrong, then, because Intelligence A is of the nature of a capacity and not of an ability and because the abilities that *are* measured by the tests are either poor candidates for what *we* want or for what the definition wants. Let us start with the latter case.

Intelligence, Heritability, and Creativity

The unmanageability of the classical conception of intelligence and its measurement is obvious in the debate on the heritability of intelligence. Since Intelligence A is *defined* as a characteristic of our biological makeup, it is reasonable to expect the abilities measured by good tests of Intelligence A to have a high heritability index (h^2)—the higher the index, the better the test. What then do we make of tests with indices that approach zero? Torrance (1977) cites a number of studies that have found no hereditary variation for tests of visual or verbal divergent production (for example, fluency, originality, flexibility). In the same studies, tests of the more traditional comprehension type (only one answer correct) obtained indices in the .80s as is customary. If we accept the classical definition of intelligence, scientific logic forces us to conclude that tests of divergent production simply do not measure intelligence. This conclusion, however, should leave even the convinced hereditarian unhappy. There is nothing obvious about the exclusion of this type of test from the ranks of the "real" tests of intelligence.

Some form of divergent production task has been included from the start in most individually administered tests of intelligence, such as the Stanford-Binet. In Cattell's theoretical model, fluency has been given the status of one of the five g factors (retrieval fluency: g_r). Twenty percent of the factors in Guilford's structure-of-intellect model are concerned with divergent production. Tests of this nature also have reliability, and for suitable criteria (mostly to be found in the general area of "creative achievement") their validity is appreciable. Torrance (1977), for instance, reports validities in the .50s for his tests of creative thinking, with creative achievement twelve years after testing as the criterion. The traditional test of intelligence did not predict nearly as well. In my own work with research scientists, tests of visual, symbolic, and verbal fluency consistently were more valid (with coefficients in the .20 to .30 range) for a criterion of scientific productivity than were the more classical tests.

The conclusion still stands, however. Good tests of Intelligence A should have a high heritability index, but tests of creative ability do not meet this criterion. In fact, I cannot think of any worthwhile and interesting intellectual achievement that, from the classical point of view, would be acceptable as a measure of intelligence, that is, of the hardware capacity. From publishing poetry to obtaining a patent for some invention to triumphing over your tax man, the conditions for equal opportunity are never met. The exception to the rule is, of course, scholastic achievement. But then the very aim of compulsory schooling, standardized by societal controls, is to equalize opportunity for learning at the highest possible level. Burt (1973) was one of the first to remark on this general rule. His interest at the time was in the fact that intellectual attainments such as the number of books and articles published are variables with extremely skewed distributions, while intelligence as he conceived it is approximately normally distributed. To explain the skewness, Burt proposed the hypothesis that attainments are a multiplicative function of intelligence and other factors, such as interest. So in Burt's view, publishing rate, like most interesting intellectual achievements, is not a reliable indicator of the innate factor, intelligence. At the root of this highly unsatisfactory state of affairs lies, of course, the one-sided emphasis on a characteristic that can only be measured under the conditions of equal opportunity.

What the classical theory lacks is a *positive* definition of the domain of real-life abilities and performances from which indicators could be selected according to the principle of equal opportunity. The only thing we are given is a rough division between abilities that provide good testing material and others that do not. The first we usually call basic mental abilities or aptitudes, the second achievements. Where at first there was only a distinction in measurement potential, this terminology suggests also a psychological distinction, and there is nothing in classical theory to put that right.

Intelligence Tests Versus Achievement Tests

The confusion that this psychological distinction leads to is nowhere so manifest as in the discussion about which is more valid in educational prediction, intelligence or previous achievement. But this whole debate is pointless. At the primary-school level, with its uniformity of curriculum, the content of an intelligence test can stay very close to the content of the achievement test. The correlations between the two types of test typically are high, and at this level the intelligence test has a slight edge on the achievement test in predictive validity (Crano, Kenny, and Campbell, 1972). This is probably because the intelligence test includes problems that ask for skills less bound to the specific educational stage than are run-of-the-mill achievement items.

At the tertiary educational level, by contrast, the situation favors the achievement test. The curricula at this level are so diverse that the constructor of a general purpose test of intelligence is forced by the doctrine of equal opportunity to rely on material that is far removed from what is taught in the schools or, if it is taught or experienced, is of a nonspecific nature. In this situation, the intercorrelations between the two types of test tend to be lower, and achievement tests have the edge in predictive validity. Whichever type of test wins this contest, however, there is no reason to treat the intellectual abilities they are supposed to measure as being psychologically different. Knowledge of what causes rain, for instance, may or may not constitute a less generally applicable type of knowledge than the ability to trace hidden figures, but a difference in applicability is insufficient ground to conclude that there is a psychological difference. Range of applicability is a matter of social ecology, not of psychology. Still, it is the fashion to think of this distinction, which was made primarily for the purpose of better measurement, as one of far-reaching psychological importance. Those who speak of the Nature of Intelligence or the Structure of Intellect seem to concern themselves exclusively with the so-called basic abilities that are measured by types of problems able to pass the criterion of equal opportunity. Everyone seems convinced that types of problems that pass the social-ecological test of equal opportunity must, by that very fact, measure something psychologically basic. But proof is never given.

Abilities connected with types of problems that fail this social criterion are invariably thought of as Intelligence plus (or times) something else, the resulting composite being qualitatively different from its intelligence component. The psychological nature of this difference remains largely unexplicated, however. Intelligence theory, classical or modern, does not provide us with a framework for understanding complex abilities (for example, the ability to debug a computer program) in relation to the so-called basic abilities that are tapped by test items. Basic abilities are supposed to be useful only in acquiring the more complex and specialized intellectual skills or in contributing to subroutines within the larger whole. Neither relation, however, justifies thinking of complex abilities as being of a different psychological nature from the abilities that are called basic.

This is fortunate because not having to make a qualitative distinction frees us from the problem: we no longer have to define what intelligence tests measure as the ability to learn and to solve problems. As Gagné and Paradise (1961) have shown, in a stretch of accumulative learning the speed of acquiring a new capability depends most on the level achieved on previously acquired capabilities, basic or complex; the closer the old skills are to the new skill, in terms of transfer, the higher the correlation. The correlation of basic abilities with Intelligence B thus decreases with the increasing complexity of the skills acquired. So it is not intelligence that has the highest validity; rather, it is the most useful abilities. In my opinion, this description is of great generality; it describes the general form of the interrelations of all sorts of intellectual performances. Together with the notion of psychological continuity, it justifies taking leave from the classical position and accepting a new definition of intelligence. Thus, intelligence may be defined as the level of our actually useful abilities, basic or complex, general or specific, depending on the demands that characterize the situation. One may think of these most relevant, directly useful capabilities as being those that define what Vygotsky (1963) has called the "zone of proximal development." This zone consists of all the problems we are *just* able to solve, all learning tasks we are *just* able to manage with our present mental equipment, both software and hardware.

Toward Tests of Intelligence-Added

What does such a redefinition achieve? Implicit in the new definition is the view that tests of intelligence and tests of achievement are of the same kind, differing in the areas of ability they cover but not in the psychological nature of what they cover. The point is whether the new definition has anything to offer that would lead to better measurement and better understanding of the phenomena of brightness and dullness. At first glance, the formulation proposed seems to be at cross-purposes with recent research designed to analyze basic abilities (by a combination of experimental and correlational techniques) into constituents that may be considered the real invariants of the information-processing system. (See, for example, Sternberg, 1977, 1979; Hunt, 1976; Dansereau, 1969; Simon and Gilmartin, 1973; Gilmartin, Newell, and Simon, 1976.)

Should this endeavor succeed in uncovering really basic processes — that is, nonprogrammed processes of invariant form that are not learned and that have constant process times — this discovery would seem to be hard to reconcile with the notion of a continuum of abilities of varying usefulness for learning and problem solving. Indeed, the classical theory would have been proven correct, and the parameters found would define Intelligence A. And again, but now with better reason, it would be necessary to distinguish between tests that measure the invariants of our mental equipment (tests of intelligence, perhaps in new formats) and tests that measure the quality of hardware and software jointly (tests of achievement). As Simon (1976) has warned, however, the aims of the research mentioned may very well be too high. At least up until now no really basic processes have been uncovered and made testable. Personally, I doubt that they ever will be, my argument being that unprogrammed behavior does not exist and that behavior is all that a test can ever measure (Elshout, 1978). Even if the original goals of this line of inquiry prove to be out of reach, however, psychological task analysis within the joint framework of general cognitive psychology and the theory of individual differences has great promise. I would be glad if the proposed redefinition of intelligence simply drew the attention of the achievement-testing community to the possibilities of psychological achievement analysis.

For very good reasons, those who construct educational achievement tests have occupied themselves exclusively with the measurement of what courses are supposed to teach and students are supposed to learn. Predictive validity generally is of no concern, nor is the basis of better performance on the test after instruction. But if educational achievement is thought of as intelligence-added, it should be very interesting, both theoretically and practically, to broaden our concern and to try to determine in a psychologically analytical way what a person can do after a certain piece of instruction that he could *not* do before. This would call for the construction of a new type of achievement test to probe the new zone of proximal development that results from a particular instructional process. Such tests would very much resemble present-day tests of intelligence in their format, especially those of an experimental nature, but would unashamedly take as their subject matter the subject matter of the course.

To conclude, let me give an example. Suppose we want to evaluate the results of a course in chess. Presumably the students following this course would study the theory of move selection in opening, middle, and end games and would be given ample opportunity to practice in actual game situations, with and without help. A typical achievement test for this course would give the student the opportunity to show what he has learned both by stating it and by applying it in representative game situations. A test like this would have high content validity and would be judged fair both by those responsible for the course and by the students. The test would presumably also have rather high predictive validity, but that would not be our concern in this context. De Groot (1965) and Jongman (1968) have shown that the single most predictive indirect measure of a chess player's actual strength is the correctness of his reproduction of a game position that he has studied for five seconds only. It was also shown that this has nothing to do with some general perceptual short-term memory ability; the superiority of better players on this task is specific to chess.

What kind of test is this test of short-term memory for chess positions? Obviously it is not a test of intelligence in the classical sense, or any aspect thereof. It is not a work-sample test such as the ones that are sometimes used in industrial selection. And it is not an achievement test, because this task was not part of the curriculum. No, it is precisely what I had in mind earlier: a test of achieved intelligence. According to Jongman (1968) and Gilmartin, Newell, and Simon (1976), what it measures is the extent of the vocabulary of codes that a person has for coding recurring perceptual patterns on the board. To have a well-developed vocabulary of this kind facilitates the short-term memory performance — one remembers the codes and not the positions of the pieces one by one — but this is a side effect; more important is that to have such an extensive coding system obviously also directly facilitates the move selection process that *is* of great interest because that is where the strength of a player lies.

It should be clear that I do not propose to replace our current achievement tests with tests such as this. What I wanted to convey is that real-life intellectual achievement and performance permit the same kind of theory-oriented psychological analysis that has recently been applied to cognitive processes at the primary-factor level. Among other things, new measurement instruments will be needed for this endeavor — tests of intelligence-added. What they measure will surely be useful.

References

Burt, C. *Ability and Income.* In H. J. Eysenck (Ed.), *The Measurement of Intelligence.* Lancaster, England: Medical Technical Publishing, 1973.

Cattell, R. B. *Abilities: Their Structure, Growth, and Action.* Boston: Houghton Mifflin, 1972.

Crano, W. P., Kenny, I., and Campbell, D. T. Does Intelligence Cause Achievement? *Journal of Educational Psychology,* 1972, *63,* 258–275.

Dansereau, D. F. *An Information-Processing Model of Mental Multiplication.* Pittsburgh: Carnegie-Mellon University, 1969.

de Groot, A. D. *Thought and Choice in Chess.* The Hague: Mouton, 1965.

Elshout, J. J. "The Characteristic Demands of Intellectual Problems." In A. M. Lesgold and others (Eds.), *Cognitive Psychology and Instruction.* New York: Plenum, 1978.

Gagné, R., and Paradise, N. "Abilities and Learning Sets in Knowledge Acquisition." *Psychological Monographs,* 1961, *75* (518).

Gilmartin, K. J., Newell, A., and Simon, H. A. "A Program Modeling Short-Term Memory Under Strategy Control." In C. N. Cofer (Ed.), *The Structure of Human Memory.* San Francisco: W. H. Freeman, 1976.

Hebb, D. O. *The Organization of Behavior.* New York: Wiley, 1950.

Hunt, E. "Varieties of Cognitive Power," In L. B. Resnick (Ed.), *The Nature of Intelligence.* Hillsdale, N.J.: Erlbaum, 1976.

Jongman, R. W. *Het oog van de meester.* Amsterdam: van Gorcum, 1968.

Simon, H. A. "Identifying Basic Abilities Underlying Intelligent Performance of Complex Tasks." In L. B. Resnick (Ed.), *The Nature of Intelligence.* Hillsdale, N.J.: Erlbaum, 1976.

Simon, H. A., and Gilmartin, K. J. "A Simulation of Memory for Chess Positions." *Cognitive Psychology,* 1973, *5,* 534–546.

Sternberg, R. J. "Component Processes in Analogical Reasoning." *Psychological Review,* 1977, *84,* 353–378.

Sternberg, R. J. "The Nature of Mental Abilities." *American Psychologist,* 1979, *34,* 214–230.

Torrance, E. P. "Creatively Gifted and Disadvantaged Gifted Students." In J. C. Stanley, W. C. George, and C. H. Solano (Eds.), *The Gifted and the Creative: A Fifty-Year Perspective.* Baltimore, Md.: Johns Hopkins University Press, 1977.

Vygotsky, L. S. "Learning and Mental Development at School Age." In B. Simon and J. Simon (Eds.), *Educational Psychology in the U.S.S.R.* London: Routledge & Kegan Paul, 1963.

Part Two

૪૨ ૪૨ ૪૨ ૪૨ ૪૨ ૪૨ ૪૨ ૪૨ ૪૨ ૪૨ ૪૨ ૪૨

Setting
Performance
Standards

Capricious, malicious, irresponsible, tyrannical, and *respectably fraudulent* are some of the words that critics of educational testing have used to describe those who devise tests and set policy for their use. In the United States, according to one view, the well-known Educational Testing Service has the power to assign people to their places in education and society and to change the way they think about their potential.* And throughout the world, those with major testing responsibilities have not escaped the charge that they are playing God with the educational and career opportunities of their nations' youth.

Although the influence of tests and testers is exaggerated in the public mind, the chapters in this section indicate that testers take their responsibilities very seriously. Better adjectives to describe them would probably be *thoughtful, sensitive, cautious, cooperative,* and

* See A. Nairn and Associates, *The Reign of ETS: The Corporation that Makes Up Minds* (Washington, D.C.: Ralph Nader, 1980).

57

humble. No aspect of testing is more humbling than the experience of trying to set standards for admission to a "closed" course of study, to certify competency, or to award a license to practice an occupation or a profession.

The three authors approach the problem of performance standards from very different perspectives. In Chapter Four, Lorrie Shepard addresses standards out of her experience at the laboratory of educational research, University of Colorado, and provides a scholarly review of standard-setting techniques and applications. Albert Maslow, in Chapter Five, discusses the implications for educational assessment practices of standard setting in the areas of occupational licensing and professional certification. Willem Hofstee, author of Chapter Six, has been involved in policy research for the minister of education in the Netherlands in response to a mandate from the Dutch parliament to propose a satisfactory solution to the problem of admission to advanced professional studies.

In spite of their diversity in background and interests, the three authors reach a striking consensus about some of the major properties of the standard-setting enterprise:

First, standard setting is an awesome responsibility, involving as it does setting the criteria by which some individuals will be labeled competent or incompetent, passing or failing, admitted or rejected.

Second, setting standards is not, and should not be, exclusively a scientific undertaking. Value systems — and conflicts — lie at its heart. It is seldom that those who would "certify" and those who would be "certified" see eye to eye. Students want to obtain the diploma with minimum effort; faculty want to ensure that students learn something — and want to confirm their own indispensability. Licensing boards may be concerned with enhancing the image or status of the occupation; government regulatory agencies may be committed to protecting the public. Affirmative action, legal issues, and plain politics all come into play when the subject of standards is broached. Somehow such competing values must be compromised (in the best sense of that word).

Third, while the notion of standards carries with it yes-no decisions, human ability is not distributed in yes-no terms. Bimodal distributions appear in psychometric models but almost never occur with real cognitive variables. We do not have spellers and non-spellers; we have better spellers and worse spellers. We do not have people who can make it into top management in the company and those who cannot; we have people who are more likely to succeed as executives and those who are less likely to survive at corporate heights. The very standard-setting process flies in the face of these natural phenomena.

Fourth, judgment is the basic tool of standard setting, even in so-called empirical investigations. What should these students know and be able to do? How many trainees should we be prepared to accept? How well do these tests measure the traits we are interested in? Whom can we hold up as the exemplars of competence? Answers to such questions as these require judgment. Thus, the choice of judges and their experience and wisdom are crucial to the process.

Fifth, we know, however, that any group of judges is fallible. Teachers in the United States tend to set standards that are unrealistically high; perhaps it is a matter of overconfidence about their aptitude for intellectual persuasion, or perhaps they long for a world in which their specialties are appropriately recognized. According to Hofstee, teachers in Holland tend to set higher cutoffs for more difficult tests, lower cutoffs for easier ones. Somehow or other, test specialists must work to increase the consciousness, flexibility, and understanding of their judges.

Sixth, one of the problems that test specialists and their consultants alike face is the apparent impasse between normative and absolute standards. Once the gurus of educational measurement had insisted on making this distinction, their followers were unable to escape from it. But Shepard points out that all standards are inherently normative and that empirical data will make absolute deliberations better informed and more realistic. Both kinds of information are essential to satisfactory fulfillment of our obligations to select people appropriately and fairly.

Seventh, the aim of any standard-setting exercise is to reduce classification errors, that is, false positives (those who are identified as "winners" but become "losers") and false negatives (the "losers" who could have become "winners"). But the importance that one attaches to the two kinds of errors varies with the setting and the kinds of decisions to be made. It would carry a serious threat to society to certify a physician who was incompetent; it would be less serious for society, if not for the individual, to turn down a person who would have made a competent physician. However, an aspiring teacher with a score on the National Teachers Examination of 600 would not seem much more able than a candidate with a score of 580.

Eighth, some doubt is cast upon the concept of mastery learning *as defined by tests,* as a driving force for educational standard setting. Hofstee is dramatic on the point: "Taking an achievement test score as a criterion or standard is to confuse learning for life with learning for school." Shepard: "Adult competence . . . cannot be captured by lists of knowledge." Maslow (quoting Orlans): "It is naive . . . to believe that competence can be 'blocked into unit, objectively measurable skills and knowledge.'"

Ninth, no single measure is likely to capture the range of competencies and characteristics that are "standard worthy."

And, finally, no single standard-setting technique is sufficient unto itself, if the decisions based on the standard are of any moment.

If these ten properties are somewhat discouraging, read on. Shepard tells us how to borrow good standard-setting techniques from a variety of sources. Maslow sensitizes us to the elegance inherent in the standard-setting enterprise. And Hofstee introduces us to the innovation of the weighted lottery. While decisions about standards are arbitrary, they need not be unreasonable — or unexciting.

4

Lorrie A. Shepard

ℜ ℜ ℜ ℜ ℜ ℜ ℜ ℜ ℜ ℜ ℜ ℜ ℜ

Standards for Placement and Certification

When tests are used to verify that an individual knows enough to pass on to the next instructional topic or to be awarded a credential, the test-score interpretation requires the imposition of a test standard or cutoff score. The purpose of this chapter is to provide an overview of the issues that govern the adequacy of standard-setting methodology. The chapter includes a summary of the relevant psychometric literature, but its focus is not primarily statistical or technical. In fact, the single most important point to be made about choosing standards is that the crucial problems are not technical and will not have technical solutions.

There are already numerous reviews that afford detailed descriptions of specific models for setting standards (Glass, 1978b; Hambleton and Eignor, 1979; Hambleton, Powell, and Eignor, 1979; Jaeger, 1976; Millman, 1973; Meskauskas, 1976; Shepard, 1980a, 1980b). These authors have listed the dozens of standard-setting techniques, categorized them by their salient features, considered their sources of invalidity, and debated their applicability for different uses of criterion-referenced and competency testing. To avoid redundancy with earlier reviews, the present chapter focuses

Note: Portions of this chapter appeared in Shepard (1980a).

on the issues that emerged from these catalogues and remain unre-
solved. Major categories of methods are discussed with special
attention to the insights they provide for identifying mastery, but
individual methods are not presented in detail since this has been
done so extensively elsewhere.

Issues in Standard Setting

Standard setting will never be a true science because it requires a dichotomy between mastery and nonmastery that does not
exist in nature. As I have noted elsewhere, "Standards are choices,
not essences" (Shepard, 1976, p. 29). For all cognitive variables you
can think of, performance is continuous; therefore, there is no
identifiable point where success or mastery turns into failure. This
issue may seem obvious, one that is easily acknowledged and then
quickly dismissed as one pursues the more practical problem of
choosing such a point as a cutoff score. But it deserves to be stressed
since many of the more technical standard-setting methods convey a
false sense of scientific precision. They sometimes resemble statistical estimation techniques in providing a cutoff score that appears to
converge on a true parameter. This impression is inaccurate; all
such methods result in an artificial dichotomy on a continuum of
performance.

Glass's (1978b) review of standard-setting techniques is the
most severe. In his view all methods are arbitrary or rest on
arbitrary premises. Not only are the methods logically flawed, but
they are inconsistent and contradictory and will lead to very different standards and very different passing rates.

Glass calculated that the differences in standards in one study
(Andrew and Hecht, 1976) would mean differences of 95 percent
and 50 percent passing the test. More recent studies comparing
different combinations of methods confirm that different methods
produce different standards (Brennan and Lockwood, 1980;
Kleinke, 1980; Koffler, 1980; Skakun and Kling, 1980). Glass
concluded that the procedures were so fallible that standard setting
should be avoided altogether.

It has always been acknowledged that all standard setting is
judgmental (Hambleton, Powell, and Eignor, 1979; Jaeger, 1976,

1978; Popham, 1978; Shepard, 1976, 1979). Since Glass's paper, the nature of the debate has shifted to attempts to justify differences in methods and to defend the use of thoughtfully chosen standards. Thus, Hambleton (1978) responded to Glass by arguing that profound differences in standards set by different methods were not surprising since the different methods reflect different definitions of minimal competence. What Hambleton means is that techniques that are based on inspection of test content imply a different *operational* definition from those based on judgments about groups. Unfortunately, the various methods do not have correspondingly different *conceptual* definitions. They seek to reflect the same construct, not different constructs. Each method uses the terms *master* and *nonmaster* as if the definitions were interchangeable across methods. Except for differences in the numbers that come out, there is no way for the user to anticipate what philosophical or conceptual differences in the understanding of minimal competence will be reflected in the different operationalizations. These anomalies and inconsistencies will have to be considered in choosing among arbitrary methods.

Popham (1978) provided a different counter to Glass: There are two meanings for the word *arbitrary*. The fact that standards are judgmental does not mean that they are capricious. Popham argued that subjective judgments can be considered and wise. Furthermore, the standard-setting process can make these decisions public rather than leaving them hidden in the grading practices of individual teachers. Popham was especially advocating that defensible standards can be set for minimal competency testing programs for high school graduation. While it is true that educators will be more thoughtful about the meaning and consequences of standards if they go through formal procedures, two cautions should nevertheless be remembered. First, a great deal is at stake when high school graduation depends on passing a single test. Individual teachers make subjective errors in assigning passing grades, but it is very unlikely that an individual will fail high school because of a succession of five unfair F's. The second caution is that even very reasonable standards will not overcome the arbitrariness of artificial dichotomies; examinees immediately on either side of the cutting point will have very similar skills.

The final rebuttal to Glass was from Scriven (1978): Imperfect standards are better than none. This presumes that it is essential to make either-or classifications of individuals. As will be discussed later, it depends on the particular use of test standards whether the benefits of having arbitrary dichotomies will outweigh the costs.

Normative Versus Absolute Values. Standard-setting issues for competency or credentialing purposes are usually cast in an absolute rather than a relative framework. Glaser (1963) introduced criterion-referenced testing and distinguished it from norm-referenced testing. He rightly pointed out that normative interpretations tell only an individual's relative standing in a group. Percentile ranks are not informative for instructional purposes because they tell nothing about what a student actually knows or doesn't know. Criterion-referenced tests were intended to solve this problem by being more carefully articulated to a behavioral domain. In this way the questions a student can answer locate him at a specific learning level. The teacher can conclude, for example, that the student knows tasks *a* through *f* but must still study *g* through *j*.

At first those who extended Glaser's work emphasized that the most important feature of criterion-referenced measurement was that it imposed absolute standards rather than relying on relative comparisons (Popham and Husek, 1969; Millman, 1970). More recently, however, Glaser's original meaning has been reexamined, and it is now generally understood that the term *criterion* refers, not to a cutoff score, but to a criterion performance dimension (as in the external criterion for test validity). The distinguishing characteristic of criterion-referenced tests is the care taken in explicating and representing the intended behavioral domain (Glass, 1978b; Hambleton and others, 1978; Popham, 1975). Cutoff scores are needed for some but not for all applications of test results.

Once it is understood that the key aspect of criterion referencing is to locate examinees accurately on a performance continuum, it is possible to consider using normative data to give additional meaning to performance levels. In practice, however, there is a great deal of resistance to allowing norms to influence standards. The insistence on absolute standards is due partly to the original association between absolute standards and the diagnostic value of tests. A second reason for eschewing norms has nothing to do with test development practices; it is a belief that norms affirm the status quo. This abhorrence of norms has created problems for standard setters, however, because all standards are inherently normative. On any topic, in any performance area, our sense of what is excellent or impoverished performance is based on our experience with the range of possible performances. We expect sixth graders to do long division because most sixth graders have done it in the past. We expect secretaries to type better than 70 words per minute because norms have established this as a reasonably good speed. But our seemingly absolute standards would no doubt change drastically if the majority of applicants had speeds of 150 words per minute or better.

Most authors now recommend at least supplemental use of normative data in the standard-setting process (Conaway, 1979; Hambleton, Powell, and Eignor, 1979; Jaeger, 1978; Shepard, 1976, 1979). I have argued that since the "experience" judges rely on in setting acceptable performance levels involves nothing more than imperfect norms, providing them with normative data only ensures that they will be familiar with typical and representative samples (Shepard, 1979). This does not mean that judges must automatically accept some median value as the standard. Empirical data will make absolute deliberations better informed and more realistic. As will be noted later, normative data are like validity evidence that can be used to cross-check goals set on the basis of test content.

Quota-Free Versus Fixed-Quota Decisions. The distinction between normatively influenced standards and absolute standards is strongly intertwined with the difference between quota-free uses and fixed-quota uses of test results. These terms derive from Cronbach and Gleser's (1965) decision theory, which relates all aspects of test development and test interpretation to the specific decisions made from the test scores.

When quotas exist for a specific application, the selection of a cutoff is not arbitrary. One has only to rank candidates from highest to lowest score and count down from the top until the quota is filled. This type of passing score does not carry with it the implication that examinees on either side of the cutoff are verifiably different, that is, competent and incompetent. Conversely, when the test decision is quota free, an absolute standard is necessary. Standard setters may sometimes wish to escape the subjectivity of their task by converting the absolute decision to a quota situation. For example, Millman (1973) suggested that the amount of resources available for providing remediation should be considered in deciding how high to set the standard. Glass (1978b) proposed that the question of acceptable passing rates be considered directly rather than being allowed to vary accidentally as a function of a substantively chosen cutoff.

At the same time, the appeal of criterion-referenced measurement is that it allows greater justice than tests where a predetermined percentage will fail. In college admissions, for example, social values might better be served by choosing at random from the top 200 candidates to fill 100 positions. In this case the decision makers would be leaving the safety of a fixed-quota decision and making a judgment that the two hundreth candidate still has sufficient ability on the trait measured by the test. Such a policy could have the effect of increasing the representation of minority group members in the selected group without altering the success rate of graduates.

Most test-based decisions will not be strictly fixed quota or quota free. The standard-setting procedures in most situations will probably require a balance of the two perspectives. For example, college admissions officers with a quota may admit an unusually large class because so many qualified applicants appear just at the cutoff point (see Shepard, 1980a). Their "absolute" sense of the quality of these candidates might be especially strong if they knew that in previous years the same characteristics would have placed these candidates much higher in the distribution of applicants. The relative emphasis to be given to the quota or the absolute judgment is essentially the same dilemma to be resolved in deciding whether normative or absolute comparisons are more compelling. If a standard were set a priori on the basis of test items and half the class from the best medical school failed, we would distrust the standard. Consider, however, a school district where students are equal to the state average in math but below it in reading. Parents unaware of this discrepancy might well set reading standards that fail a surprisingly large number of students.

Test Uses. In previous work (Shepard, 1980a, 1980b) I have proposed that the adequacy of standard-setting methodology depends on test purpose, just as the validity of a test depends on how it is used (American Psychological Association. . . , 1974; Cronbach, 1971). Three different uses have been identified that are distinct enough to affect the validity of the dichotomous interpretations made from the test cutoff score: pupil placement decisions in the classroom, certification of individuals, and program evaluation.

In the classroom, tests are used for diagnostic purposes. Various approaches to objectives-based instruction, including mastery learning (Bloom, 1968, 1971; Block, 1971) and individually prescribed instruction (Glaser, 1968; Lindvall and Bolvin, 1967), involve testing to decide whether a student is ready to go on to the next topic or needs further instruction. The features of competency testing in a classroom setting are that (1) testing is proximal to the instructional decision; (2) the test content covers only those objectives for which the teacher is uncertain of the pupil's mastery; and (3) classification errors are not very serious and are easily corrected.

Certification uses of criterion-referenced or competency tests include professional licensure examinations and proficiency tests required for high school graduation. Although high school competency programs with remediation classes may resemble mastery-learning instructional programs, the tests still serve primarily a credentialing function. Certification tests are distinguished from diagnostic tests in that (1) testing is distant from the instructional use (at the end of the year or the end of the course of study); (2) test coverage must be comprehensive, that is, representative of the full certification domain; and (3) errors are more costly and less easily redressed, because so much rests on the result of a single test.

Program evaluation uses of test results involve judging the effectiveness of an educational program on the basis of aggregated scores from pupils participating in it. In contrast to the use of testing for individual placement or certification, reports of group performance for program evaluation do not require dichotomous classifications of individual pupils. When standards are used to reflect the achievement levels for an entire school or program, a great deal of information is lost. For example, knowing that 60 percent of the students "passed" a reading test does not tell us how much the best students know, only what the minimally passing students know. Furthermore, as soon as educators try to interpret whether 60 percent is a creditable showing or a very poor one, they find that the value of this result depends very much on the difficulty of the material, the stringency of the standard, and how effective other programs have been with the same type of student. Because dichotomous classifications are not essential for this purpose, other more interpretable ways of reporting results will be recommended.

Nature of the Criterion. The success of standard-setting methods will also depend on the nature of the trait being measured by the test. Although it will always be difficult to say how much knowledge is sufficient in a given area, identifying a cutoff point on a continuum is even more perplexing when the continuum is poorly defined and only crudely measured. Some standard-setting methods that require matching test results to criterion performance are simply not applicable in instances where a criterion (other than the test itself) cannot be specified. This is true for high school graduation tests currently being implemented in the United States. Both Linn (1979) and Madaus (1978) describe the enormous validity difficulties that would be encountered if competency scores were expected to predict successful adult functioning. Jaeger (1978) and Hambleton, Powell and Eignor (1979) fault numerous decision-theoretic models for setting cutoffs on competency tests because the models presume that the fundamental problem of defining a "competent" high school graduate has already been solved. Much of the intensity of arguments by Glass (1978b) and Burton (1978) against ever setting standards comes not just from the artificiality of the classifications but also from the impossibility of identifying just what combination of skills is essential for a successful and happy life.

The more that the content of a test is limited to circumscribed academic skills, the more likely it is that the trait measured by the test can be well understood and delineated. We can most easily demonstrate content validity for basic skills tests of academic achievement, though even here there are inferences made about underlying constructs such as "comprehension" and "problem-solving ability." The content of professional licensure examinations is also more clearly understood than "adult competence"; but, even more than with basic skills, there will be aspects of professional expertise that cannot be captured by lists of knowledge. For example, as Tukey (1977, p. 682) has said, "Medical and surgical practice have always depended more on skilled professional opinion than on knowledge." The adequacy of standard-setting techniques will depend on the particular purpose of the test and on the test's construct validity. When the ability to be measured by the test is elusive, standard setters will find that the cutoff score problem merges with ambiguities in defining test content.

Standard-Setting Methods

Different methods of setting standards result in different standards. No single method can be viewed as the most valid or logically correct. All methods are fallible because, when performance is continuous, there is no true dichotomy for the methods to approximate. Therefore, it is more appropriate to consider standard-setting methods as strategies for thinking about what the cutoff score should be. Different methods provide different insights to improve our judgments.

Standards Based on Judgments of Test Content. The only way to set an absolute standard is to examine the test content and decide which questions a "passing" candidate must know. Given the emphasis on absolute standards for criterion-referenced tests, the most obvious and widely used standard-setting methods are those that facilitate inspection of test content. This approach is especially satisfying when judges can point to a specific item and say, "It is absolutely essential that every doctor know that insulin should not be administered to a patient who is in insulin shock." Usually, however, each item is not so clearly mandatory, and competence will be reflected in adequate performance on an acceptable proportion of the items. The various judgmental methods are strategies for assigning probabilities to items that will lead to an overall proportion of correct answers that are acceptable.

Perhaps the most straightforward technique for inspecting test content is the Angoff (1971) approach. When using this method as well as other judgmental methods, standard setters are asked to imagine a minimally qualified individual. A mental picture of what skills the just-barely-passing candidate must have is necessary whether the test is meant to certify high school graduates or medical doctors. Even masters of a topic will make a small number of errors, and judges must have an image of such an individual that differs from their image of the person whose error rate is indicative of nonmastery. Examples will help develop these images. Judges might, for example, think that the mistakes they themselves make are consistent with mastery. But, in the mind's eye, there is a point where the errors become too numerous to excuse, and the judge says to herself, "The individual with this score is similar to the obvious incompetent, the illiterate, or the physician who unwittingly administers lethal drugs."

The validity of judgmentally set standards depends on the definition of the minimally qualified examinee. Discussion with, and training of, the judges can increase the amount of thought that is given to the problem and improve the agreement among judges. Of course, there is still no way to remove either the subjectivity of this crucial definitional stage or the variability in judges' operational definitions. The subjectivity of this process is both its strength and its weakness. By ignoring normative data, the judges are able to assert what should be rather than what is. At the same time, the many different standards that are produced by the different expectations of the judges make all their separate standards defensible; hence, there are always challenges or alternatives to the final cutoff point.

Once judges have defined mastery, then using the Angoff method they read all the test items and assign each one a probability value. The probability value is a subjective estimate of the likelihood that the just-barely-qualified person will answer correctly. The sum of all test-item probabilities becomes the cutoff score. So, for example, if a judge thinks that a minimally competent individual will have an 80-percent chance on each of ten items, the passing score on the test will be eight.

Other methods provide standard setters with slightly more complicated formulas for weighing item difficulty. The Nedelsky (1954) method is the oldest procedure and is still widely used, especially in the health professions. Judges arrive at item probabilities indirectly by eliminating the wrong choices that they believe a minimally competent individual would know are clearly wrong and then applying a correction-for-guessing formula. Using the Nedelsky procedure creates some practical problems because the task of eliminating wrong choices is unfamiliar to most judges. Furthermore, in new competency-testing programs, with content curtailed to test only for minimal skills, judges might feel that *all* the distracters should seem clearly wrong to the minimally competent examinees or that they will be guessing between the correct answer and the next best answer. Because the Nedelsky procedure limits the probabilities to discrete steps (see Brennan and Lockwood, 1980), the resulting standard will either be an unrealistic 100 percent (eliminate all the wrong answers with certainty) or a very generous 50 percent. Empirical studies have found consistently that the Nedelsky procedure produces lower standards than do other methods based on judgments of test content (Andrew and Hecht, 1976; Brennan and Lockwood, 1980; Kleinke, 1980; Koffler, 1980; Skakun and Kling, 1980).

The Ebel (1972) method for deciding on standards is like the Angoff approach, with the additional complexity that judges are first asked to categorize items by relevance and difficulty. This particular categorization scheme tends to break down in practice because the dimensions tend to be correlated in the judges' minds; that is, they think everyone should know a highly relevant item. However, some sorting procedure is recommended since consistent probabilities can then be assigned to clusters of items similar in importance and difficulty. For example, when implementing the Angoff method with the National Teachers Examination, the Educational Testing Service (1976) asked judges to locate items on a probability continuum.

All the judgment methods are commonsense approaches for wrestling with the standard-setting task. The Angoff procedure is favored here primarily because it is simpler than other methods. Simplicity has the advantage of not obscuring the basic subjectivity of the decisions; judges more clearly have the sense that they are pulling the probabilities from thin air. This uneasiness is essential for dealing properly with the limited validity of the cutoff score.

Glass's (1978b) indictment of standard-setting techniques was based not only on their subjectivity but also on the serious discrepancies in the standards they produced. A more fundamental problem is the disagreement among individual judges even when the same approach is used. In a recent work (Shepard, 1980a), I offered the following advice for coping with the threat to validity implied by extreme ranges in judges' standards: First, ensure that different value positions and areas of expertise are systematically represented when judges are impaneled. This is more important for high school competency programs than for classroom tests or professional certification examinations, because in the first instance the issues are political and there are more relevant audiences who hold stakes in the testing process (see Jaeger, 1978; Shepard, 1976, 1979). Second, rather than hide variability with the group average, collect evidence on important differences of opinion and consider their significance for validity. Brennan and Lockwood (1980) suggested a reconciliation procedure in which judges would meet and arrive at a final standard. In this way the reason for choosing a particular version of the standard would become more explicit. In Kleinke (1980), the judge who specialized in a particular area had the greatest weight; for the North Carolina high school competency test, Jaeger (1978) advised that the final standard be the lowest one set by groups representing different constituencies.

The final recommendation for dealing with subjective and varied standards is to collect validity evidence. Several of the methods that follow can be thought of as alternative strategies for providing different insights into the problem of standards *or* as strategies to check on the reasonableness of cutoffs established by a logical study of the test.

Standards Based on Empirical Validation. Judgments based on test content may be internally inconsistent; sometimes they may also be obviously wrong. This happens when many individuals we believe are competent fail a test (or conversely, when no one fails the test, but we know there were nonmasters present). Schoon, Gullion, and Ferrara (1979) noted the tendency of experts to set minimum levels that are unrealistically high: "In our experience with expert committees which set minimum criterion levels, using the [Ebel and Nedelsky] methodologies presented herein, levels are often set that would have failed more than half the candidates. These candidates have all completed accredited educational programs and fieldwork experience under close supervision, and our subjective prior probabilities are that the great majority of these candidates are competent to practice at the entry level" (p. 199). Sometimes other evidence of mastery is more compelling than our belief in the validity of the standard.

As a way to avoid the problems of standards that do not jibe with our recognition of competence in individuals, standards can be based directly on judgments about the performance of mastery and nonmastery groups. The contrasting-groups method was proposed by Zieky and Livingston (1977). Teachers or judges are asked to identify individuals who are clearly masters and clearly nonmasters (using information gained apart from the test); then the test-score distributions for the two separate groups are examined to select the cutoff score that best distinguishes them. Figure 1a illustrates a standard set where the curves cross; this choice minimizes the overall classification errors. As will be discussed in a later section, the authors also allow for the cutoff to be moved up or down to selectively reduce false positive or false negative errors.

This procedure for finding a dividing score between mastery groups and nonmastery groups is analogous to "known-groups" validation. Just as the validity of a personality instrument is enhanced when it discriminates between clinically identified populations, so the contrasting-groups method is intended to select the cutoff score that best separates the criterion groups.

Although the additional validity evidence of this method adds an important perspective not provided by judgments of test content, the contrasting-groups method does not avoid the subjectivity and arbitrariness of standard setting. The simplicity and precision of Figure 1a are misleading. The point of overlap between the curves can vary tremendously depending upon the judges' definitions of mastery. For example, if judges are stringent and tend to classify marginal students as nonmasters, the standard would drift upward because of a greater range of test scores for the nonmastery group. Figure 1b illustrates how the standard for Figure 1a would change if uncertain cases were sorted as nonmasters rather than cast into the two groups equally. Even if the instructions to judges improve the certainty of the classifications by suggesting that marginal cases be discarded, the standard will still shift depending upon different

Figure 1. Changes in the Contrasting-Groups Standard Caused by Differences in the Stringency of Nonmastery Classifications.

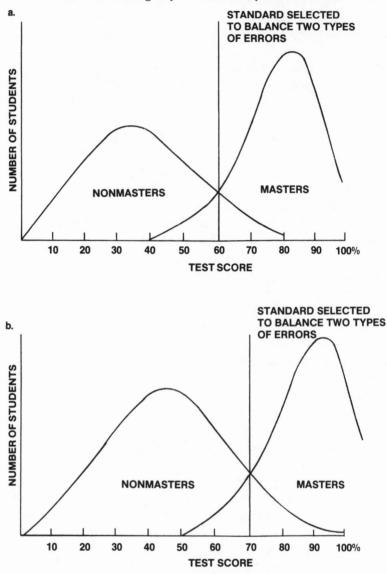

conceptualizations of marginal performance and how marginal cases are handled. Another factor influencing standards is whether the two samples are equal in size or are selected to represent their populations proportionately. Nevertheless it will be important to compare standards that result from judging groups with those determined by judging test content.

Normative percentile ranks are an alternative way to use validity data to arrive at a standard. For example, judges might operationalize their conception of competence and incompetence by saying that roughly 20 percent of the examinees deserve to fail. This may be as accurate as assigning probabilities to test items. In fact, if judges have had experience with representative groups of examinees, asking judges to name an acceptable failure rate is the same first step as is found in the contrasting-groups method. In essence, judges are being asked to name what percentage of their students or which particular students have not mastered the material.

There are other empirical methods for "discovering" standards that are similar to the contrasting-groups method but that were intended by their authors to avoid subjectivity in identifying masters and nonmasters. These methods do not add much, however, since they either hide inherent judgments or require relationships among variables that are not found in practice. For example, Berk (1976) proposed an empirical method nearly identical to the contrasting-groups method. However, he sought to eliminate the problem of defining (and judging) mastery and nonmastery by selecting two criterion groups: one instructed and the other uninstructed. The cutoff score that maximizes the agreement between the test classifications and criterion groups is then selected.

Berk's original intent was to use this approach with short criterion-referenced tests in instructional settings. Hambleton and Eignor (1979) concluded that Berk's method is promising for this purpose. However, even in the situations for which the method is most appropriate, there will not be a "true" standard to be discovered. The optimal cutoff score identified will depend on the degree of nonmastery in the uninstructed group, as well as on the duration and effectiveness of the instruction received by the group expected to be masters. The standard could vary widely, depending on how much more the average master knows than nonmasters. For minimum-competency testing, the method is not applicable at all: It is impossible to identify instructed and uninstructed groups for the competencies tested since the skills are presumably acquired during twelve years of schooling. Moreover, the presumption that an instructed group will be composed predominantly of masters is hardly valid; if instruction guaranteed mastery, the need for minimum-competency testing programs would not have arisen in the first place.

Block (1972b) developed a standard-setting model called *educational consequences*, which was named for its attempt to maximize subsequent learning or some other valued outcome. The method depends on there being a functional relationship between performance on the test and level of attainment on the criterion variable. The curve is expected to look like a learning curve, as illustrated in Figures 2a through 2d. Experimental studies using different mastery cutoffs must be carried out to determine the nature of the relationship; then the cutoff score on the test (C) is selected to maximize performance on the outcome dimension.

Glass (1978b) severely criticized this method, which was intended to discover an appropriate standard scientifically. Unless the relationship between the test and the valued outcome is nonmonotonic (that is, unless it increases and then decreases), a 100-percent test standard will be optimal. This is obviously unrealistic and hardly worth the extensive investment in field trials to determine. Figures 2a and 2b illustrate the kinds of functions that would have to occur to make the desired standard obvious. Curve 2a is nonmonotonic, but this means that increasing your score beyond a certain point on the criterion-referenced test actually diminishes performances on the subsequent task or criterion variable. It is hard to imagine a cognitive task for which this relationship would occur. Curve 2b is a step function; although it is more plausible than 2a, it will rarely occur in practice. Curves 2d and 2e are more gradual and better resemble real data (in Block, 1972a, actual slopes were flatter than 2e). But these more realistic relationships require judgments to arrive at a cutoff point. Someone has to decide how much of the criterion variable is "good enough." Block hoped to escape this ambiguity by using multiple-valued outcomes. If one could find an attitude variable with a decreasing relationship to test

Figure 2. Hypothetical Relationships Between a Criterion-Referenced Test (CRT) and a Valued Outcome.

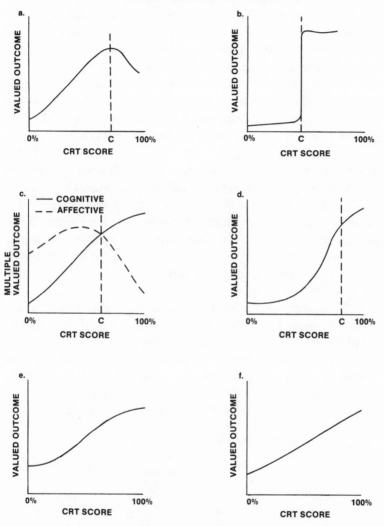

performance, then the composite criterion would create the desired nonmonotonic curve, as shown in 2c. However, even if such a graph were obtained, it is still a matter of choice whether the outcome variables should be weighted equally in arriving at a composite; the standard will shift as the weights shift.

Finally, it should be noted that if performance on a test and on a subsequent task are not hierarchically related, there may not be any interesting or informative bends in the curve at all, as in Figure 2f. Given the very limited success of research intended to demonstrate the existence of learning hierarchies, it is unlikely that this approach will solve the standard-setting dilemma even in narrow classroom subjects. The method is even less likely to work for minimum-competency testing programs, where it is virtually impossible to operationalize the criterion variable. As Hambleton and Eignor stated: "One can't maximize a valued outcome if the outcome can't be defined in any reasonable manner" (1979, p. 385).

External Standards and Utility Functions. In recent works, (Shepard, 1980a, 1980b), I have referred to this last category of methods as "empirical methods for adjusting standards." They do not address the problem of selecting a standard. Rather, if a standard already exists on an external criterion, these methods will translate that cutoff into a passing score on the test. As Jaeger (1978) commented: "By reverting to an external criterion measure, we merely transfer the arbitrary standard-setting task from one measure to another" (pp. 4–5).

These methods for locating the passing score on the test are based on decision theory (see Cronbach and Gleser, 1965; Hambleton and Novick, 1973). The object is to match the test dichotomy to the criterion dichotomy to ensure that the smallest possible number of classification errors will be made. The familiar fourfold table shown in Table 1 represents the two kinds of correct decisions and the two kinds of incorrect decisions that can be made in any place-

Table 1. Possible Decision Outcomes.

		External Criterion	
		Nonmaster $\pi < \pi_0$	*Master* $\pi > \pi_0$
Test-Based Decision	*Fail* $X < C$	Correct nonmasters	False negatives
	Pass $X > C$	False positives	Correct masters

ment or certification situation. This conceptualization is the same as that offered by other authors as a model for decision validity; given the standard on the criterion, the cutoff on the test is selected to maximize validity. The approach is not very different from the contrasting-groups method, except that the validation variable must have a specific demarcation point instead of two overlapping groups.

Huynh's (1976) empirical Bayesian approach is one of the better known procedures for setting cutoff scores, given the existence of an external criterion. Huynh was initially interested in situations where criterion-referenced tests would be used to determine when a student's mastery of a topic was sufficient to allow him to progress to the next topic. Success on the next unit of instruction, called the referral task, is used as the criterion. The reasoning is also the same as for Block's educational consequences method, except that there is already somehow a standard for success on the outcome variable. Given the cutoff score for success on the criterion task (π_0), the cutoff score for the test (C) is chosen so that in the fourfold table the average loss, $P(\pi < \pi_0, X \geq C) + P(\pi \geq \pi_0, X < C)$, is the smallest. Other methods following the same paradigm are those of Davis and Diamond (1974), Kriewall (1969, 1972) and Livingston (1976). Glass (1978b) called these methods "bootstrapping on other criterion scores" and faulted the authors for taking at face value the standards that must already exist — for example, the commonly found standard of 80 percent on criterion-referenced tests and the traditional 70 percent on competency tests. Hambleton and Eignor (1979) also found little to recommend these methods for minimum-competency testing programs since no agreed-upon criterion measure or standard of adult success is likely to be found.

Several of the decision-theoretic methods have an additional feature that may be the most useful contribution of this approach. Several authors have given special attention to weighing the differential costs of two types of classification errors. Originally, Millman (1973) recommended techniques for adjusting a cutoff score to protect against the more serious type of error. For example, in an instructional context, the possibility of failing on the next learning unit has to be balanced against the boredom and annoyance involved in repeating a task one has already mastered. In minimum-competency testing programs the consequences of decision errors are more serious. There are different opinions about whether standards should be set high and examinees given three chances or set low to prevent unfair failures.

Various mathematical models are available for reducing either false positive or false negative errors on the basis of assigned utilities. Procedures proposed by Livingston (1975) and Van der Linden and Mellenbergh (1977) use linear functions to quantify the expected loss from the two kinds of error. The loss function to be minimized is like Huynh's equation to minimize the proportion of incorrect classifications, but now weights have been assigned according to the type and extent of the loss. The Bayesian method introduced by Novick and Lewis (1974) adds the use of prior information on examinees as well as specifying utilities in the form of loss ratios. (Loss ratios simply express whether the cost of one type of error is one-and-one-half times as great or two times as great as the cost of the other type.) Although this approach is wonderfully complete, it is difficult to know under what conditions it would be useful practically. In classroom situations it would probably be too cumbersome. In minimum-competency testing applications it would probably be worth the extra complexity and cost, but it is unlikely that prior data on examinees could be introduced without raising more validity issues than does the test itself. Novick and Lindley (1978) gave further attention to the appropriate form for the utility function; the normal distribution and other families of distributions are probably an improvement on simple linear functions for representing the gains and losses associated with decision errors.

All these methods still presume that the standard-setting problem has already been solved for the criterion variable. They also presume that the teacher or administrator will know how to assign the necessary utilities (and choose the right shape for the utility function). Virtually no advice is given about how to begin to quantify both financial and psychological costs and benefits—for example, how to balance the job-getting potential of a high school diploma for a marginal student against the cost to society when the diploma is devalued by unqualified graduates. These discussions have probably been avoided because there is very little that can be offered concretely except to say that one has to choose numbers that roughly reflect one's values. The use of loss ratios, "one type of mistake is twice as bad as the other," conveys the global and subjective nature of the judgments. Because administrators will usually be pulling such numbers out of thin air, they are urged to pay particular attention to how changes in credible loss ratios, two to one or three to one, will affect the passing rates.

Selecting Methods for Specific Uses

Classroom Uses. Classroom passing scores for instructional placement are frequently set informally, because classroom teachers do not have the resources to make use of elaborate standard-setting methods. Furthermore teachers can tolerate a certain number of errors in judgment because misclassifications can easily be detected and corrected. If a nonmaster is accidentally moved on to the next topic because of a low standard, his incomplete knowledge will be noticeable in his difficulties with the new material. If the material is not hierarchical, the next review test should catch the error.

The best advice for the teacher is to keep in mind both absolute and normative conceptualizations of mastery. For example, what are the expectations for a passing essay about the causes of the Civil War? But also, what are typical experiences with essays written by eighth graders considered to be masters? In formal terms, this means reconciling the insights provided by judgments about test content and by judgments about groups.

When subject matter is sequential, teachers could also benefit from an understanding of the empirical validation methods. What Block (1972a) did with experimental variation of the mastery score, teachers can do by trial and error. If there is a noticeable number of apparent nonmasters struggling on a new unit, the previous standard was probably too low and can be adjusted to see if more reasonable placements result. What we are seeking is a standard like Huynh's (1976) that will ensure success on the referral task. There are always some classification errors; but if the teacher's impression is that too many students are being held back or too many passed on with incomplete mastery, then the passing score should be changed.

For objectives-based instructional programs, implemented for an entire school district, it would be possible to set standards formally and to systematically collect validity data. Meanwhile, researchers should continue to try to establish the existence of learning hierarchies and discover whether perseverance by students on the first task will improve success on the second. A simpler question to be addressed by research is what level of mastery assures long-term retention. No matter how fruitful these inquiries are, however, it is certain that the optimal passing score will be different for each test and each learning context. The only generalizable findings are likely to be procedures for gathering validity data and adjusting cutoff scores accordingly.

Use of standard-setting methods may cause teachers to think more about their decisions to review a subject or to go on to the next topic. These methods will not provide a means of determining when to push ahead despite students' incomplete knowledge.

Certification. Certification standards for high school graduation or professional licensing require a composite approach to protect against the fallibility of separate methods. This strategy is analogous to using multiple measures for triangulation when operationalizations of research outcomes are imperfect (Webb and others, 1966). Measurement specialists may wish to think of the necessity for several perspectives as comparable to the process of construct validation.

At a minimum, standard-setting procedures should include a balancing of absolute judgments with direct attention to passing rates. All the embarrassments of faulty standards that have ever been cited are attributable to ignoring one or the other of these two sources of information. If absolute judgments are ignored, incompetent doctors could pass tests if they were members of a weak class. High school seniors are sometimes graduated without basic skills because norms are so low. Since criterion-referenced testing was invented to overcome the problems of relative judgments, this kind of mistake is not usually made with criterion-referenced tests. Instead, out of loyalty to absolute standards, examining boards have made the opposite mistake of setting standards without norms— standards that fail half a medical school class or that pass all the high school graduates in an entire state. Direct attention to passing rates will allow standard setters to reconcile their beliefs about the required competencies (items on the test) and their beliefs about how many individuals are qualified.

The Angoff (1971) and Jaeger (1978) methods for judging test content are recommended as the most practical ones. As part of their deliberations, judges should have normative data to consider (Conaway, 1979; Hambleton, Powell, and Eignor, 1979; Jaeger, 1978; Shepard, 1976, 1979; Zieky and Livingston, 1977). In addition, I have proposed that judges make independent estimates of anticipated failure rates (Shepard, 1980b).

When the standard setters are teaching experts for a particular profession, they may have a good sense of how students they know will perform on the test. When judges are removed from the population of test takers — as they may be when political constituencies set the standards for high school competency tests — additional validity data may be needed to confirm the wisdom of the standard. The contrasting-groups method (Zieky and Livingston, 1977) is the preferred method for verifying whether the dichotomy on the test corresponds to the distinction between individuals who are judged to be masters and those who are considered to be nonmasters. Beyond this, however, for certification purposes, the empirical methods for discovering standards (Berk, 1976; Block, 1972b) add nothing to the method based on judgments about groups, because no valued outcome or criterion dimension can be operationalized. Similarly, the various statistical techniques that presume the existence of a standard on an external criterion (Huynh, 1976; Livingston, 1975, 1976; Van der Linden and Mellenbergh, 1977) are not applicable. However, the methods that propose utility functions to quantify loss ratios (Novick and Lewis, 1974; Novick and Lindley, 1978) may be helpful in conceptualizing adjustments in the cutoff to compensate for differences in the costs of classification errors. Taking all these methods into account, the best composite approach will reconcile absolute judgments with empirical data, as well as provide some additional consideration for weighing the two types of error.

Program Evaluation. Standards are subjective and variable. They are arbitrary cutting points along a continuous performance scale. Because standards impose an artificial dichotomy, they obscure information about individuals along the full performance continuum. Therefore, standards should not be used to interpret test data regarding the worth of educational programs. For other uses of criterion-referenced tests it could be argued that pass/no-pass results are essential to serve educational decisions, but for program evaluation purposes there are other more appropriate ways to attach value to the "goodness" or "badness" of the test results. Dichotomous classifications of individuals are not needed.

Program evaluation interpretations tend to compound the errors in separate standards. For example, if 10 percent of the students fail the reading test and 35 percent fail the math test, there is no way to tell whether this discrepancy is due to better teaching in reading or a more lenient standard in reading (see Glass's, 1978a, criticism of the Florida Functional Literacy Test interpretations). Variability in the stringency of the standards will be mistaken for program strengths and weaknesses. When standards are further layered to require that 80 percent of the students attain the mastery criterion on at least 80 percent of the objectives, less and less light is shed on whether the program is better than other programs or whether the students are learning as much as they should be.

When group achievement is reported only as percentage passing the standard, the reader has no sense of whether this is an unusually good or unusually bad rate. Popham (1976) suggested that normative data be added to criterion-referenced test results to supply comparative meaning. But comparisons can better be made with means or even quartile scores than with percent passing. Using passing rate as a group statistic means that achievement gains will be reflected only if they occur near the cutoff. The effects of the program for those already above the standard are ignored. For some time, evaluators have been concerned that gains in the group mean could occur because of growth in only one subgroup — for example, teaching only the brightest students could raise the group average considerably yet leave most of the students at their original level. To ensure that the program is effective for the full range of students, gains can be mapped at quartile points as well as at the mean. For example, when a program is improving achievement, we should expect to see that test scores at the 25th percentile go up just as they do at the mean and at the 75th percentile. But with percent passing as an index of program quality, there is no way to compensate for the index's insensitivity to changes in performance that are not near the cutoff.

The choice of standard-setting method will depend on test use. If a test is to be used for program evaluation, fallible standards should not be used at all because differences in the stringency of the standards will be mistaken for program effects. There are other sources of comparisons that can be used to decide whether group achievement levels are good or bad.

When test results will be used to make pass-fail decisions about individuals, cutoff scores must be set. A combination of standard-setting methods will best protect against the shortsightedness of any one method. How elaborate this standard-setting process should be will depend on how serious the consequences of invalid standards are. In classroom settings where placement errors can be readily corrected, less formal procedures can be used.

For professional licensure and competency testing, however, more thorough deliberations are necessary to arrive at defensible standards. The most complex procedure would borrow from all the major categories of standard-setting methods: (1) judgments of test content, (2) norms and passing rates, (3) known-groups validation, and (4) costs associated with the two types of error (false positives and false negatives). Implicit in a composite approach for setting standards is the need to reconcile both absolute and normative perspectives on mastery with both fixed-quota and quota-free interpretations of test-based decisions.

References

American Psychological Association, American Educational Research Association, and National Council on Measurement in Education. *Standards for Educational and Psychological Tests.* Washington, D.C.: American Psychological Association, 1974.

Andrew, B. J., and Hecht, J. T. "A Preliminary Investigation of Two Procedures for Setting Examination Standards." *Educational and Psychological Measurement,* 1976, *36*, 35–50.

Angoff, W. H. "Scales, Norms, and Equivalent Scores." In R. L. Thorndike (Ed.), *Educational Measurement.* Washington, D.C.: American Council on Education, 1971.

Berk, R. A. "Determination of Optimal Cutting Scores in Criterion-Referenced Measurement." *Journal of Experimental Education,* 1976, *45,* 4–9.

Block, J. H. "Operating Procedures for Mastery Learning." J. H. Block (Ed.), *Mastery Learning: Theory and Practice.* New York: Holt, Rinehart and Winston, 1971.

Block, J. H. "Student Evaluation: Toward the Setting of Mastery Performance Standards." Paper presented at annual meeting of the American Educational Research Association, Chicago, April 1972a.

Block, J. H. "Student Learning and the Setting of Mastery Performance Standards." *Educational Horizons,* 1972b, *50,* 183–190.

Block, J. H. 'Standards and Criteria: A Response." *Journal of Educational Measurement,* 1978, *15,* 291–295.

Bloom, B. S. "Learning for Mastery." *Evaluation Comment.* Vol. 1. Los Angeles: Center for the Study of Evaluation, University of California, 1968.

Bloom, B. S. "Mastery Learning." In J. H. Block (Ed.), *Mastery Learning: Theory and Practice.* New York: Holt, Rinehart and Winston, 1971.

Brennan, R. L., and Lockwood, R. E. "A Comparison of the Nedelsky and Angoff Cutting-Score Procedures Using Generalizability Theory." *Applied Psychological Measurement,* 1980, *4,* 219–240.

Burton, N. W. "Societal Standards." *Journal of Educational Measurement,* 1978, *15,* 263–271.

Conaway, L. E. "Setting Standards in Competency-Based Education: Some Current Practices and Concerns." In M. A. Bunda and J. R. Sanders (Eds.), *Practices and Problems in Competency-Based Education.* Washington, D.C.: National Council on Measurement in Education, 1979.

Cronbach, L. J. "Test Validation." In R. L. Thorndike (Ed.), *Educational Measurement.* (2nd ed.) Washington, D.C.: American Council on Education, 1971.

Cronbach, L. J., and Gleser, G. C. *Psychological Tests and Personnel Decisions.* Urbana: University of Illinois Press, 1965.

Davis, F. B., and Diamond, J. J. "The Preparation of Criterion-Referenced Tests." In C. W. Harris, M. C. Alkin, and W. J. Popham (Eds.), *Problems in Criterion-Referenced Measurement.* Monograph Series in Evaluation, No. 3. Los Angeles: Center for the Study of Evaluation, University of California, 1974.

Ebel, R. L. *Essentials of Educational Measurement.* Englewood Cliffs, N.J.: Prentice-Hall, 1972.

Educational Testing Service. *Report on a Study of the Use of the National Teachers Examination by the State of South Carolina.* Princeton, N.J.: Educational Testing Service, 1976.

Glaser, R. "Instructional Technology and the Measurement of Learning Outcomes." *American Psychologist,* 1963, *18,* 519–521.

Glaser, R. "Adapting the Elementary School Curriculum to Individual Performance." In *Proceedings of the 1967 Invitational Conference on Testing Problems.* Princeton, N.J.: Educational Testing Service, 1968.

Glass, G. V. "Minimum Competence and Incompetence in Florida." *Phi Delta Kappan,* 1978a, *59*(9), 602–605.

Glass, G. V. "Standards and Criteria." *Journal of Educational Measurement,* 1978b, *15,* 237–261.

Hambleton, R. K. "On the Use of Cutoff Scores with Criterion-Referenced Tests in Instructional Settings." *Journal of Educational Measurement,* 1978, *15,* 277–290.

Hambleton, R. K., and Eignor, D. R. "Competency Test Development, Validation, and Standard Setting." In R. Jaeger and C. Tittle (Eds.), *Minimum Competency Testing.* Berkeley, Calif.: McCutchan, 1979.

Hambleton, R. K., and Novick, M. R. "Toward an Integration of Theory and Method for Criterion-Referenced Tests." *Journal of Educational Measurement,* 1973, *10,* 159–170.

Hambleton, R. K., Powell, S., and Eignor, D. R. "Issues and Methods for Standard Setting." In *A Practitioner's Guide to Criterion-Referenced Test Development, Validation, and Test Score Usage.* Laboratory of Psychometric and Evaluative Research Report No. 70. (2nd ed.) Amherst: School of Education, University of Massachusetts, 1979.

Hambleton, R. K., and others. "Criterion-Referenced Testing and Measurement: A Review of Technical Issues and Developments." *Review of Educational Research*, 1978, *48*, 1–47.

Huynh, H. 'Statistical Consideration of Mastery Scores." *Psychometrika*, 1976, *41*, 65–78.

Jaeger, R. M. "Measurement Consequences of Selected Standard-Setting Models." Paper presented at annual meeting of the National Council on Measurement in Education, San Francisco, April 1976.

Jaeger, R. M. "A Proposal for Setting a Standard on the North Carolina High School Competency Test." Paper presented at spring meeting of the North Carolina Association for Research in Education, Chapel Hill, 1978.

Kleinke, D. J. "Applying the Angoff and Nedelsky Techniques to the National Licensing Examinations in Landscape Architecture." Paper presented at annual meeting of the National Council on Measurement in Education, Boston, April 1980.

Koffler, S. L. "A Comparison of Approaches for Setting Proficiency Standards." *Journal of Educational Measurement*, 1980, *17*, 167–178.

Kriewall, T. E. "Application of Information Theory and Acceptance-Sampling Principles to the Management of Mathematics Instruction." Unpublished doctoral dissertation, University of Wisconsin, 1969.

Kriewall, T. E. "Aspects and Applications of Criterion-Referenced Tests." Paper presented at annual meeting of the American Educational Research Association, Chicago, 1972.

Lindvall, C. M., and Bolvin, J. O. "Programmed Instruction in the Schools: An Application of Programming Principles in 'Individually Prescribed Instruction.'" In P. C. Lange (Ed.), *Programmed Instruction.* Chicago: National Society for the Study of Education, 1967.

Linn, R. L. "Issues of Validity in Measurement for Competency-Based Programs." In M. A. Bunda and J. R. Sanders (Eds.), *Practices and Problems in Competency-Based Education.* Washington, D.C.: National Council on Measurement in Education, 1979.

Livingston, S. A. *A Utility-Based Approach to the Evaluation of Pass/Fail Testing Decision Procedures.* Report No. COPA-75-01. Princeton, N.J.: Educational Testing Service, 1975.

Livingston, S. A. *Choosing Minimum Passing Scores by Stochastic Approximation Techniques.* Report No. COPA-76-02. Princeton, N.J.: Educational Testing Service, 1976.

Madaus, G. F. "Measurement Issues and Consequences Associated with Minimal Competency Testing." Paper presented at spring membership conference of the National Consortium on Testing, Arlington, Va., May 1978.

Meskauskas, J. A. "Evaluation Models for Criterion-Referenced Testing: Views Regarding Mastery and Standard Setting." *Review of Educational Research,* 1976, *45,* 133–158.

Millman, J. "Reporting Student Progress: A Case for a Criterion-Referenced Marking System." *Phi Delta Kappan,* 1970, *52,* 226–230.

Millman, J. "Passing Scores and Test Lengths for Domain-Referenced Measures." *Review of Educational Research,* 1973, *43,* 205–216.

Nedelsky, L. "Absolute Grading Standards for Objective Tests." *Educational and Psychological Measurement,* 1954, *14,* 3–19.

Novick, M. R., and Lewis, C. "Prescribing Test Length for Criterion-Referenced Measurements." In C. W. Harris, M. C. Alkin, and W. J. Popham (Eds.), *Problems in Criterion-Referenced Measurement.* Monograph Series in Evaluation, No. 3. Los Angeles: Center for the Study of Evaluation, University of California, 1974.

Novick, M. R., and Lindley, D. V. "The Use of More Realistic Utility Functions in Educational Applications." *Journal of Educational Measurement,* 1978, *15,* 181–191.

Popham, W. J. *Educational Evaluation.* Englewood Cliffs, N.J.: Prentice-Hall, 1975.

Popham, W. J. "Normative Data for Criterion-Referenced Tests?" *Phi Delta Kappan,* 1976, *58,* 593–594.

Popham, W. J. "As Always Provocative." *Journal of Educational Measurement,* 1978, *15,* 297–300.

Popham, W. J., and Husek, T. R. "Implications of Criterion-Referenced Measurement." *Journal of Educational Measurement,* 1969, *6,* 1–9.

Schoon, C. G., Gullion, C. M., and Ferrara, P. "Bayesian Statistics, Credentialing Examinations, and the Determination of Passing Points." *Evaluation and the Health Professions,* 1979, *2,* 181–201.

Scriven, M. "How to Anchor Standards." *Journal of Educational Measurement,* 1978, *15,* 273–275.

Shepard, L. A. "Setting Standards and Living with Them." *Florida Journal of Educational Research,* 1976, *18,* 23–32.

Shepard, L. A. "Setting Standards." In M. A. Bunda and J. R. Sanders (Eds.), *Practices and Problems in Competency-Based Measurement.* Washington, D.C.: National Council on Measurement in Education, 1979.

Shepard, L. A. "Standard-Setting Issues and Methods." *Applied Psychological Measurement,* 1980a, *4,* 447–467.

Shepard, L. A. "Technical Issues in Minimum Competency Testing." In D. C. Berliner (Ed.), *Review of Research in Education.* Vol. 8. Itasca, Ill.: Peacock, 1980b.

Skakun, E. N., and Kling, S. "Comparability of Methods for Setting Standards." *Journal of Educational Measurement,* 1980, *17,* 229–235.

Tukey, J. W. "Some Thoughts on Clinical Trials, Especially Problems of Multiplicity." *Science,* 1977, *198*(4318), 679–684.

Van der Linden, W. J., and Mellenbergh, G. J. "Optimal Cutting Scores Using a Linear Loss Function." *Applied Psychological Measurement,* 1977, *1,* 593–599.

Webb, E. J., and others. *Unobtrusive Measures: Nonreactive Research in the Social Sciences.* Chicago: Rand McNally, 1966.

Zieky, M. J., and Livingston, S. A. *Manual for Setting Standards on the Basic Skills Assessment Tests.* Princeton, N.J.: Educational Testing Service, 1977.

5   Albert P. Maslow

ℜ ℜ ℜ ℜ ℜ ℜ ℜ ℜ ℜ ℜ ℜ ℜ ℜ

Standards in Occupational Settings

Of the thirty or so dictionary definitions of the term *standard,* the one most fitting reality is that a standard is "anything, [such] as a rule or principle, that is used as a basis for judgment." A "rule or principle," as Shepard points out in Chapter Four, should serve as the basis for purposeful rather than capricious actions. Thus, a useful perspective on techniques for standard setting for occupational and professional entry might start with some overview of the many uses of standards.

I will not presume to deal with standard-setting problems throughout the world of work. The crucial issues will, I believe, become clear if I concentrate on those occupations and professions in which relatively formal entry requirements exist and are applied and monitored by a board with legal authority (as in licensing) or with professional support (as in certification or registration). Furthermore, these fields of work tend to be closely identified with particular academic curricula; therefore, the standard-setting issues have direct implications for educational assessment practices. Rather than present an exhaustive review of the literature, I will concentrate on a number of contemporary developments for dealing with standard-setting issues. It is worth noting here that colleagues in Europe and elsewhere are also grappling with the problems that arise from the interaction between academic preparation and work entry requirements.

Background of Standard Setting

In the United States, entry into more than 2,000 occupations and professions is regulated. Perhaps a fourth of the work force is in jobs guarded by licensing, certification, or registration standards. Each year more groups seek the status and protection against competition provided by such standards. It is a fact that, in essentially every instance, the decision as to one's readiness for entry into such an occupation or profession is based, not on a single test, but on a very complex set of information, measures, and judgments. These include academic credentials, self-testimony in personal history and work experience records, testimony of others, tests of all sorts, work simulations, interviews, medical examinations, apprenticeships, and legal requirements for residence and citizenship, as well as investigations of morality and character. Often the first cut, perhaps the unkindest one of all, is in the process of self-selection, the career choices that individuals make for a host of reasons, valid or otherwise.

These "standards" are embedded in a maze of systems. Some systems involve sequential steps and multiple "cut scores." Others — such as assessment centers — apply a multidimensional/multimethod approach in a controlled judgmental setting. Most often, the final decision is an outcome of many "cut scores" in a system having both sequential and compensatory features. Classical validation precepts as to the optimum ways to apply standards to such a melange are, needless to observe, rarely honored. For most applications, psychology today can offer little theory or technical guidance that has research support.

It is regularly ignored that, in any interdependent system, a change in one member affects standards for other members. For example, removing a restrictive educational requirement may bring into competition people who differ from those on whom a test has been standardized. This will not only unsettle normative expectations but will most likely change, in useful ways, beliefs about who can do the work and how it should be performed.

I should also observe that, as Sarason reminds us in Chapter

Seven, few standard-setting systems are designed for the benefit of the candidate. They are not meant to be growth experiences. The assumption is that candidates are in a highly charged situation and therefore will be highly motivated. The curvilinear relationships that Atkinson cites in Chapter Two are not considered. If any conditions *are* optimized, they are likely to be those that help the decision makers, who must ultimately tell the candidate whether he is judged competent or, if not, why not. It follows that, unless the role of each requirement and standard is reasonably well defined, the rejected candidate must conclude that his rejection was the work of either knaves or fools.

It is probably the case that few systems make full or best use of the information available. Most systems could, of course, be improved by additional, nonredundant measures that would contribute to validity. But perhaps the most urgent need is for articulation of the purposes and procedures of the standard-setting process. Standards serve many ends:

1. To protect the health and welfare of the public (this is a basic rationale for regulation, and such standards usually call for minimal competence).
2. To improve the quality of service to the public.
3. To make recruiting more effective by supporting self-selection decisions.
4. For crowd control in a loose labor market.
5. To protect those already on the job from competition, by controlling access and restricting mobility.
6. To convince the public of the equity and values of restrictive requirements, so that the public will support these standards in the political arena.
7. To carry out national employment policies—for career opportunities for women, minorities, the handicapped.
8. To enhance the image or status of the occupation or profession and so to maintain status with professional peers and with agencies responsible for accrediting academic institutions and curricula.
9. To comply with specific laws and regulations—for example, laws dealing with licensing or certification.
10. To support or rationalize classification and pay structures.

11. To influence education and training curricula.
12. To support career development and continuing competence requirements.
13. To reduce training costs.
14. To recognize and reward expertise or specialization.
15. To reduce the cost of applying standards.

This list could go on. The point is that licensing boards, certifying agencies, and academic bodies usually have a number of purposes to serve — some they admit to, others they pursue without open acknowledgment. It is to serve these divergent interests that the responsible agents set requirements, choose and array measurement procedures, and decide on the amount or kind or level of performance that they will equate with "competence."

An interesting study would be to examine, perhaps by a policy-capturing research model, how standard setters do, in fact, balance their competing pressures. Visualize a scale. Toward one end are the standard setters concerned with protecting the interests of their institutions, the public, or their professions; they are likely to err on the high side in defining minimal competence. Toward the other end are those who value individual opportunity, open access to careers, and minimal barriers; they are likely to press to lower or discard traditional educational credentials and performance requirements.

But standards, once set, are quickly subject to demands for change. In the case of physicians, for example, efforts to achieve balance and equity in selection bring with them demands for uniformity of professional competence. But standards that are rigid and inflexible make it difficult to achieve balance. The degrees of uniformity imposed must be adapted over time to changing perceptions of what is equitable (National Board of Medical Examiners, 1978). This, in turn, requires continuing reappraisal and adjustment of the criteria and the procedures used to define competence.

Just as standards themselves need continuing review, so does the *continued* competence of professionals and other specialists. But attempts to ensure current competent performance are complicated by issues that cannot be made part of the assessment at the time of original entry. For example: Under what conditions should a practitioner be denied the right to continue to work? For relicensing or requalification, should the practitioner be examined over the broad range of his field, or just in the area in which he has specialized? To what extent should consumer reaction become a part of the assessment process? Should the recheck on competence be voluntary or mandatory? What is the role of formal education in the maintenance of competence? A variety of approaches is under study or in use — for example, periodic self-assessment or assessment by peers, participation in "continuing education" programs, and work simulation exercises. So far, each of these has been beset with technical and policy controversies.

It is not possible to set standards without hurting someone. To balance the pressures, standard setters must decide *who* is at risk — individuals, institutions, or society. Then they must evaluate how serious the risks are in each case and weigh the risks against the benefits the standards will provide.

Standards on Tests and Other Structured Assessment

From a measurement perspective, standard setters must also consider and choose among a variety of models. Jaeger (1979) provides a useful summary of current models and of the "threats" each presents to the validity of the inferences drawn.

Written Tests. The literature provides several summaries of procedures for setting cut scores for tests (see, for example, Krueger and Werner, 1979; Buck, 1977; and Rock, 1979). And we also have the benefit of Shepard's review in Chapter Four. Available procedures include those based on criteria *internal* to the test (for example, the well-known Ebel, Angoff, and Nedelsky procedures), as well as those based on the performance of identifiable reference groups. The latter procedures cover familiar options for setting cut scores. Scores can be set:

1. To meet predetermined quotas.
2. By comparison to current "satisfactory" employees. But the experienced researcher will take care to inquire about turnover rates and exactly who these "satisfactory" employees are. If they are the ones *not* promoted, then to use them as models must

result over time in driving down the effectiveness of the organization.

3. To distinguish between two or more groups of different standing — for example, professionals and trainees.

4. At gaps in score distributions — typically a function of small sample size or of the mixture of two classes. (For example, trainees and journeymen in the same sample.)

5. On the basis of external criterion methods, including regression models, stochastic approximation (Livingston, 1976), and a Bayesian approach (Gullion, 1979).

Since the decision to be made is typically categorical, it follows that special methods for assessing reliability and validity are needed. Rock (1979) observes that "any decision reliability index is a function of not only the psychometric characteristics of the test items and 'cutting score' but also of the type of decision strategy being used to compare an individual observed score (or true score) with the 'cutting score.' [I]n 'cutting-score' decisions about minimally qualified vs. not qualified, . . . the decision maker is making decisions about individuals, and the benefits of extreme selection ratios are not present to compensate for the moderate validities usually found. [D]ecision strategies that compare an individual's true score with the 'cutting score' and also utilize Bayesian loss function strategies will prove to be the most promising decision-making procedures" (pp. 31 – 32).

But consider that many professionals and other practitioners do *not* work under supervision. Difficulties in validating tests and cut scores against external criteria heighten interest in models for content-oriented test construction to support claims of content validity. Several procedures involve judgments of item difficulty and importance or relevance (Lawshe, 1975). Robert Lockwood, while at ETS, was developing a technique for deriving, from relevance and difficulty judgments, a single index that could be useful in item selection, in setting cut scores, and in describing the content validity of the test. The extension of these judgmental processes to other kinds of competence measures should find an eager audience.

The judgments made in the current cutting-score models are beginning to attract research interest. For example, reliability can be improved by increasing the number of expert judges, and the relevance of their judgments can be studied by comparison of judged differences and observed differences in a group of minimally qualified candidates (Rock, 1979). How differences in the background of judges affect cutting-score decisions has also been examined (Rock, Davis, and Werts, 1979; Lockwood, 1979). Such research is constructive, but it does not deal directly with the judgmental process, which is critical to setting minimal test scores and vital to the use of nontest standards procedures.

Judgments about test data also need to be related to other factors external to the test. A useful scheme for relating two of these factors—the judged degree of societal risk and the supply of applicants—is found in a paper by Temp and others (1979). If we consider just three degrees of societal risk and three labor market conditions, nine situations exist—and each produces some special problems in setting cut scores. For example, with low risk and too many qualified applicants, standards should be minimal; all those scoring above chance should be considered. Unless the test validity justifies ranking of applicants, then all should be considered, and selection based on other factors (Temp and others, 1979). Obviously this plan may protect the sanctity of the test; in reality, it simply unloads on the test user the burden of applying and defending some other bases for discriminating among applicants.

We take another cell from this analysis—the case of medium societal risk with a large supply of candidates. Here it might be argued that employers should resist raising test standards, openly or not, and should add other job-relevant measures to the assessment plan so that the burden on the test will be lightened and those with lower-than-top test scores will not be summarily rejected. An example of such a design is found in a certification examination for social workers. All candidates met academic requirements and the requirement of two years of relevant experience. Then achievement test scores were used to identify a "gray" zone around a tentative cutoff score. For candidates within that zone, references supplied judgments about the candidate on a specially prepared form covering fourteen job-relevant scales. These were then evaluated as a basis for final certification decisions.

Schemes such as this, I believe, provide a very useful template for analyzing the interaction of critical factors in setting standards for tests and will lead to better decisions about the technology that fits given cases.

Other Measures. In recent years, measurement research and development have produced both improved ways to define competence and innovations in its measurement (see, for example, Menges, 1975). Procedures other than written tests do not provide such convenient units as "test items" as a basis for standard setting of the kind reviewed earlier. Nevertheless, it is possible to apply to other measures the same concern for standardization, reliability, and control of the judgmental process.

An example is provided by a study of standard setting in a proficiency examination for dental auxiliaries (technicians) (Livingston, 1979). Here, performance in a standardized situation by the technician was observed by two dentists who used a specific checklist to score the observed behavior. The scores were then "validated" against an overall judgment of proficiency. Statistical decision theory was applied to setting a "cutoff score" so as to minimize the probability of misclassifications (false positives or false negatives) in terms of their perceived relative importance. In some respects, this procedure is superior to the judgmental process applied to test items. It captures the direct observation of the behavior of the candidate by the trained observer; it does not depend on the inference that must be made from item responses.

It is safe to infer that the focus in linking test performance to job competence is shifting from test *scores* to test *items*. The question being asked is: In what way is the item a sign, not a sample, of the behavior to be measured? The test constructor needs to know not just the skill or knowledge applied but also the setting — the constraints, the time pressures, the environmental presses — found on the job, as well as the kind of performance valued for the purpose.

It is predictable that test constructors will come to attend more carefully to *how* skills and knowledges are applied at work. It is also predictable that, for many purposes, traditional multiple-choice knowledge tests will give way to procedures — videotape, in-baskets, simulations, performance measures, and so on — that reflect more closely the content of work behaviors. But these alternatives are likely to depend even more on judgmental processes in test development and in setting standards.

One organized appraisal system deserves special mention. An assessment center provides for observation of candidates in a variety of work simulations and for careful attention to the process by which trained assessors reach their conclusions. The key features are as follows: (1) the definition of job-relevant behavioral dimensions and behavioral standards of competence; (2) the design of individual and group exercises in which the candidate has the opportunity to behave as he or she should on the job; (3) the intensive training of assessors; and (4) procedures to guide the consensual evaluation process.

A recent summary of research (Assessment Center Research Group, 1980) concludes that such centers (1) are valid for assessment of competence in a wide variety of careers — executives, clergymen, police captains, foreign service officers, and school principals; (2) achieve comparable results across different assessor teams; (3) minimize differences in performance among gender, racial, age, and other subgroups; and (4) show good agreement among raters.

Assessment centers are not limited to the marketplace of jobs. At least one college — Alverno, in Michigan — is fully committed to applying these concepts to its admission practices, to individualized curriculum planning, and to evaluation of the progress of students and their readiness to deal with society and work. Their transcripts are not the familiar grades and points; rather, they are an assessment report covering a range of competences — for instance, problem-solving ability, interpersonal skills, and even "awareness of the contemporary world" and "esthetic sensitivity" (see Loacher and Mentkowski, 1980).

The assessment concept has had a broad impact on that institution: The organization of instruction has shifted from traditional academic subject matter to the development of the target competencies. Faculty behavior has adapted to the role of providing opportunities for learning, rather than teaching. Performance assessments by observations over time have replaced achievement tests. Grading practices have yielded to observation and evaluation of performance. And individual development has come to override mastery as the purpose of education.

The cutting-score problem in an assessment center involves defining the differences in kind, quality, or results of observed behavior that should distinguish the competent from the incompetent. In a typical center, the assessors may spend a full day in observation, then spend half the next day organizing and evaluating their notes and making preliminary ratings on each performance dimension. They then meet as a group to discuss each candidate in terms of predetermined behavioral standards (avoiding normative comparisons as far as possible) and to agree on a final rating. Finally, the assessors' conclusions are presented and discussed with the candidate in a constructive, career-planning context. The job relevance and fairness of the process, as well as the soundness of the assessors' decisions, are reportedly attested to by candidates and accepted by U.S. courts.

Credentials as Standards

The dependence on credentials in turn warrants some attention to those factors — social and economic — that determine both who gets into college or graduate school and who succeeds. The demands for competently trained employees are clearly rising. Education and training institutions, along with their standards for admission and graduation, increasingly affect access to careers and the related economic rewards and social mobility. Orlans (1974) and others (for example, Huff, 1974) have pointed out the "fatuity of credentialing everyone and everything." In the regulated professions and occupations, licensing boards depend upon the testimony of the educational institution. Many employers seek comfort in credentials as a standard testifying to at least minimal competence.

Some research results suggest that the intellectual abilities and personal characteristics sought by admissions officers are those also valued by employers. Although the pattern of relevant abilities changes over time during employment, success at work remains dependent on the same competences present at entrance. This suggests that approaches such as the one at Alverno may produce more useful information than the traditional transcript. The validity of academic achievement records in terms of grade point average is, at best, limited (Miller and Mills, 1978).

We should distinguish the simple requirement for *completion* of a prescribed course of study or academic degree from the requirement for a specified *level* of achievement — for example, a B average or a 2.5 grade point average or some other standard. In either case, whatever the record measures or implies about competence is adopted as a standard. Thus, in a sense, the criteria used by accrediting agencies become an integral part of the standard-setting process.

The impact, in the United States at least, of policies and laws promoting fair employment have made employers and others more sensitive to the limitations of academic credentials. Thus many people responsible for assessing candidates for entry into technical and managerial occupations and professions are concerned not just with evidence of specific knowledge; they also look for skills in analyzing and processing information, problem-solving abilities, interpersonal skills, communication skills, and "motivation." These kinds of concerns lead to the use of a wide variety of measurement procedures to complement or add to educational credentials.

The demand for specific academic credentials is perceived by many as arbitrary. In tune with legal and social policy commitments to fair and open access to careers, such requirements are under attack. In U.S. courts, a series of cases is establishing the precedent that employers *may* impose special education and training requirements when they are clearly job related. Job relatedness can be construed broadly, however; thus, the requirement for a bachelor's degree for the position of health program representative is justified in part because of the "maturity" that accrues to a college graduate but not so surely to a nongraduate. But to reject a candidate without the credential generally demands strong evidence that the work cannot reasonably be done by persons who do not have the specified credential. This is often difficult to prove.

An interesting extension of credentialing processes is found in the assessment of experiential learning. Here, experiences outside the classroom — whether sponsored by an educational institution or not — are accumulated in a dossier. This record is then the basis for review and for granting of academic credit for the competencies gained. A variety of techniques is used to assess the claimed competence. These include appraisal of products, interviews, and, occasionally, tests. A key step is the organization and reporting of this mass of information in such a way that other institutions can understand and evaluate the novel transcripts.

Some of the consequences of such educational innovations are emerging. With the spread of alternative routes to competence

—open universities, experiential learning, on-the-job training—
standard setters must now try somehow to equate the competence of
candidates who come up through a variety of pathways. The emphasis will inevitably begin to shift somewhat to ways of assessing
experience and training that are not condensed and coded into
familiar credentials.

A second consequence, for those academic institutions that
grant specialized credentials and their implied warranty of competence, is that employers may look to them for *evidence* of the reliability and job relevance of those records. So, these institutions may be
stimulated to look more critically at their own standards and criteria. But, before reliance on such new forms of credentials becomes epidemic, it may be well to heed Orlans's (1974) warning.
These new approaches—credit for work experience, nontraditional
programs, and so on—"lean heavily on the frail reed of scientific
measurement and share the social sciences' proclivity to cloak, ro-
manticize, or sterilize, and thereby distort humdrum reality" (p. 4).
It is naive, Orlans argues, to believe that competence can be
"blocked into unit, objectively measurable skills and knowledge";
this notion is also artificial, since "in omitting what cannot be measured, it omits most of the things that give education and work,
society and the individual, their distinctive character" (p. 14).

Experience as a Standard

Judgments about the competence of candidates almost always
are based in large part on an assay of their experience and training.
Thus, assuming adequate documentation is on hand, the familiar
questions again are: What identifiable experience is likely to be
relevant and important to assessing job competence (that is, can be
assumed to have provided job-relevant skills, knowledge, and abilities)? How much experience, or what kind, marks the competent
from the less competent?

In regulated fields of work in the United States, experience
requirements are normally set by state laws. As a result, widespread
differences exist among states in both educational and experience
requirements, as well as in the tests used to verify them. The same
may be true within other countries, and it is certainly the case both

within and between countries. We do not have a common market in the regulated fields of work.

Where an accredited course of training is a prerequisite, the need for experience over and above this training may be questioned. As other traditional requirements (for example, citizenship, moral character, age) are deleted and the decision comes to rest on fewer variables, chiefly tests and credentials, there will be intensified challenges to their rationality and validity. It would be a real contribution to law and policy if psychology were to develop a more general theory and more general procedures for establishing experienced-based standards.

How do you reach the first decision — is prior experience really necessary? A scheme proposed for assessing the need for prior experience looks at such factors as the seriousness for the public's health and welfare of allowing inexperienced persons to practice and the difficulty of independently exercising necessary discretion in the job without previous practical experience. But when this analysis is applied to current programs, very few can justify their experience requirements (Cathcart and Graff, 1978). In many standards, it is simply the *number* of years of experience that is counted. Here the experience requirement operates much like an academic credential. Some standards emphasize the nature or *quality* of experience. We can generalize by saying that, to the extent that they are structured and contain rules for crediting kinds and amounts of experience, such rating procedures can be adequately reliable.

A particularly promising systematic approach is based on the concept of behavioral consistency (Schmidt and others, 1979). The emphasis is on past achievement rather than past exposure; the procedure seeks out the candidate's major behavior patterns that are stable across time and in various settings. Assessment procedures are developed on the basis of these principles:

1. Only those behavioral dimensions that differentiate between minimally competent and superior performers are evaluated.
2. The relevant behavioral dimensions must be defined by those who have had firsthand experience with performers at the various levels.

3. The candidate is the primary source of information—thus, it becomes critical to define what is needed and to provide for accurate reporting of relevant and verifiable material that shows past achievements for each dimension.
4. Job experts and trained personnel specialists can "scale" the achievement record with adequate reliability.

This approach has been reported to have greater reliability than older procedures and, probably, higher validity.

Basic Research Needs

Common to all the technologies of measurement development and standard setting, and indeed to policy preferences and purposes, are two fundamental issues. The first of these is an understanding of the process of human judgment and of the ways in which it can function optimally in standard-setting applications. Much of the research attention so far has dealt with the *outcomes* of the judgments made in setting standards. There is as yet little research-based guidance as to the psychological *processes* at work— for example, the processes involved in forming first impressions, in selective attention by observers to different behavioral data, in the retention and recall of observed behavior by judges, and in the tendency to match candidates with stereotypes. Contributions to these issues may be more forthcoming from personality research and social psychology than from psychometric studies. In any case, knowledge in these areas is basic to improving practice in standard-setting, as we ponder:

- Whom should we select as judges for our particular purpose?
- What is the optimal size and structure of the group of judges?
- How can instructional material for judges best be introduced?
- What are the best ways to arrange for the observation of candidates?
- How can bias, set, and various rating errors be dealt with?
- What rules for consensus should apply, and how can we enforce them?
- How can assessors be helped to improve and share their percep-

tions of the behavioral meaning of competence, minimum performance, and superior levels?

- How can information from different measures be integrated?
- Should we display and use descriptive data about candidates, such
  as personal history records and test scores? If so, when should it
  be done? How might that affect the judgment process?
- What records should be made? In what kind of language? Using
  what scales?
- How can the process be made more useful to the candidate?

These are the practical questions that must be settled. The research
literature gives only brief and unsteady guidance here.

The other fundamental issue is that of the adequacy of the job
analysis. A number of methods share professional respectability.
The procedures used vary with the purpose, as they should. For
assessing competence, particularly, it is important that the method
used result in a statement of the work behaviors that are relevant in
some eventful way to the concept of competence. Whether these
behaviors are identified by factor or cluster analysis of task questionnaires, by critical incident studies, or by observational techniques is
less important than that the description of the behavior include not
just what things are done but expectations as to the manner, impact,
quality, or consequences of the work. In my judgment, these latter
criteria comprise the core of standards. It follows, then, that a job
analysis for choosing assessment methods and setting cutting scores
must focus on those behaviors that are, in fact, *critical* to minimally
competent performance or to the level of competence desired.
Note also that, to the extent these critical behaviors are independent,
that is, call for different characteristics, the assessment model too
must be multidimensional.

I have not dealt with a number of psychometric problems that
are common to all measures used in competence decisions. Reliability and validity concerns, of course, apply across the board. Some
special problems, such as the equivalence of test forms, amenability
of measures to special coaching efforts, and anxiety, have been
studied primarily with respect to written tests. There is no reason
why these should not be systematically investigated for other measures. Finally, as we look at the question of generalizability, we

should consider the probability that the constructs that define competent performance may be more readily generalized than the specific tests and measures of those constructs.

Perhaps a fitting way to end this chapter is to quote Lerner's (1979, p. 28) statement that "reasonable applications of standards require reasonable cutoff scores, and the cutoff-score problem is one that seems to daunt most contemporary psychometricians. Line drawing . . . is, in essence, a question of balance. Democracy . . . is also a question of balance. So is civilization."

References

Assessment Center Research Group. "What Do We Know About Assessment Centers?" Report to the International Congress on the Assessment Center Method, Toronto, June 1980.

Buck, L. S. *Guide to the Setting of Appropriate Cutting Scores for Written Tests: A Summary of the Concerns and Procedures.* PRDC Technical Memo 77-4. Washington, D.C.: U.S. Civil Service Commission, 1977.

Cathcart, J. A., and Graff, G. "Occupational Licensing: Factoring It Out." *Pacific Law Journal,* 1978, *9,* 147–163.

Gullion, C. M. "Setting the Pass-Fail Point on a Credentialing Examination: An Application of the Bayesian Approach." Paper presented at International Personnel Management Association Assessment Council Conference, San Diego, Calif., June 1979.

Huff, S. "Credentialing by Tests or by Degrees: Title VII of the Civil Rights Act and *Griggs* v. *Duke Power Company.*" *Harvard Educational Review,* 1974, *44*(2), 246–269.

Jaeger, R. M. "Measurement Consequences of Selected Standard-Setting Models." In M. A. Bunda and R. J. Sanders (Eds.), *Practices and Problems in Competency-Based Measurement.* Washington, D.C.: National Council on Measurement in Education, 1979.

Krueger, K., and Werner, E. *Development and Evaluation of Strategies for Setting Written Test Cutoff Scores on Content Valid Tests.* Sacramento, Calif.: Selection Consulting Center, 1979.

Lawshe, C. H. "A Quantitative Approach to Content Validity." *Personnel Psychology,* 1975, *28,* 563–574.

Lerner, B. "Tests and Standards Today: Attacks, Counterattacks, and Responses." In R. T. Lennon (Ed.), *New Directions for Testing and Measurement: Impactive Changes on Measurement*, no. 3. San Francisco: Jossey-Bass, 1979.

Livingston, S. A. *Choosing Minimum Passing Scores by Stochastic Approximation Techniques*. Princeton, N.J.: Center for Occupational and Professional Assessment, Educational Testing Service, 1976.

Livingston, S. A. *The Development of a Proficiency Examination for Dental Auxiliaries*. Princeton, N.J.: Center for Occupational and Professional Assessment, Educational Testing Service, 1979.

Loacher, G., and Mentkowski, M. "Establishing Educational Competency Using Assessment Center Methodology at Alverno." Paper presented at International Congress on the Assessment Center Method, Toronto, June 1980.

Lockwood, R. E. "Application of Generalizability Theory to the Issue of Agreement Among Raters in Setting Cutting Scores." Paper presented at annual meeting of the Mid-South Educational Research Association, Little Rock, Ark., November 1979.

Menges, R. J. "Assessing Readiness for Professional Practice." *Review of Educational Research*, 1975, *45*(2), 173–207.

Miller, J. W., and Mills, O. (Eds.). *Credentialing Educational Accomplishments*. Washington, D.C.: American Council on Education, 1978.

National Board of Medical Examiners. "Uniformity and Diversity: Challenge to Examination Systems in Medicine." In *Proceedings of Annual Conference of National Board of Medical Examiners*. Philadelphia: National Board of Medical Examiners, 1978.

Orlans, H. "The Fatuity of Credentialing Everyone and Everything." Paper presented at 57th annual meeting of the American Council on Education, San Diego, Calif., 1974.

Rock, D. A. "The Setting of Standards or Cutting Scores." Unpublished report, Educational Testing Service, 1979.

Rock, D. A., Davis, E. L., and Werts, C. "An Empirical Comparison of Standard-Setting Procedures." Unpublished manuscript, Educational Testing Service, 1979.

Schmidt, F. L., and others. *The Behavioral Consistency Method of Unassembled Examining*. Washington, D.C.: Personnel Research and Development Center, U.S. Office of Personnel Management, 1979.

Temp, G. E., and others. "Issues Associated with Setting Standards in Civil Service Systems." Unpublished paper, Southern Regional Test Development Center, Educational Testing Service, 1979.

6   Willem K. B. Hofstee

ℛ ℛ ℛ ℛ ℛ ℛ ℛ ℛ ℛ ℛ ℛ ℛ ℛ

The Case for Compromise in Educational Selection and Grading

In 1975, the Dutch parliament invited the minister of education to propose a satisfactory solution to the problem of selection for "closed studies" such as medicine, dentistry, and veterinary science. The advisory committee established by the minister opened its first report by stating that a solution satisfactory to all persons involved does not exist and that the choice between alternatives is ultimately a political, not a scientific, matter. Decisions about grading or selection policies are, in fact, based on two classes of premises, one political and the other cognitive. The term *political* does not here refer to national or party politics. It is used rather to denote actions that promote certain values at the expense of other values. In contrast to these political values, the validity of "cognitive" premises can be assessed analytically or empirically. What contributions can be expected from the educational researcher in this interplay of values and facts?

    In many cases, there will be pressure on the researcher to provide "automatic" solutions in which the necessity of choosing between values is obscured. The researcher may be tempted to give in to this pressure, since doing so will enable him or her to make a personal choice between values and thus to exert power. The temptation should be resisted, however, because ignoring values or obscuring the distinction between values and facts is bad for both science and politics. Rather, the researcher should expose the value component of the problem so that it can be subjected to constructive political discourse. The selection and grading models to be discussed here attempt to do just that. They are called *compromise models*, in that seemingly opposing policies appear as special cases of the same model. More appropriately perhaps, the models may be described as *generative* or *superordinate*.

For purposes of illustration, let us say that a decision between two clearly opposed and mutually exclusive policies has to be taken. Each alternative has its partisans, and there is a certain balance of power between the two parties. The difference between the alternative policies is usually perceived as a difference of principle — in other words, a difference that touches on very fundamental values. Emotions may run high in the debate.

The contribution of a general model in this situation is as follows: First, it shows that the two alternatives may be thought of as special cases — usually, extreme cases — on a continuum of possible policies. The inescapable implication is that a difference of principle can be reduced to a difference of degree, which in turn may be solved through bargaining. The presentation of the general model is usually met with less than complete enthusiasm. It takes the sting out of the debate, to the disappointment of many. The presenter is usually accused of cynicism, and the model is found to be iconoclastic. Both parties will tend to focus on the fact that the other party's principle is incorporated in the model and will thus react negatively.

On second thought, however, both parties may come to realize that every conceivable solution to the debate amounts to choosing parameter values for the model and that a whole continuum of solutions exists — solutions that are at least preferable to the other party's proposals. Thus, sooner or later, depending on the pressure under which the debate takes place, the model may become a tool for finding a pragmatic solution to the conflict. The solution is going to make everybody unhappy, but the balance of unhappiness may be such that each party is satisfied with the other party's unhappiness. The sustained and clamorous proclamation of one's objections to the compromise therefore becomes a vital element in maintaining the balance.

Three such models, one pertaining to admission policies, a second to setting cutoff scores, and a third to the combination of grades, will be discussed. But certain reservations must first be made. The approach to applied problems through generative models has nothing to do with empirical science. Of course, one may use these models to find out how well they capture spontaneous choices between policies and to establish parameters in an empirical manner. But in the applications that I have in mind the models are simply put forward, and their parameters result from bargaining. In the bargaining, simulations of past decisions may provide an argument for one party or another, but it would be a grave mistake to believe that an objective empirical solution to the debate can be found. So the scientific contribution here is purely analytical. This is an unfamiliar situation in the behavioral sciences.

Another reservation is that the models to be discussed are very simple and unsophisticated. We all are familiar with far more elegant models. I even plead guilty to the charge that the models, in order to do their job, should be simple enough to be understood by the lay parties involved. But designing such models does require at least a touch of creativity.

A last reservation is that a plea for compromise models seems itself to be indicative of a particular system of values. Strictly speaking, that is not true. The models do not dictate a compromise; they just widen the scope of possible solutions and provide the tools for negotiating a solution. Psychologically, however, it is probably true that a person who believes in radical solutions would not ask that consideration be given to compromise models. That interpretation is not contested here. Compromises are obviously in the interest of the weaker party, which is why they agree very well with my definition of democracy.

Restricted Admission

The first example, which will be discussed at some length, is the weighted lottery model for admission of students to closed (*numerus clausus*) studies, such as medicine, dentistry, and veterinary science. One particular solution under this model was proposed by Vermaat, a Dutch professor of mathematics and member of parliament, and the general model is easily derived from that proposal. It states that in cases of restricted admission, an applicant's chances of being admitted—that is, the number of lottery tickets he or she receives—is a monotonically increasing function of his or her score (for example, a secondary school grade point average). Clearly, the model fills the gap between straight lottery selection and comparative selection.

The model may be formalized to a certain extent as follows: An applicant with score x receives a chance of admission $f(x)$ where f is a monotonically increasing function such that

$$\Sigma f(x)p(x) = R$$
or
$$\int f(x)p(x)dx = R,$$

with R the selection ratio and $p(x)$ the empirical score distribution summing to 1.

In the special case of a straight lottery,

$$f(x) = R \text{ for all } x,$$

whereas in the case of comparative selection,

$$f(x) = 1 \text{ for } x > a$$
and
$$f(x) = 0 \text{ for } x < a,$$

the cutoff point a being defined by

$$\int_a^{x_{\max}} p(x)dx = R.$$

Figure 1 illustrates the model. Weighted lottery selection has been applied in The Netherlands on a national scale as an admission policy for studies such as medicine. In practice, applicants are classified according to grade point average, and ratio weights representing the relative proportion admitted to each class are established a priori.

Figure 1. Illustration of the Effects of Weighted Lottery with Overall Selection Rate of .45.

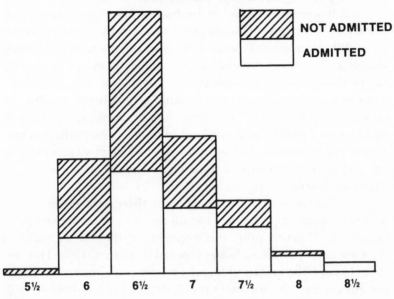

Weighted lottery selection has been discussed in other countries; the Germans have even coined their own term, *Leistunggesteuertes Losverfahren* or *performance-guided lottery procedure.* But the compromise model does not seem to have caught on in countries other than The Netherlands, and even there it may have been abolished by the time this is printed. It may be questioned how useful the model is. In most countries there is ready acceptance of the notion of comparative selection. The problem arises, therefore, when the comparative selection procedure includes a lottery component that is unacceptable. There is little use for models that mediate between alternatives when one of the alternatives would generally be considered illegitimate or inappropriate.

The lottery alternative has been extensively debated in The Netherlands over the past few years. The arguments that have been brought forward may be classified according to the fourfold table containing false positive, false negative, valid positive, and valid negative arguments. An attempt will be made here to give a balanced, if incomplete, account of these discussions.

Advocates of admission by lottery have often stated that grade point averages are invalid predictors anyway. This is patently false. What is true is that because of favorable base rates and modest validities, the expected payoff of selection by grade point average rather than by random admission is not impressive. The more ultimate the criteria, the more "fleeting" (Humphreys, 1968) is the expected payoff. Finally, the distinction between expected payoff and observed payoff should be kept in mind. The institution may appear resistant to improvements because of adaptive processes on the part of both faculty and students that annihilate the effects of selection (Aiken, 1963).

As for the false negative argument, there is the highly sophisticated view that a probability has no meaning when applied to an individual. Theoretically, this argument is difficult to maintain since adequate rules have been proposed (Naerssen, 1961; Hofstee, 1979) to assess the validity of singular stochastic propositions. In the present context, the argument is as farfetched as it is sophisticated; for, if an individual probability had no meaning, the distinction between two tickets representing chances of admission of .99 and .01 would also be meaningless.

Probably the most important and valid negative argument against random admission pertains to what is sometimes called the immoral impact of the lottery method; that is, it does not reward achievement. The principle that achievement should be positively sanctioned is intuitively compelling. Selection by lottery undermines that principle. It should be noted, however, that the lottery rule is not unconditional. An applicant has to qualify himself or herself by demonstrating an appropriate level of performance in secondary school. For those who have little difficulty in fulfilling the minimum requirements, lottery admission is probably demotivating. However, comparative selection is probably demotivating to the majority of students — that is, average students — since it reduces their expected payoff relative to the random admission situation.

The prime valid positive argument for lottery admission is that it is the closest approximation to equal distribution of a scarce

commodity. The right of admission to higher education is achieved
through certain secondary school diplomas under Dutch law. In a
restricted situation, equal probability of admission for qualified
applicants may be found to be the most equitable policy.

There are secondary arguments in favor of the lottery
method. One is that the intellectual pecking order among studies is
disturbed by selection, not by lottery. Back in the 1960s, a colleague
and I (Hofstee and Wijnen, 1968) compared intelligence scores with
choice of study at Groningen University. The natural intellectual
order was clearly visible, starting with mathematics and physics and
ending with some of the more obscure studies. Psychology, I am
happy to say, was above average. More to the point, the studies that
became "closed" in the 1970s were not characterized by high intellectual status in the unrestricted situation. Medicine was above
average but clearly below biology, and dentistry attracted quite
mediocre students. Naturally, these professions will profit to some
extent by comparative selection and even by the use of weighted
lotteries. There is probably no such thing as being too intelligent to
be a doctor. But from a societal point of view, one may have
reservations about this redistribution of talent. It is difficult to see
why the field of study that happens to have the most unfavorable
selection rate — in The Netherlands, veterinarian studies — should
consequently have the highest intellectual status. It may even be
argued that problems of restricted admission are not likely to develop in studies requiring high intellectual ability and that the
popularity of the restricted studies is caused in part by the restricted
intellectual demands they impose upon students.

Another side effect of selection as opposed to the lottery
method is that the former results in devaluation of secondary school
diplomas. To the extent that one is satisfied with a secondary school
system, the lottery method should be preferred, since it backfires
least upon that system. Interestingly, however, secondary school
teachers have been predominantly opposed to this method. One
interpretation is that, in the discussions, *numerus clausus* and admission procedures were confused, and objections to admission restrictions were carried over to the weighted-lottery rule.

A final argument in favor of using lotteries is that they are
more acceptable than comparative selection, at least to Dutch sec-

ondary school students.   In a study by Hofstee and Trommar
(1976), secondary school students in their last year were asked the
following question: If you could advise the government on admission
policies, which would you recommend? Since the investigation was
carried out under the auspices of the advisory committee referred to
earlier, our respondents were indeed indirectly advising the government. The straight lottery method received 40 percent of the votes,
comparative selection only 10 percent; the remaining 50 percent
went to weighted lottery. These results have been replicated in at
least three other unpublished studies. One might hypothesize that
the mediocre students were primarily responsible for the results.
Figure 2, however, shows that this is only partially the case. The
relationship between scholastic standing and preference is by no
means perfect. Most notably, comparative selection received only
some 25 percent of the votes even in the highest scholastic performance category.

**Figure 2. Relationship Between Scholastic Standing and Preference for
Admission Procedures.**

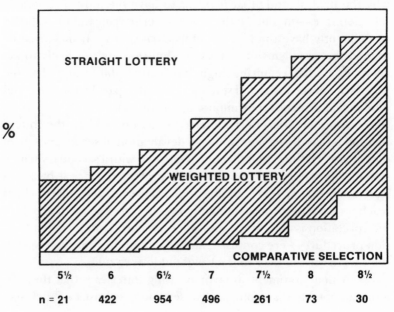

If we leave complications aside, the kernel of the discussion between the extremes of comparative selection and selection by straight lottery consists of two opposing political principles: rewarding achievement and providing equal opportunity. Many other political problems could be adequately captured in those terms, and many solutions consist of a weighted compromise between the two principles. Compromise models such as weighted lotteries may facilitate construction of the least unacceptable solution.

One feature of compromise models that was touched upon in the introduction has come up repeatedly in the discussion of admission policies. It is the "dirty hands" feature; that is, the very situation to which the compromise applies is found unacceptable by some. Any attempt to solve the problems created by *numerus clausus* can only prolong the existence of that undesirable state of affairs, according to this reasoning. I have little sympathy with the consequences that are usually drawn from this argument, but I think it should be acknowledged that compromises do compromise.

Cutoff Points

The second model (Hofstee, 1977) to be discussed here applies to the situation in which a cutoff score on an achievement test is set for the first time. The expression "for the first time" means that no agreed-upon prior or collateral information is available on the difficulty of the test, the quality of the course, or the amount of preparation by the students.

The following example illustrates the concept of setting a standard for the first time. In 1979, I gave a course on methodology to some 160 second-year psychology students. The passing score on the test had to be lowered to 45 percent mastery, and even then only 55 percent of the students passed. In 1980, the passing score was set at close to 60 percent, and over 90 percent of the students passed. The learning materials were essentially the same; the teachers and the test items were essentially the same; and in view of the large numbers it would be difficult to ascribe the discrepancy to a cohort effect. The discrepancy was probably caused by a shift in administrative regulations that enabled the students to spend more time on the subject. I know of no other standard-setting policy that could have handled these two testings in a coherent and still more or less acceptable way; the compromise model to be described did so, by treating both testings as "first tests."

The model is best explained by referring to Figure 3. The vertical axis there represents percentage of "knowledge" k — in the case of a multiple-choice test, it represents the percentage of right answers corrected for guessing. The horizontal axis represents percentage of failures (f) on the test, that is, the percentage of students scoring below the cutoff point.

The model consists of the locus of admissible cutoff points and is represented by the straight line $k + af = c$. The parameters a and c may be established as follows: First, the maximum required percentage of mastery, k_{max}, is established. This may be defined as

Figure 3. Illustration of Compromise Model for Establishing Cutoff Points.

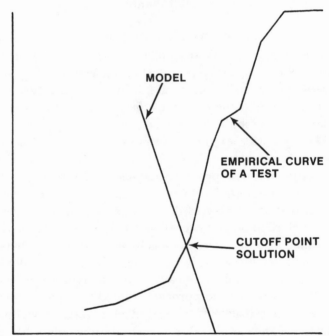

the cutoff score that would be satisfactory even if every student attained that score at the first trial. Second, the minimum acceptable percentage of mastery, k_{min}, is determined. This level may be defined as the cutoff score below which one would not go even if no student attained that score at the first trial. Third, the maximum acceptable percentage of failures, f_{max}, is established. Fourth, the minimum acceptable percentage of failures, f_{min}, is established. In our student-centered times, it may seem obvious to set this percentage at zero, but one might argue that this solution is unrealistic since the next cohort of students will quickly adapt to such a lenient state of affairs and will turn it into a self-defeating policy.

The points (f_{min}, k_{max}) and (f_{max}, k_{min}) are now considered admissible solutions and are substituted into the model to determine the model parameters. For example, if $f_{min} = 0$, $k_{max} = 70$, $f_{max} = 60$, $k_{min} = 40$, the locus of admissible cut-off scores is $k + .5f = 70$.

To find the actual cutoff score for a test, the empirical relation between k and f within the test is determined over all possible cutoff scores. An example is given by the curved line in Figure 3. The cutoff point is the point of intersection between the model and the empirical curve. Clearly, the model compromises between "absolute" and "relative" norms. Objections to the model are to be expected from the proponents of mastery learning and would run as follows: Norms should be absolute and should be set at about 85 percent; there is absolutely no need for compromise models; all they will do is take us back to the days when misguided psychometricians were busy mixing up selection and education.

In response, it should be noted that the 85 percent norm is not sacred. It is a compromise between the ideal of 100 percent and the realization of the old psychometric truth that item validities are usually somewhat less than perfect, so that even a "master" may choose an attractive distracter for his or her answer. So there seems to be room for bargaining within the mastery-learning philosophy.

There are, of course, some doubts about whether mastery learning is such a good idea after all (Crombag, 1979). I should like to submit that taking an achievement test score as a criterion or standard is to confuse learning for life with learning for school; that uniform high standards can usually only be met through capitalization on chance, outright coaching, and contempt for cost-benefit considerations; and that there is nothing very progressive about creating the false illusion of equal attainment. I should add that many school systems on the Continent have practiced mastery learning all along in the sense of having students repeat examinations that they fail, and little can be said in favor of that policy (Wilbrink, 1980). I could also make scathing remarks about other policies. But that would only support a plea for compromise models.

A second, more serious competitor to the present model is the decision-theoretic approach to establishing norms (Mellenbergh, 1979). In this approach, a loss function is defined as the discrepancy between observed score and criterion score. The criterion may be a true-score estimate or an external criterion. The cutoff score is the test score that minimizes the expected loss.

A minor criticism of the decision-theoretic approach is that so far too much attention has been given to linear and threshold loss functions. On the one hand, threshold or binary loss is realistic only if examination scores are combined in a strictly conjunctive, multiple-cutoff manner and if credits are the only thing that counts, not grades. My department experimented with such a system but abolished it, and I know of no other examples. Linear loss, on the other hand, is appropriate only when scores are combined in a strictly compensatory manner; that is, when there is no such thing as failing a course. Pure compensatory policies are probably even rarer than pure conjunctive policies. For most of the existing educational systems with their mixed policies, some S-shaped loss function is required, such as the normal or beta ogive or a polynomial function.

A more important source of uneasiness with the decision approach comes from the powerful nature of the assumptions that have to be made (Glass, 1978; Shepard, Chapter Four). In the first place, a cutoff score should be set on the criterion. Even if a certain level of required mastery can be agreed upon, this level cannot be directly translated into a required true-score level. There is simply no objective way to represent course objectives by test items, except in a trivial sense; and, in practice, the difficulty of a test is probably more indicative of the disposition of the item writer than of the difficulty of the course content. So it is always unreasonable to set standards in an a priori way without any regard for the number of passes and failures.

A second problem is the establishment of the utility parameters. It is customary to distinguish between direct assessment and indirect assessment of such parameters. Through use of indirect assessment, parameters are selected on the basis of tangible consequences. In many settings, and probably also in the educational setting, indirect assessment is a superior approach: If a discrepancy arises between directly chosen parameters and those that are indirectly derived, persons will change their direct utilities to avoid unacceptable consequences in terms of the proportion of knowledge and proportion of failures associated with the cutoff score. All this takes us back to my compromise model for setting cutoff scores. Whether the two approaches can to some extent be integrated, and especially whether the crudity of the compromise model could thus be alleviated, are open questions at this moment.

Before we leave the discussion of the decision-theoretic approach, a final comment on utilities should be made. In all applications to educational settings that I am aware of, policies are judged by their effects in the average individual case. No separate utility is placed on the global effect of a policy. There is some naiveté about this. If a norm is chosen that maximizes the utility with respect to the average individual, very high or very low percentages of failures may be the result. These extreme percentages may themselves have a negative utility. I am cynical enough to suspect that extremely low or extremely high failure rates may have a corrupting influence both on the next generation of students and on the instructional staff.

It should be stressed that the compromise model for establishing a first-generation cutoff score does not apply to subsequent occasions, that is, to situations in which no systematic differences are intended or expected. For the problem of equating or adapting norms, Gruyter (1978) has proposed very satisfactory solutions of a Bayesian type. His model, of which an earlier solution by Hofstee (1973) appears to be a degenerate case, compromises between maintaining a knowledge percentage and a failure percentage. Naerssen (1979) has shown that it makes little difference whether the equating of subsequent norms is carried out in a relative or absolute manner, that is, by maintaining a knowledge percentage or a failure percentage. His conclusion that there is little use for "hybrid models" needs to be qualified, however. By "little difference" Naerssen means difference in institutional utility. But if utility, as a function of cutoff score, has a flat optimum, a small shift may make a good deal of subjective difference to several students. Second, Naerssen uses linear utility. It remains to be seen what happens if this assumption is varied. Third, even if hybrid models are uncalled for in the context of equating norms, it would not follow that they can be dispensed with when the first standard is set in a situation where prior information is lacking.

Turning now to the compromise model itself, let us consider precisely what the compromise is about. A clue can be found in a study by Zegers, Hofstee, and Korbee (1978). We presented subjects with several frequency distributions of raw achievement test scores and asked them to establish a cutoff point. On the basis of these judgments, an attempt was made to capture their individual grading policies with the compromise model. The most relevant result was that students displayed more relative grading, whereas staff members tended to prefer absolute grading. This suggests that the model compromises between student-centered and staff-centered value systems. In fact, the model was derived to facilitate staff-student bargaining in educational policy committees, so the differences in strategy were not unexpected. In discussing these differences, I shall not use the high-toned and idealistic arguments that make the reading of educational literature so pleasant, if not particularly rewarding. Instead, I will focus on the differential interests of students and staff. The offensive proposition that, compared to interests, ideals have little motivating power will serve as a guideline.

A priori or absolute standards are in the interest of the institution and its officials for obvious reasons. More status is associated with absolute than with relative norms, not only because in practice relative norms tend to come out lower but also because absolute norms have a sacrosanct quality that relative norms lack. Teaching is a secondary profession in the sense that it does not produce a tangible product, so the teacher is subject to feelings of unimportance. This may well be a reason why educational philosophies advocating absolute norms of 85 percent and higher have become so popular. Absolute norms also provide a more apt vehicle for acting out irritation with "ever duller" generations of students, upon whose performance the teacher depends — perhaps not materially but for his or her own sense of accomplishment.

The prime interest of the student, in contrast, is to obtain passing grades. Students are probably well aware of the virtual absence of correlation between educational and real-life criteria, so their interest is in obtaining a diploma rather than in mastering what is taught. Since at their age they have other interesting things to do, they will try to obtain the diploma with minimal effort. Thus, they may be expected to have little sympathy for the kind of surprises that result from absolute grading. They know where they stand relative to their group, so that with normal study effort they can predict their grades if relative norms are used. They are probably also aware that absolute grading is usually associated with a higher failure rate, which is directly against their interests.

Of course, there are exceptions to this picture. Some teachers are more student oriented than the students themselves, and some students have a keener interest in the learning material than the teacher has. But the student-oriented teacher is subject to collegial pressure, and the intrinsic motivation of a student can hardly extend to everything that he or she is taught. The mere proclamation that all interests are equal — usually followed by the corollary that staff interests are more equal than student interests — is not going to produce a healthy learning environment. The realization that there is an ongoing and structural conflict of interests and that bargaining and compromises are honorable facts of life may in the end lead to better solutions.

An interesting ramification of the cutting-score model was suggested by findings in the study by Zegers, Hofstee, and Korbee (1978) — findings that appeared anomalous at first. Some judges chose to set higher cutoffs for the more difficult tests and lower cutoffs for easier tests. An interpretation of this policy may be constructed by referring to cooperative grading systems (see, for example, Fraser and others, 1977; Beaman and others, 1977). With a relative policy, an individual's chances of passing are higher as the others perform worse; under a cooperative policy, his or her chances are higher as the others perform better. This interpretation of the grading behavior of the judges in the study by Zegers, Hofstee, and Korbee (1978) is a bit farfetched, since cooperative grading makes sense only when students are actually encouraged to cooperate, and the judges had no reason to suppose that this was the case. But the point is brought up because cooperative grading is an interesting possibility in itself, and because the compromise model can easily be extended to cover all intermediate policies between absolute and cooperative grading.

Combining Grades

Having discussed student admission and the grading of single tests, let us now turn to the topic of combining grades for an examination decision. A special case is the problem of setting standards for a single course when students who fail have to repeat the test until they reach a passing level. Some people may not think of this as a combination problem, but there are good reasons to do so.

The specific problem of setting a standard for a single course with repeated testings is almost invariably solved by a disjunctive policy; that is, the student passes as soon as a passing score is obtained on one out of two or more testings. In most cases there are no restrictions on the number of testings, though there may be restrictions on the intervals between testings. The disjunctive policy has at least two weaknesses. In the first place, it capitalizes on chance because of the unreliability of the tests. Naerssen (1976) calculated that inserting an extra testing per year would result in many false positives if the norm was not raised. Second, the disjunctive policy elicits a "reconnaissance effect" (Brink, 1977); since students can fail a test with impunity, some will take a test just to see what it looks like. This is a costly state of affairs, for several obvious reasons.

An alternative that would solve these problems is a compensatory policy in which the obtained grade for a single course is the average over repeated testings; a person passes as soon as his or her average is above the norm. Both capitalization on chance and reconnaissance strategy would be effectively counteracted by the averaging policy. Unfortunately, this policy is in conflict with most people's feelings (or sentiments) about justice. In the moral atmosphere that characterizes educational rhetoric, failing a test is a sin, so the student should be given the benefit of the doubt, even if that amounts to capitalization on chance.

The compromise model for this dilemma is easily constructed through application of the Minkowski r metric (see, for example, Coombs, Dawes, and Tversky, 1970), as illustrated in Figure 4. The

Figure 4. Minimal Required Score on Second Testing as a Function of Score on First Testing.

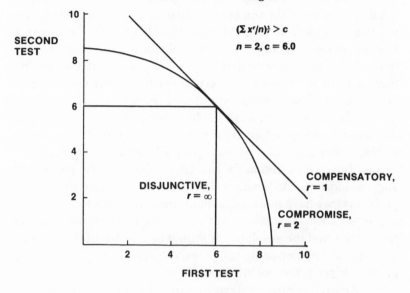

individual student is represented as a point in an n space; the coordinates of the point represent his or her scores on the n repeated testings. A student passes if the average distance between the point and the origin is greater than the norm distance. In general:

$$\left[\left(\frac{1}{n}\right) \sum_{g=1}^{n} x_g^r\right]^{1/r} \geq c, r \geq 1,$$

where x_g is the score on test g and c is the norm. Setting the Minkowski parameter r equal to infinity gives the disjunctive model; setting $r = 1$ gives the averaging model. An intuitively appealing compromise is the quadratic or Euclidian model, in which higher grades are given more weight than lower grades (Coombs, Dawes, and Tversky, 1970). I know of no present applications, but I hope that presentation of the compromise will lead to practical applications in the future.

With respect to the combination of scores for *different* courses, the debate is usually between conjunctive and compensatory policies. Compromise models between the two are easily constructed through a translation of axes in the Minkowski model. Here also,

the compensatory policy deserves more attention for both psychometric and pedagogical reasons than it usually receives. The personal investment of the teacher in a particular course is probably the
most serious obstacle to compensatory policies. To the marginal
student, however, compensatory combination is threatening since,
beyond a certain point, it may be practically impossible to attain a
passing average. The interaction between these motives may form a
powerful conspiracy against educational change.

Three compromise models have been discussed here in relative isolation: weighted lottery for the problem of student selection,
a compromise model for setting a pass-fail standard on a single test,
and a Minkowski solution for merging disjunctive, compensatory,
and conjunctive combination policies. But the models and the
problems may have more in common than their isolated treatment
suggests. Formally, their main theme is the counterpoint between
the relative and the absolute. It should be possible to find a superordinate, all-encompassing compromise model; however, such integrative elegance was not attempted here.

An even greater challenge is offered by the heterogeneity of
values and motives that dominate the discussion to which the models
pertain. Would a global classification into absolutist versus relativist
value systems make sense, or would it only obscure the substantive
issues? Maybe the distinctions should be drawn along quite another
dimension: between those favoring clear-cut solutions, either relative or absolute, and those who are looking for compromises.

References

Aiken, L. R. "The Grading Behavior of a College Faculty."
    Educational and Psychological Measurement, 1963, *23*, 319–322.
Beaman, A. L., and others. "Effects of Voluntary and Semivolun-
    tary Peer-Monitoring Programs on Academic Performance."
    Journal of Educational Psychology, 1977, *69*, 109–114.
Brink, W. P. van den. "Het Verken-Effect." *Tijdschrift voor Onder-
    wijsresearch*, 1977, *2*, 253–261.
Coombs, C. H., Dawes, R. M., and Tversky, A. *Mathematical Psychol-
    ogy*. Englewood Cliffs, N.J.: Prentice-Hall, 1970.
Crombag, H. F. M. "ATI: Perhaps Not Such a Good Idea After
    All." *Tijdschrift voor Onderwijsresearch*, 1979, *4*, 176–183.

Fraser, S. C., and others. "Two, Three, Four Heads Are Better than One: Modification of College Performance by Peer Monitoring." *Journal of Educational Psychology,* 1977, *69,* 101–108.

Glass, G. V. "Standards and Criteria." *Journal of Educational Measurement,* 1978, *15,* 237–261.

Gruyter, D. de. "A Bayesian Approach to the Passing Score Problem." *Tijdschrift voor Onderwijsresearch,* 1978, *3,* 145–151.

Hofstee, W. K. B. Een Alternatief voor Normhandhaving Bij Toetsen." *Nederlands Tijdschrift voor de Psychologie,* 1973, *28,* 215–227.

Hofstee, W. K. B. "Caesuurprobleem Opgelost." *Onderzoek van Onderwijs,* 1977, *6,* 6–7.

Hofstee, W. K. B. "'Jan Heeft een Kans van .70. . . .': Drogredenen met Betrekking Tot Individuele Kansuitspraken." *Kennis en Methode,* 1979, *3,* 433–445.

Hofstee, W. K. B., and Trommar, P. M. "Selectie en Loting: Meningen van VWO-Eindexaminandi." *Heymans Bulletin,* No. 251, Department of Psychology, University of Groningen, 1976.

Hofstee, W. K. B., and Wijnen, W. H. F. W. "Intelligentieonderzoek Eerstejaars 1968." *Mededelingenblad Rijks Universiteit Groningen,* 1968, *2*(8).

Humphreys, L. G. "The Fleeting Nature of the Prediction of College Academic Success." *Journal of Educational Psychology,* 1968, *59,* 375–380.

Mellenbergh, G. J. "De Beslissing Gewogen." In G. J. Mellenbergh, R. F. van Naerssen, and H. Wesdorp (Eds.), *Rede als Richtsnoer.* The Hague: Mouton, 1979.

Naerssen, R. F. van. "A Scale for the Measurement of Subjective Probability." *Acta Psychologica,* 1961, *17,* 159–166.

Naerssen, R. F. van. "Het Derde Tentamenmodel, met een Toepassing." *Tijdschrift voor Onderwijsresearch,* 1976, *1,* 161–170.

Naerssen, R. F. van. "Absolute of Relatieve Aftestgrens: Een Verkenning met Simulatie." *Tijdschrift voor Onderwijsresearch,* 1979, *4,* 8–17.

Wilbrink, B. "Caesuurbepaling." COWO-Rapport, University of Amsterdam, 1980.

Zegers, F. E., Hofstee, W. K. B., and Korbee, C. J. M. Een Beleidsinstrument M.B.T. Caesuurbepaling." Paper presented at Ondernijs Research Dagen, Utrecht, 1978.

Part Three

⌘ ⌘ ⌘ ⌘ ⌘ ⌘ ⌘ ⌘ ⌘ ⌘ ⌘ ⌘ ⌘

Anxiety and
Test Performance

To the extent that test anxiety differentially affects individual test scores, we obtain information that distorts a true measure of achievement or ability. Consequently, anything we can do to alleviate or control test anxiety or to understand the way it functions will improve our interpretation and use of test information. In Part Three, Irwin Sarason provides an introduction to the subject of test anxiety and discusses ways of moderating its effects, while the chapter by Heinz Krohne and Paul Schaffner, as well as the one by Willy Lens, examine various interrelations of test anxiety, motivation, and performance.

In Chapter Seven, Sarason looks at test anxiety from an information-processing point of view, considering it as a tendency to produce task-irrelevant responses under conditions of awareness that performance is being evaluated. There are wide individual differences in this tendency, and, while specific to the situation, it still shows substantial generality within the individual. Test anxiety is usually measured through the use of one of several questionnaires, and the scores so obtained typically show low but significant correlations with school grades. Numerous experimental studies have manipulated variables to determine their effect on the performance of high- and low-anxious persons, and some of these are reviewed. A variety of interventions is suggested for reducing anxiety (or its effects): reassurance, modeling, attentional training, relaxation, and social support. A supportive environment and social sharing are two ways of moderating test anxiety, and the results of work to date suggest that a reduction of the social evaluative component would be important in the organization of school and society.

Krohne and Schaffner concentrate in Chapter Eight on the influence of motivation on performance, noting that anxiety can have either a positive or a negative effect on motivation. They point out that most studies have focused on the effect of anxiety only during examinations or testing situations. To understand the full process, however, it is also necessary to consider the effect of motivation on preparation. They view two variables as important in the preparation phase, namely, the degree to which the task is structured and the opportunity available to prepare for it. The typical laboratory study uses highly structured tasks, and the opportunity to prepare is controlled. In real life, however, tasks are not always well structured, and preparation is under the individual's control. Evidence is presented to show the way in which structure and opportunity interact with anxiety and ability to produce different levels of performance. Anxious individuals may be motivated to devote more effort to preparation and hence to perform at least as well as the less anxious. An experimental study using a more nearly real-life situation supports, through correlations, multiple regression, and path analysis, the authors' deductions from their theoretical position.

In Chapter Nine, Lens is also primarily interested in the relation between test anxiety and motivation and the consequent effect on performance. He starts with Atkinson's theory of achievement motivation that posits opposed needs to achieve success and to avoid failure (see Chapter Two). The dynamics of action are such that, other things being equal, the fear of failure (test anxiety) will reduce the motivation to succeed, resulting in a negative effect on performance. Evidence supports three hypotheses from this relationship. Those high in the need to succeed and low in fear of failure will prefer achievement tests at intermediate difficulty levels, will perform more efficiently on achievement tests that are labeled as requiring important abilities than will those with strong test anxiety, and will be less persistent in solving difficult tasks when given alternatives. Of particular importance is the finding that additional incentives can reduce performance. This is explained by reference to the Yerkes-Dodson hypothesis that the relation of performance to motivation is represented by an inverted U-shaped curve. If motivation is too high, performance will suffer. In that case, test anxiety, through its reduction of motivation toward an optimal level, will actually improve performance. The general conclusion is that the effect of test anxiety on performance depends on the exact shape of the relationship of motivation to performance and on the overall level of motivation.

Taken together, these chapters provide an unusually clear look at test anxiety in its various manifestations. Ample evidence establishes that there are some individuals who express feelings of anxiety about taking tests and who also do less well in them, and often in schoolwork, than might otherwise be expected of them. But test anxiety is not a simple phenomenon operating in an either-or or unidimensional fashion. And it is certainly more complicated in real-life situations than in controlled laboratory studies. The challenge for testers, researchers, and educators is to predict test anxiety in evaluative situations in the real world, where it operates in association with motivation and other variables, and then, if possible, to control it or harness it in the service of better performance.

7　Irwin G. Sarason

ℜ ℜ ℜ ℜ ℜ ℜ ℜ ℜ ℜ ℜ ℜ ℜ ℜ

Understanding and Modifying Test Anxiety

Tests are not just assessment devices. They play important roles in the lives of those who take them. Performance on them can be influenced by personal characteristics in which the tester may have no interest. Test anxiety is an example of such a personal characteristic. Teachers and educational institutions want to know how skilled their students are in mathematics or biology, not how upset they become at the thought of taking tests. Yet test anxiety must be taken into account when it intrudes upon performance.

Anxiety is a very personal experience that involves anticipations of danger, harm, and inability to meet challenges. In the case of test anxiety, these anticipations are linked to evaluational situations. Test anxious people see evaluational situations as difficult, challenging, and threatening and themselves as ineffective in coping with academic challenges. They focus—sometimes obsessively—on the undesirable consequences of personal inadequacy. Their self-deprecating thoughts are strong and interfere with orderly problem solving. Test anxious people frequently expect and anticipate failure and loss of regard by others.

One useful approach to the study of test anxiety is the information-processing point of view. From this perspective, it is important to identify the cognitive events that influence overt behavior inasmuch as they determine the personal meaning that a particular situation has for the individual. Test anxiety has been conceptualized as a tendency to emit personalized task-irrelevant responses when individuals experience heightened awareness that their performance is being evaluated. Highly test anxious individuals are especially attentive to cues concerning the evaluative component of performance. Their fear of failure involves self-centered thoughts that interfere with concentration on the task at hand. Although evaluative cues seem to motivate persons low in test anxiety, the same cues may be quite threatening danger flags for those who are highly anxious.

The range of reactions to tests extends from virtual immobilization in the face of potential criticism to exhilaration at the prospect of receiving accolades. The person who freezes up on a final examination seems preoccupied with self-doubt and the consequences of failure, whereas the accolade seeker seems confident and approaches the examination as an opportunity for receiving recognition. This chapter begins with a discussion of test anxiety as a personal characteristic, how it is assessed, and the relationship of test anxiety to performance. Later in the chapter, relevant theoretical, research, and educational issues will be discussed.

Assessment and Correlates of Test Anxiety

Why has interest in test anxiety not only persisted but actually increased over the years? All researchers know how difficult it is to come to grips with such global concepts as anxiety, aggression, and dependence. But concepts rooted in specific classes of situations are more manageable. The anxious football player may not be an anxious public speaker or anxious parent. Evaluational situations are relatively specific and are experienced by everyone. At the same time, their universality makes them significant educational, social, and clinical problems. They are also scientifically valuable because they provide a specific situation for the study of stress and how people cope with it.

Research on test anxiety has flourished because testing situations are considered personally important by most people. This is particularly true for those who go to school or who may be subjected to evaluations of intellectual skills and performance. This immediate personal relevance is not seen in all areas of psychological research. Anyone who has ever taught the introductory psychology course in a college or university is well aware of the question all too often asked by students when they serve as subjects in the experiments that usually go along with that course: "What in the world do these experiments have to do with real life?" But individuals know from personal experience that performance evaluations take place all the time and that these evaluations can be of great personal importance. It is not surprising, therefore, that many researchers find the performance evaluation situation a useful one for studying the effects of anxiety. It is also not surprising that the clinical and educational aspects of test anxiety have received growing attention.

For many years, theories of anxiety were rooted primarily in the experiences of the clinical worker and the insights of the sensitive observer of people going about their day-to-day activities. Important scientific papers appeared during the 1930s and 1940s, when increasing efforts were made to study the problem of anxiety from an experimental perspective. Psychologists were in the forefront of these efforts — efforts that often took the shape of analogues of psychoanalytic concepts. During the 1950s, researchers took another step forward in their attempts to assess anxiety quantitatively. Although some work along these lines had been done earlier, the 1950s saw a flowering of anxiety scales, questionnaires, and measures (Sarason, 1960).

Because of the desirability of rooting the study of anxiety in a definable situational context, some researchers turned their attention from the generalized concept of anxiety to specific sources of anxiety, such as social anxiety, anxiety over public speaking, and test anxiety. Test anxiety has become the most widely studied of these specific sources of anxiety, and there are now available a number of indexes of persons' anxieties about being examined and having their performances evaluated.

Test anxiety is usually assessed by means of self-reports, with questionnaires and rating scales being the most commonly used

assessment instruments. There are many measures of test anxiety.
The Test Anxiety Scale for Children, constructed by Seymour
Sarason and his associates (Sarason and others, 1960), was the first
index of test anxiety to be used widely by researchers. It continues
to be a popular and valued instrument. The Test Anxiety Questionnaire (Mandler and Sarason, 1952) provides a series of graphic
rating scales on which subjects can indicate the degree of discomfort
they experience while taking tests. Liebert and Morris (1967)
devised the Worry-Emotionality Questionnaire to assess the degree
to which worry and emotionality intrude upon task performance.
The Achievement Anxiety Test (Alpert and Haber, 1960) was
developed on the assumption that anxiety can be either debilitating
or facilitative. The Test Anxiety Scale (Sarason, 1978) consists of
thirty-seven true-false items, many of which deal with what people
think about before, during, and after tests. The Test Anxiety
Inventory by Spielberger and others (1978) uses many Test Anxiety
Scale items but employs a 5-point scale. Tryon (1980) and Anderson and Sauser (in press) have recently reviewed the large number of
instruments available for the measurement of test anxiety.

A number of researchers have correlated test anxiety with
academic indexes. In general, significant negative correlations have
been reported between test anxiety and grades; that is, high test
anxious students tend to obtain lower grades. However, the magnitude of these correlations has been low. I found that the Test
Anxiety Scale correlated negatively with grades only during the first
two years of college. For the last two years, there were no significant
correlations (Sarason, 1957). It is possible that over time students
somehow come to terms with their test anxiety. This might occur
through greater expenditure of effort (for example, more study
time) or a gradual change in attitudes toward self and schoolwork.
It may be that the relatively high intellectual level of college students
is a limiting factor that helps to account for the low correlations of
test anxiety with grades obtained at the college level. Further
research is needed into the effects of test anxiety on the performance
of groups differing more widely in aptitude and ability.

College entrance examinations differ from course examinations in that the content of the former is usually less predictable by
the student than is the latter. In this regard, it is interesting that the

relationship of test anxiety to entrance examinations was found to be of greater magnitude than the relationship between test anxiety and course examinations (Sarason, 1957).   Further research is also needed into the effects of situational factors on the relationship between test anxiety and performance.

Experimental Study of Test Anxiety

The view of test anxiety taken in this chapter is a cognitive one because it directs attention to what the individual is thinking about when confronted with evaluative stressors.   Through cognitive appraisal, individuals define for themselves the opportunities and dangers connected with tests.   They also appraise their abilities.   For the test anxiety researcher, the challenge is to relate individual differences in cognitive appraisals of tests, self, and outcomes to objective elements of testing situations.   From this perspective, individual differences in test anxiety are important factors in how persons process information.

Laboratory experiments carried out by many researchers have added to our knowlege about the deleterious influence of high levels of test anxiety on information processing and performance. There is considerable evidence that the performance of highly test anxious persons on complex tasks is adversely affected by evaluational stressors.   An example of an evaluational stressor is achievement-orienting instructions that either inform subjects that some kind of evaluation of their performance will be made or provide some other rationale for the importance of performing well.   The less complex and less demanding the task, the weaker the effect of the evaluational stressor.   When persons are reassured that a negative evaluation of their performance will not be made, highly test anxious persons often perform as well as or better than those who are typically less worried.

Effects of Test Anxiety.   An experiment carried out by Sarason and Stoops (1978) illustrates how the effects of test anxiety can be studied under experimental conditions.   The index was the Test Anxiety Scale (TAS) (Sarason, 1978).   Table 1 contains five of the TAS items.   Sarason and Stoops used the TAS in testing hypotheses about both performance and cognitive processes.   The investigation

Table 1. Selected Test Anxiety Scale (TAS) Items.

(T)	1.	While taking an important exam, I find myself thinking of how much brighter the other students are than I am.
(F)	15.	When I am taking a test, my emotional feelings do not interfere with my performance.
(T)	17.	I seem to defeat myself while working on important tests.
(F)	27.	I really don't see why some people get so upset about tests.
(T)	28.	Thoughts of doing poorly interfere with my performance.

Note: Keyed answers are in parentheses.

comprised a series of three experiments concerning subjective judgments of the passage of time. After being given either achievement-orienting or neutral instructions, subjects waited for an undesignated period of time before performing an intellective task. The achievement-orienting manipulation involved telling the subject that the task was a measure of intelligence. The dependent measures were subjects' estimates of the duration of the waiting and performance periods and their scores on the assigned task.

The experiments were aimed at providing information about the way individuals who differ in anxiety fill time. It was predicted that, in the presence of achievement-orienting cues, time would pass more slowly for high than for middle and low TAS scorers. When these cues are not present, there should not be a significant gap in estimates of time duration among groups differing in test anxiety. Furthermore, it was felt that the effects of an achievement orientation should be as noticeable while the individual is waiting to perform as during performance itself.

The findings of the first two experiments supported the conclusion that not only is the performance of TAS subjects deleteriously affected by achievement-orienting instructions but subjects also tend to overestimate both the duration of the test period and the period during which they wait to have their ability evaluated. This appears analogous to the tendency of many people to exaggerate time spent waiting for what they anticipate will be an unpleasant experience — for example, the time spent in the dentist's waiting room. Anticipating and going through unpleasant, frightening, or threatening experiences seem to take up a lot of time. If this interpretation is correct, the question arises: Do individuals differing in anxiety fill time periods in similar or dissimilar ways? The third experiment dealt with this question.

In this experiment, sixty female undergraduates worked on a digit-symbol task prior to a waiting period and then were asked to solve a series of difficult anagrams. Following this, the subjects responded to a questionnaire dealing with their cognitive activity during the anagrams task. The experimental design encompassed two factors: (1) high, middle, and low TAS scores; and (2) achievement-orienting and neutral instructions. Each subject worked on the digit-symbol task for four minutes. This was followed by a four-minute waiting period. At the end of the waiting period, subjects performed for eighteen minutes on the anagrams. The experiment concluded with subjects responding to the Cognitive Interference Questionnaire, estimating the time they had spent waiting, and working on the anagrams task (see Table 2).

There were two significant factors in an analysis of variance performed on waiting-period time estimates, those for Test Anxiety ($p < .002$) and those for Test Anxiety $\times$ Conditions ($p < .05$). High anxious subjects made the highest estimates. This significant interaction was attributable to the higher time estimates mean obtained by the high TAS group that received achievement-orienting instructions rather than the estimates of all other groups. Table 3 presents the means of the four dependent measures for all groups in the experiment. The analysis of estimates of duration of the anagrams task also yielded two significant factors, those for Test Anxiety and for Test Anxiety $\times$ Conditions (each at the .05 level). Again, the significant results were explicable largely in terms of the relatively large estimates given by the high TAS achievement-oriented group (see Table 3).

When the analysis was performed on the number of correct responses to the anagrams task, only the Test Anxiety factor was statistically significant. As the means in the third column of Table 3 show, this effect was due mainly to the relatively poor performance of the high TAS group that received the achievement-orienting instructions. There were two significant results in the analysis of Cognitive Interference Questionnaire scores. These were the factors for Test Anxiety ($p < .0001$) and for Test Anxiety $\times$ Condi-

Table 2. Cognitive Interference Questionnaire.

I.[a]   We are interested in learning about the kinds of thoughts that go through people's heads while they are working on a task. The following list includes some thoughts you might have had *while doing the task that you just completed.* Please indicate approximately how often each thought occurred to you while working on this task by placing the appropriate number in the blank provided to the left of each question.

Example: 1 = never
2 = once
3 = a few times
4 = often
5 = very often

—— 1.   I thought about how poorly I was doing.
—— 2.   I wondered what the experimenter would think of me.
—— 3.   I thought about how I should work more carefully.
—— 4.   I thought about how much time I had left.
—— 5.   I thought about how others have done on this task.
—— 6.   I thought about the difficulty of the problems.
—— 7.   I thought about my level of ability.
—— 8.   I thought about the purpose of the experiment.
—— 9.   I thought about how I would feel if I were told how I performed.
—— 10.   I thought about how often I got confused.
—— 11.   I thought about things completely unrelated to the experiment.

II.   Please circle the number on the following scale that best represents the degree to which you felt your mind wandered *during the task you have just completed.*

Not at all   1 : 2 : 3 : 4 : 5 : 6 : 7   very much

[a] The score on Part I is obtained by summing the subject's responses to all eleven items.

tions ($p < .05$). As column four of Table 3 shows, most of the interaction effects were due to the high scores obtained by the high TAS achievement-oriented group. Results for separate analyses of individual items were, in every case, in the same direction as the results presented for the questionnaire as a whole.

An item appended to the questionnaire asked the subject to indicate on a 7-point scale the degree to which her mind wandered while working on the anagrams task. An analysis of variance of these scores yielded significant factors for Test Anxiety ($p < .05$)

Table 3. Mean Waiting Time and Task Time Estimates, Anagram Performance Scores, and Cognitive Interference Scores.

	Waiting Time Estimate (seconds)	Task Time Estimate (seconds)	Anagrams Score	Cognitive Interference Score
H-E[a]	357.0	1354.1	3.3	33.2
H-C	286.5	1114.0	4.8	24.6
M-E	266.3	1031.5	5.5	18.2
M-C	274.4	1103.5	5.7	21.6
L-E	266.5	1172.0	5.0	19.8
L-C	265.0	1140.5	5.0	21.4

[a] H, M, and L refer to levels of test anxiety (high, medium, and low); E and C refer to experimental (achievement-orientation) and control conditions.
Source: Sarason and Stoops (1978).

and for Test Anxiety $\times$ Conditions ($p < .05$); the directions of these results resembled those in the other analyses.

Results from the time estimation tasks indicated that individuals for whom tests are noxious experiences (high TAS subjects) apparently tend to overestimate, to a greater degree than do others, both the duration of their performance evaluation period and the time spent waiting for the evaluation to take place. In addition, highly test anxious subjects performed at significantly lower levels than did low and middle TAS scorers when emphasis was placed on the evaluational implications of performance.

The evidence obtained from the Cognitive Interference Questionnaire is enlightening from the standpoint of what people think about while working on a task. Highly test anxious scorers, more so than low and middle scorers, are preoccupied with how poorly they are doing, how other people are doing, and what the examiner will think about them. It is difficult not to interpret these preoccupations as appreciably complicating the task at hand. Although a measure of cognitive interference during the waiting period was not obtained, it seems likely that similar preoccupations would also have characterized highly test anxious subjects during that period.

Reducing the Effects of Test Anxiety. We have seen how experimental manipulations can be used to heighten test anxiety. Can test anxiety be reduced under controlled laboratory conditions? A number of studies suggest that this can be done (Kaplan, McCordick, and Twitchell, 1979). In an early study, I showed that reassuring instructions ("don't worry about how you are doing") differentially influenced the performance of groups who varied in test anxiety. Reassuring instructions facilitated the performance of high, but not of low, TAS scorers (Sarason, 1958). In a later investigation, college students were tested on a series of difficult anagrams (Sarason, 1973). Subjects differing in test anxiety were given the opportunity to observe a model who demonstrated effective ways of performing the task. Using a talk-out-loud technique, the model displayed several facilitative thoughts and cognitions. The major finding was that high TAS subjects benefited more from the opportunity to observe such a cognitive model than did low TAS scorers.

It seems possible that an analysis of behavior in terms of its cognitive substrate will lead to interventions that teach people both overt adaptive responses and better ways of controlling the objects of their attention. When one is working on a task, it is obviously more adaptive to pay attention to the task at hand than to oneself. Research on cognitive modification has shown that focalized instruction and practice in attending to relevant external cues and in ignoring internal responses that interfere with task performance have a significant facilitating effect on anxious people (Sarason, 1980; Wine, 1980). The following interventions have been found in controlled research to be helpful in reducing the deleterious effects of test anxiety:

1. *Reassurance.* Communications that encourage the individual to (1) focus attention on the task at hand and (2) not worry about their performance level contribute to reducing the tension experienced by highly test anxious people.
2. *Modeling.* The opportunity to observe someone cope with a task or think through a problem can provide clues to solving problems that have existed for weeks, months, and even years. Adaptive models provide valuable information in usable forms.
3. *Attentional training.* Skill at attending to the task at hand can be learned and represents an important aspect of self-control.
4. *Self-monitoring and self-control.* People can learn to monitor and control both their behavior and their thoughts.

5. *Relaxation.* Knowing how to relax under specifiable conditions can be especially valuable for people who must work under tension, personal threat, and danger. The literature on systematic desensitization has much to contribute to lowering anxiety in people so that they can learn needed coping skills.

6. *Practice and reinforcement.* Whether the person is performing a task or thinking about a problem to be solved, practice, together with reward, is needed in shaping adaptive psychological functioning.

7. *Information.* People often are woefully ignorant of basic information about themselves, others, their jobs, and their responsibilities. At present, it is difficult to estimate how much human maladaptation, inefficiency, and unhappiness is due largely to poor information. At a minimum, test anxious persons need applicable information about study and test-taking skills.

8. *Social support.* Feeling that one is part of a mutually supportive group facilitates task-relevant thought and inhibits self-preoccupation.

Test anxiety can be interpreted as the tendency to view with alarm the consequences of inadequate performance in an evaluative situation. In a sense, the highly test anxious person creates his or her own problem by processing too much information. The job of processing task-relevant information is complicated by maladaptive personalized feedback ("I'm dumb." "What if I don't pass this exam?"). We have seen that the deleterious impact of this feedback can be countered either through manipulating cues external to the individual (for example, the no-risk test) or through fostering better cognitive and self-control skills. Cognitive and self-control approaches to anxiety seem especially valuable because everyone at one time or another is forced to react to circumstances over which he or she has little or no control. Practical training programs directed toward improving attention and thought may prove to be feasible, convenient, and effective.

Moderators of Test Anxiety. A supportive environment may exert its impact on behavior by strengthening what Bandura (1977) calls *self-efficacy* and White (1959) *effectance motivation.* High anxiety and low self-efficacy in any individual can either be specific to a particular situation, such as academic performance, or pervade many aspects of life. The belief that others have similar interests and concerns and that help is available may contribute to a decrease in anxiety level. Although it was not especially concerned with performance, Schachter's (1959) research also suggests that social affiliation has anxiety-reducing effects.

In addition to teaching anxious subjects to alter their cognitions concerning fear of failure and comparisons with others, another approach has been to alter the individual's perception of social support. Social support refers to persons' feelings that others care about them and that they have people to turn to if they need either reassurance or direct assistance.

Because the anxious person often reports feeling alone and "on the spot," it seemed possible that social support might have a salutary effect in situations that would ordinarily arouse high levels of tension and self-preoccupation in people prone to test anxiety. Hence, I recently studied this possible relationship between social support and test anxiety by performing three experiments in which it was predicted that highly test anxious subjects under stress-arousing conditions who received social support would perform at a higher level than highly test anxious, stressed subjects not exposed to support (Sarason, 1981).

In one of these experiments, subjects differing in TAS scores performed on difficult anagrams under either neutral or achievement-orienting experimental conditions. The second experimental variable was the opportunity for social support. Half the subjects did not engage in a preperformance activity. They performed only on the anagrams. Subjects under the social support condition were told they would perform in two unrelated experiments; they participated in a twenty-minute group discussion prior to the anagrams task. Each discussion group was composed of six subjects who were asked to discuss a series of questions about their academic experiences. This is what they were told:

We are bringing together groups of students to discuss the problem of anxiety and worry over exams. Typically, students suffer in silence and keep their academic concerns to themselves. As a result, there isn't much opportunity for sharing views and joining together socially to identify problems and consider possible solutions. That's unfortunate because it helps to be aware of what we have in common.

While I will ask you to talk about some specific topics, how you approach them in this discussion will be up to you. From past experience, I know that the twenty or so minutes we have for discussion is often not enough. If that happens, you might want to continue on your own later on.

The subjects were asked to give their names and briefly introduce themselves. Following this, the experimenter said: "Let's start with the most basic questions. Are stress and anxiety about exams important problems here at the University of Washington?" Other questions that were asked included:

How often do you share your worries about tests with other students?

What are the barriers to this sharing of personal concerns?

What steps might be taken at the University of Washington to lower tension levels about academic standing?

Do you think discussions such as the one we have had are useful?

Do you feel this discussion has brought you closer to people who otherwise would just be "other" students?

Except for the experimeter's suggestion of the specific topics, the discussions were freewheeling. All groups discussed all topics, and the amount of time devoted to the several topics seemed roughly comparable across groups. In addition to the six subjects, two confederates were present at each discussion. Their roles were to (1) stimulate discussion and keep it going if necessary, (2) positively reinforce comments made by participants and build group feeling and a sense of sharing, and (3) at the end of the discussion suggest that group members might meet again. The last condition was designed to heighten the sense of social association and shared values among group members. So, at the end of the discussion period, one of the confederates commented:

I can only speak for myself, but I really appreciated this chance to get to know some students who are more like me than I would have thought. Would any of you like to get together again in the next day or so? [At least one person (the other confederate) was certain to say yes.] Well, why don't we meet for a minute after the second experiment is over and see if we can set up a time and place to get together.

In every case, the group members agreed to meet briefly at the conclusion of the second experiment to set up a meeting. Pilot work on the social support manipulation and informal comments by subjects at the end of the experiment suggested that they valued the opportunity to share experiences and opinions with peers.

As each group discussion came to an end, the experimenter said, "I hope you don't mind having two experimenters. We are doing different things, but it seemed a good idea to share you for this hour." This was said cheerfully and with a smile. The first experimenter left after the second experimenter entered the room. The second experimenter then proceeded with what appeared to be unrelated experimental tasks.

The results of this experiment, and two additional studies, showed that, consistent with previous research, high TAS scorers performed at a lower level under stressful conditions (achievement-orienting instructions) than did high TAS control subjects and low TAS subjects under less stressful conditions. However, the special contribution of this series of social support experiments was the demonstration that social support can serve as a moderator variable. This means that, while social support does not influence the performance of subjects with low test anxiety, it does moderate the effect of stressful instructions on the performance of those who are high in test anxiety. Social support enhanced the performance of highly test anxious subjects, reduced their tendency to become self-preoccupied while taking tests, and generally seemed to strengthen their capacity to cope effectively with stress.

The results were consistent with the idea that the problem of anxiety is, to a significant extent, a problem of interfering cognitions and the direction of attention. Stress becomes maladaptive when it evokes, in susceptible individuals, self-preoccupying thoughts that interfere with attention to the environment and to tasks that must be dealt with. Social support may be effective because the presence of another interested person reduces the individual's concern that he or she must face a challenge alone.

This chapter has emphasized the contribution of experimental studies to understanding and modifying test anxiety. Considerable evidence supports the validity of an *attentional theory of test anxiety*. According to this theory, persons high in test anxiety experience increases in personalized, task-irrelevant cognitions under conditions that heighten the testlike features of situations that require performance. This tendency toward self-preoccupation under stress interferes with problem solving and performance. Experimental research has shown that the interfering effects of stress on highly test anxious people can be countered through several types of interventions—for example, reassurance, modeling, and social support.

To a certain extent, test anxiety is a product of the way in which industrialized societies and their schools are organized. The evidence presented in this chapter may have some important educational and social implications. If task-irrelevant worry is a major factor in test anxiety and if poor performance is significantly related to what test takers are thinking (or not thinking) about, then efforts to (1) improve their cognitive strategies and (2) remove impediments to adaptive problem solving make sense. To accomplish these goals, Wine (1960) has suggested reducing the evaluative emphasis in schools.

Perhaps students are spending too much time worrying about how their work will be evaluated and not enough time absorbed in intrinsically interesting academic pursuits. If there is validity to this suggestion, teachers should make special efforts to provide feedback to students that focuses on skill acquisition and skill strengthening rather than skill evaluation. Research with young elementary school children supports this approach (Nottelmann and Hill, 1977; Wine, 1979). In other words, it may be desirable to reduce the social evaluative component in school. This does not mean that grades must be abolished. Evaluations can be of great value in providing students with feedback concerning their performance. However, a person who receives low global evaluations of his or her work finds it all too easy to conclude that "I'm dumb" or that "my teacher doesn't like me." If feedback included information both about the tasks being performed and about the specific strengths and weaknesses people bring to the tasks, the process of evaluation might make for more self-actualization and less test anxiety.

Such teacher-student interaction is also likely to be higher in the social support component than in the more traditional grading or ranking of students. In addition, work with highly anxious students to help them learn more adaptive cognitions should be of value in enabling them to cope more adequately with the many evaluative situations they will inevitably encounter, no matter what modification can be achieved in grade-giving procedures.

References

Alpert, R., and Haber, R. N. "Anxiety in Academic Achievement Situations." *Journal of Abnormal and Social Psychology*, 1960, *61*, 207–215.

Anderson, S. B., and Sauser, W. I., Jr. "The Measurement of Test Anxiety: An Overview." In C. D. Spielberger and P. R. Vagg (Eds.), *The Measurement and Treatment of Test Anxiety*. New York: McGraw-Hill, in press.

Bandura, A. "Self-Efficacy: Toward a Unifying Theory of Behavioral Change." *Psychological Review*, 1977, *84*, 191–215.

Kaplan, R. M., McCordick, S. M., and Twitchell, M. "Is it the Cognitive or the Behavioral Component Which Makes Cognitive-Behavior Modification Effective in Test Anxiety?" *Journal of Counseling Psychology*, 1979, *26*, 371–377.

Liebert, R., and Morris, L. W. "Cognitive and Emotional Components of Test Anxiety: A Distinction and Some Initial Data. *Psychological Reports*, 1967, *20*, 975–978.

Mandler, G., and Sarason, S. B. "A Study of Anxiety and Learning." *Journal of Abnormal and Social Psychology*, 1952, *47*, 166–173.

Nottelmann, E. D., and Hill, K. T. "Test Anxiety and Off-Task Behavior in Evaluative Situations." *Child Development*, 1977, *48*, 225–231.

Sarason, I. G. "Test Anxiety, General Anxiety, and Intellectual Performance." *Journal of Consulting Psychology*, 1957, *21*, 485–490.

Sarason, I. G. "The Effects of Anxiety, Reassurance, and Meaningfulness of Material to be Learned on Verbal Learning." *Journal of Experimental Psychology*, 1958, *56*, 472–477.

Sarason, I. G. "Empirical Findings and Theoretical Problems in the Use of Anxiety Scales." *Psychological Bulletin*, 1960, *57*, 403–415.

Sarason, I. G. "Test Anxiety and Cognitive Modeling." *Journal of Personality and Social Psychology*, 1973, *28*, 58–61.

Sarason, I. G. "The Test Anxiety Scale: Concept and Research." In C. D. Spielberger and I. G. Sarason (Eds.), *Stress and Anxiety*. Vol. 5. New York: Halsted, 1978.

Sarason, I. G. (Ed.). *Test Anxiety: Theory, Research, and Applications*. Hillsdale, N.J.: Erlbaum, 1980.

Sarason, I. G. "Test Anxiety, Stress, and Social Support." *Journal of Personality*, 1981, *49*, 101–114.

Sarason, I. G., and Stoops, R. "Test Anxiety and the Passage of Time." *Journal of Consulting and Clinical Psychology*, 1978, *46*, 102–109.

Sarason, S. B., and others. *Anxiety in Elementary Schoolchildren*. New York: Wiley, 1960.

Schachter, S. *The Psychology of Affiliation: Experimental Studies of the Sources of Gregariousness*. Stanford, Calif.: Stanford University Press, 1959.

Spielberger, C. D., and others. "Examination Stress and Test Anxiety." In C. D. Spielberger and I. G. Sarason (Eds.), *Stress and Anxiety*. Vol. 5. New York: Halsted, 1978.

Tryon, G. S. "The Measurement and Treatment of Test Anxiety." *Review of Educational Research*, 1980, *50*, 343–372.

White, R. W. "Motivation Reconsidered: The Concept of Competence." *Psychological Review*, 1959, *66*, 297–333.

Wine, J. D. "Test Anxiety and Evaluation Threat: Children's Behavior in the Classroom." *Journal of Abnormal Child Psychology*, 1979, *7*, 45–59.

Wine, J. D. "Cognitive-Attentional Theory of Test Anxiety." In I. G. Sarason (Ed.), *Test Anxiety: Theory, Research, and Applications*. Hillsdale, N.J.: Erlbaum, 1980.

Heinz W. Krohne

8   Paul Schaffner

૭૨ ૭૨ ૭૨ ૭૨ ૭૨ ૭૨ ૭૨ ૭૨ ૭૨ ૭૨ ૭૨ ૭૨ ૭૨

Anxiety, Coping Strategies, and Performance

The ability of educational measurement to obtain an accurate estimate of an individual's underlying ability is impeded by the influence
of motivational factors on performance. Among these motivational
factors anxiety is of central importance, its influence on the resulting
performance level being both positive and negative, which means
that, dependent on certain conditions, the performance level is
either increased or reduced. (For an overview, see Gaudry and
Spielberger, 1971; Heinrich and Spielberger, 1980; Krohne, 1975,
1976, 1980a; Sarason, 1980; Sieber, O'Neil, and Tobias, 1977;
Spielberger, 1966b.)

In this chapter recent theoretical conceptions regarding the
relationship between anxiety and performance are presented and
criticized. The central point of our criticism will be the fact that,
nearly without exception, these approaches discuss the influence of
anxiety *in* the actual exam or testing situation and neglect the
significance of anxiety during preparation. Since — at least in real-
life situations — performing includes more than the period of actual
evaluation, a model is presented that also conceptualizes the role of
anxiety in the *preparation period.*

Conceptualizing the Relation Between
Anxiety and Performance

For analysis of the relationship between anxiety and performance, stimulus-response (S-R) theoretical approaches following the tradition of the Spence-Taylor theory (see Spence and Spence, 1966) are more and more being replaced by cognitive conceptions. These two orientations, however, not only present different models for explaining the observed anxiety-performance relationships but also emphasize different aspects within these relationships. Whereas S-R approaches consider anxiety as a uniform factor and, in exchange, emphasize the different degrees of complexity of the task to be solved, cognitive models center on analyzing anxiety and its components as they are evoked in a performance situation. Thus, in relevant experimental designs, the distinction between trait anxiety as a disposition of longer temporal extension and state anxiety as a temporally shorter, situation-dependent reaction of the organism has been accepted (Spielberger, 1966a, 1972). In addition, from the initially rather unstructured field of anxiety, test anxiety has been differentiated as a situation-specific anxiety, that is, as a disposition to experience anxiety in ego-involving situations (Sarason, 1972, 1975; Wine, 1971, 1980).

Most of the recent approaches distinguish two processes or anxiety components evoked in an ego-involving stress situation such as an examination: a *cognitive* process (self-centered cognitions frequently expressing self-doubts, such as worry about results and their consequences) and a process of *autonomic arousal* (emotionality) (Doctor and Altman, 1969; Morris and Liebert, 1969, 1970).

The impact of cognitive analyses lies in the field of worry cognitions. It is generally assumed that an interference takes place between those processes that make up the cognitive component of test anxiety and the processing of task-relevant information in a performance situation. This interference is supposed to have a negative effect on the resulting performance level. The theoretical basis of the assumed interference is a so-called attention hypothesis (Sarason, 1972; Wine, 1971, 1980), according to which task-irrelevant cognitive processes are supposed to require a great deal of the attention that ought to be devoted to solving the task. For the

emotional component of test anxiety, no such effect and no performance debilitating influence are assumed (Deffenbacher, 1977; Doctor and Altman, 1969; Morris and Liebert, 1969, 1970).

This concept of the relation between anxiety and performance presents a number of problems that we will list and then discuss
in some detail:

1. The empirical evidence for the hypothesis that the cognitive
   anxiety component has a debilitating effect on performance
   becomes ambiguous as soon as artificial tasks instead of real-life
   situations are investigated.
2. The assumption of one single definable class of task-irrelevant
   cognitive activites (self-centered worry cognitions) in ego-involving situations is too simplistic.
3. Just as the assumption of one single class of task-irrelevant
   cognitive activities is too simplistic, the concept of one single
   autonomic process evoked in a stress situation (emotionality)
   also seems to be an inadmissible simplification.
4. The concept of an interference between the processing of
   task-relevant and task-irrelevant information (attention hypothesis) remains largely descriptive. It does not explain which
   processes determine the performance debilitating effect and
   how they operate.
5. Cognitive approaches, in particular the attention hypothesis,
   primarily conceptualize the incidents *during* a performance
   situation. Anxiety-related factors that are activated *prior* to this
   situation and thus influence the performance level are rarely
   discussed — for example, such factors as effort, study habits,
   strategy formation for problem solving, and person-specific
   stress-coping systems.

Empirical Evidence. A survey of the empirical investigations
of the anxiety-performance relation yields an ambiguous picture
with respect to confirmation of the attention hypothesis. The hypothesis can be significantly supported in the case of rather artificial
tasks such as solving anagrams (see Holroyd and others, 1978) and in
the case of performance requirements without adequate preparation

conditions. The latter includes intelligence tests (see, among others, Deffenbacher, 1977; Morris and Liebert, 1969) and school ability tests (see Cowen and others, 1965; Hodapp, 1979; Lissmann, 1977; Paul and Eriksen, 1964). As we abandon these modes of performance measurement and approach tasks involving real-life achievement, the degree of confirmation of the hypothesis of the debilitating effect of anxiety decreases. (For a review of positive and negative findings, see Krohne, 1980b.)

Lack of Distinctiveness of the Cognitive Component. Cognitive anxiety theories describe the cognitive processes occurring in a test anxious person as "cognitive concern about the consequences of failing" (Liebert and Morris, 1967), "preoccupation with performance" (Doctor and Altman, 1969), "a cognitive response marked by self-doubt, feelings of inadequacy, and self-blame" (Sarason, 1978), or "anxious self-preoccupation" (Sarason, 1975). However, it is by no means certain that these are the only anxiety-relevant cognitions occurring in an exam situation and affecting the performance level. Heckhausen (1980), on the basis of his process model of motivation (Heckhausen, 1977), has described at least three different kinds of cognitions, each with varying functions, beyond those related to the actual task-solving behavior: (1) cognitions that monitor and govern the activity process, (2) self-doubt cognitions, and (3) cognitions that are neither task centered nor self-centered.

In our opinion, all these cognitions can be seen within the context of test anxiety or, as we prefer to call it, "defensive motivation" (Cronbach and Snow, 1977) in ego-involving situations. Thus, we maintain that the performance level is decisively determined by the processes of monitoring and governing the activity process (*control process*).

Lack of Distinctiveness of the Emotional Component. The question arises whether, in analogy to the cognitive component of test anxiety, functionally different autonomic processes of the emotional component can also be identified. Investigations observing different kinds of relations between the autonomic component and performance suggest that the system is probably not uniform. In fact, at least two processes (Kahneman, 1973), and probably even three (Pribram and McGuinness, 1975), have to be distinguished in the autonomic field: information intake (arousal), readiness to respond (activation), and, possibly, the activity of the control and coordination system (effort).

Each of these autonomic processes probably bears a different functional relation to performance. The self-report instruments frequently used for the operationalization of the emotional component—(for example), the relevant subscales of the Test Anxiety Questionnaire (Mandler and Sarason, 1952) or of the Test Anxiety Inventory (Spielberger, 1980)—presumably do not measure any of these autonomic processes precisely enough, since they refer only to the cognitions of arousal or activation. In other words, the emotional state on which the self-perceptions are based probably represents a combination of these two or three autonomic processes. This might possibly explain not only the ambiguous findings concerning the relationship between emotionality indicators and performance but also the inconsistent results concerning the relation between self-descriptions of emotionality and the relevant physiological indicators. A series of relevant positive findings—for example, Bronzaft and Stuart (1971); Harleston, Smith, and Arey, (1965); Haywood and Spielberger (1966); Kissel and Littig (1962)—must be viewed in the context of at least as many studies that could not observe any relationship between the two indicators (Doctor and Altman, 1969; Holroyd and others, 1978; Katkin, 1965; McGuigan, Calvin, and Richardson, 1959; Scott and Kessler, 1969).

Problems with the Attention Hypothesis. As already mentioned, the attention hypothesis suggests that, during increased state anxiety, part of the attention that ought to be directed to solving the task is preempted by self-centered cognitions. In this context it is not quite clear where the debilitating effect originates. One explanation might be that there is not sufficient attention left for solving the task efficiently. This view is held, for example, by Wachtel (1968) and reflects the widely shared belief in a fixed cognitive capacity. As Neisser (1976) pointed out, however, the empirical evidence for this view is not convincing.

In another conception, the performance-debilitating effect results from an interference between the processing of the task-irrelevant (self-centered) information and the processing of task-relevant information (Sarason, 1975). This conception is also shared by

M. Eysenck (1979), who, on the basis of the concept of "working memory" (Baddeley and Hitch, 1974), assumes that the information created by self-centered cognitions ("I'll flunk this exam") competes with the simultaneously existing task-relevant information for a position in the information-processing system.

It seems, however, that at least the following question cannot satisfactorily be answered by this argument: Why does the self-perceived arousal scarcely exercise any interfering influence? As shown by the relevant operationalizations of this arousal, we are here also assessing a cognition that refers to autonomic processes. After all, if distraction (or competition) is the crucial factor in performance debilitation, it should not make a difference whether a person's attention is distracted by thinking "I can't cope with it" (cognitive component) or "my heart beats faster" (emotional component). Doctor and Altman (1969), as well as Wine (1971), argue that autonomic processes, provided they are not extremely vigorous, do not require as much attention as cognitive events. Apart from the fact that this argument is not sufficiently empirical, the "emotional" subscale of relevant test anxiety questionnaires does not assess autonomic processes per se, but rather the perceived emotionality, that is, the emotionality that already requires attention.

Anxiety-Related Processes Prior to the Exam or Testing Situation. A series of investigations illustrates that the generally held assumption that anxiety exercises its influence primarily during the exam situation (for example, the attention hypothesis in Wine, 1971, 1980) has to be reformulated. Obviously, the anxiety-related processes preceding an exam or testing situation are of equal importance for the resulting performance level. These associations become evident when two factors are analyzed: (1) the influence exercised by the *degree of structure of a preceding learning situation* on the performance on an exam and (2) the influence of the *opportunity to prepare for a task* on the performance level.

As for degree of structure, Dowaliby and Schumer (1973) trained a group of students for one term in a student-centered manner; that is, the activity was left to the students (according to student ratings, this was a low-structured learning situation). A second group was trained in a teacher-centered manner, that is, in a highly structured learning situation. Anxious students profited for their final exam more from the highly structured situation, whereas nonanxious students experience a performance-debilitating effect because of the high degree of structure of the instructional situation.

Similarly, Grimes and Allinsmith (1961) found that a highly structured learning situation can compensate for the handicap of high test anxiety. On the one hand, the authors observed that the performance of anxious children was poorer than that of their nonanxious peers if the learning situation preceding this perform-ance had little structure. In the investigation, the whole-word method for learning to read represented the less structured learning situation. If, on the other hand, the learning experience was highly structured—for example, if students were taught to read by the phonics method—both anxious and less anxious children achieved the same good results, which means that anxious children made relatively better progress under a structured learning situation.

Peterson (1977) argued that highly structured learning mate-rial may possibly be of help only to those pupils who are anxious and whose abilites are above average. Anxious persons with lower abilities would feel overstrained by elaborate instructional material and would react with avoidance. But low-anxious pupils who are less able are particularly supposed to require structured material for their progress in learning, whereas nonanxious persons with high ability should profit most by exposure to material that has little structure. An investigation of pupils in the ninth grade supported the hypothesis of a three-way interaction of learning situation, anxi-ety, and ability level.

With respect to opportunity to prepare for a task, many authors are now assuming that the performance of anxious persons is not poorer than that of nonanxious individuals when anxious per-sons are able to compensate, by means of increased effort, for the handicap produced by their cognitive anxiety processes (M. Eysenck, 1979). Such an effort, for instance, could take the form of more intensive preparation. Vagt and Kühn (1976) observed a longer preparation time for anxious compared to nonanxious pupils for normal lessons, but not for a specific test. Contrary to this, in some of our own unpublished work, we have noticed that anxious persons prepared more intensely for a test, but not for normal lessons. For anxious students, Culler and Holahan (1980), as well as Jacobs (1980), found a longer preparation time for an exam. However, these investigations are subject to some criticism since they rely only on self-reported preparation time, a measure that probably tends to be somewhat biased. Therefore, direct observation of the preparation behavior ought to be used in future investigations. Moreover, investigators should consider whether the quantity of preparation is as decisive as is the quality of preparation.

If investigators want to observe the influence of intensified preparation on performance, the relevant test or exam situation should be easy to prepare. Thus, the degree to which subjects can prepare for an exam should influence the distinctiveness of the anxiety-performance relationship. Prell (1973) found a significant relation between test anxiety of students and grades on an essay test ($r = .50$, $p < .01$) when the learning material of the preceding term did not prepare students for this kind of test. Contrary to this, the results of a multiple-choice test for which subjects could prepare well showed no relation to anxiety ($r = -.12$).

Thus, the degree of structure of the learning material and the opportunity to prepare for an achievement situation obviously represent prerequisites that anxious individuals can use to compensate for a possible performance deficit. This illustrates that anxiety (or "defensive motivation") not only influences processes during the immediate performance situation but also can affect the preparatory process. A theory of the anxiety-performance relation thus should include assumptions about the processes that comprise task preparation and the materials that are used. Such a theory could be based on Kahneman's (1973) analysis of the increased information-processing effort as a source for improving performance. The distinction between *efficiency* (the performance level achieved) and *effectiveness* (the relationship between efficiency and effort) suggested by M. Eysenck (1979) would also be part of this context. According to this assumption, it can be predicted that anxious individuals, under certain circumstances (for example, good preparation conditions), could be as efficient as nonanxious persons. Their effectiveness, however, would be inferior, since they would invest a larger amount of effort than nonanxious persons.

A theory of the anxiety-performance relation that included the preparatory phase could also be based on a more exact analysis of the temporal conditions in information processing. Perhaps anxious persons may already have difficulty selecting material in the early stages of information processing. Brower and Mueller (1978), for instance, argue that anxious persons do not encode certain characteristics that might be relevant for further task solving. If one assumes that submitted material (for example, certain words) can be encoded on different levels (Craik and Tulving, 1975), anxious individuals seem to employ "shallow" processing methods (using physical cues to remember the words), whereas nonanxious persons process on "deeper" levels (that is, they rely on semantic features).

It may also be that anxious individuals generally have more difficulties in deciding *which* material should be processed and what may be neglected as being less important. Thus the anxious person is supposed to suffer more from an overload of the information-processing system (see Dornic, 1977). The inferior study skills observed for anxious persons compared to those of nonanxious individuals (Culler and Holahan, 1980) probably could also be a manifestation of their prevailing decisional difficulty. Perhaps the positive effect of prestructuring is that it provides anxious persons with aids for their decisions. Several investigations demonstrate that the performance of anxious and nonanxious persons can be equalized by providing an "external storage" or "memory support" (Sieber, Kameya, and Paulson, 1970) that reminds the individual of the relevant material during task processing. These studies may also support the assumption that, without these aids, the information-processing system of the anxious person frequently becomes overloaded.

These considerations demonstrate that laboratory tests are generally bound to yield a distinctly negative relation between anxiety and performance. Tests of this kind usually neither allow a longer time of preparation for task solving nor provide aids for structuring the material. Contrary to this, a number of real-life performance situations are marked by extended preparation time. Here the association between anxiety and performance should be weaker or completely disappear.

Coping and Performance

To measure performance, it is essential to consider both the preparation phase with its inherent processes and the actual evaluation or testing phase and its processes — "confrontation" is the term that Krohne and Rogner (1980) use for this latter phase. In this context, Krohne (1980b) postulated that the performance level is decisively determined by processes of coping and of behavioral regulation, the kind of influence (performance facilitation or debilitation) depending both on the type of process and the moment of occurrence (during preparation or confrontation).

One can argue that the period of preparation for a test or exam situation is characterized by features that evoke threat experiences and anxiety and, it is hoped, lead to "intrapsychic" modes of coping, that is, modes of coping that do not manifest themselves in overt reactions (Lazarus, 1966). These include (1) working under announced performance evaluation (so-called ego-threat); (2) an ambiguous threat situation — lack of "informational control" or uncertainty as to the exact performance requirements and the ability to comply with these requirements (Averill, 1973); and (3) blocking of responses to immediately abolish danger (restricted "behavioral control"). The coping process evoked during the period of preparation is supposed to extend into the confrontation phase and to decisively affect the performance level achieved. If persons do not construct a coping system during preparation — for instance, if they avoid the threatening aspects of a performance situation — they might as a consequence inefficiently cope with anxiety during confrontation and thus show inferior test results (see Krohne and Rogner, 1980).

Apart from situational determinants, the way a person copes with the cognitions and emotions evoked in a threat situation is supposed to depend largely on this person's learning history and the cognitive structures set up thereby. On the basis of a number of empirical investigations, these various structures can be assigned to a unidimensional bipolar personality dimension, *repression-sensitization* (see Bell and Byrne, 1978; Byrne, 1964; Krohne, 1978). The fundamental differences between repressive anxiety coping and sensitive anxiety coping are to be found (1) in the direction of attention in threat situations (sensitizers focus their attention on danger-related information, while repressers divert their attention from this information); (2) in the degree of anticipation of future dangers (increased degree for sensitizers); and (3) in the way that control of the situation and behavior is exercised (sensitizers exercise intensified and abundant control over information and their own activities). Repression sensitization is an acquired behavioral tendency from which the actual (repressive or sensitive) coping strategies effected in a situation (for instance, redefinition) have to be distinguished. (For the assessment of actual coping with anxiety, see, for example, Houston, 1977, 1980; Krohne, in press.)

Repressers and sensitizers cope with anxiety in different ways. Repressers try primarily to defend themselves against the perceived arousal and this process is already underway during the period of preparation. Contrary to this, the arousal perceived by sensitizers evokes a controlling process over the danger situation. Here, arousal is not being defended during preparation but is used as a cue to evoke and control behavior. Accordingly, sensitizers show an increased degree of arousal during this stage (Monat, Averill, and Lazarus, 1972; Niemelä, 1974). It can be said that it is the goal of the sensitive plan to facilitate, by means of an increased arousal during preparation, the construction of an internal coping system that can be put to use during confrontation (see Janis, 1958). Such a mode of coping could be accomplished by means of habituation (Maltzman and Wolff, 1970) or cognitive processes such as "threat redefinition" (Holmes and Houston, 1974). The sensitve plan can only be realized, however, if sufficient preparation time and adequate situational possibilities are available.

In performance situations, length of preparation time and task structure should be crucial for constructing the coping systems and for the resulting performance level. Since the sensitive system requires a comparatively large amount of time and the opportunity for actively mastering the situation in order to cope successfully with a threat experience, it should prove nonadaptive in the absence of these prerequisites (see, for example, Houston, 1977; Houston and Hodges, 1970). Then the sensitizer would still respond during confrontation in the same way (with intensified control of information and behavior and with increased autonomic arousal) as, according to our considerations, he generally is supposed to during the preparation phase. So, in a sense, it would be too late to construct the sensitive system needed to solve the task efficiently.

Our consideration concerning the regulatory functions of different modes of coping with anxiety in threat situations can thus

be summarized as follows: From the standpoint of personality, repression-sensitization is the basic dimension determining the actual
process of coping with anxiety under threat. The result of this
coping (that is, the performance level) is, however, determined by
the interaction between personality dimensions and situational characteristics (provided factors such as intelligence and knowledge level
are ignored). Here "length of preparation time" and "opportunity
of preparing for a task solution" are particularly relevant for performance situations. We therefore hypothesize that, given sufficient time and good preparation conditions, the extent of sensitive
coping during preparation should be positively associated with the
performance level. This positive relationship should not exist if
tasks are not easy to prepare for or if preparation time is too short.
The sensitive mechanisms evoked under confrontation would then
have a performance-debilitating effect. Several studies have been
conducted to evaluate the validity of our assumptions. One sutdy,
performed in the classroom, is reported in the next section.

Empirical Investigation

Fifty boys and forty-four girls from four classes in grades 8
and 9 (mean age 14.5 years) participated in the investigation. In a
first ("neutral") situation (a regular English lesson), these subjects
were asked to respond to questionnaires for measuring state anxiety,
especially self-perceived arousal. The questionnaires used were the
German version of Spielberger's (1973) State-Trait Anxiety Inventory for Children (STAIC) (Krohne, Schaffner, and Spielberger, in
press), the Repression-Sensitization Scale (RSS) (Krohne, in press),
and the "cognitive" subscale of the German version of the Test
Anxiety Inventory (TAI) (Hodapp, Laux, and Spielberger, in press).
Ten days later, two classes took classroom tests, one class
under good preparation conditions and the other under poor ones.
Both tests were announced one week prior to administration. Following the advice of English teachers, we used a grammar test as an
exam situation for which the subjects could prepare well. In this test
the subjects ($N = 45$) had to complete sentences according to rules
practiced in the preceding lessons. Correspondingly, a test on
which they had to produce English sentences was administered

under the bad preparation condition; here the subjects ($N = 49$) had to rely on their wider knowledge of English vocabulary and grammatical rules. The number of mistakes (for the grammar test) and the quotient of mistakes to words used (for the production test) transformed into T values served as performance measures, with a high score representing a low performance. Immediately after having taken one of these tests, the subjects again answered questionnaires referring to state anxiety, actual sensitive versus repressive coping (RSS), and disturbance of task solving by irrelevant cognitions (a newly constructed "cognitive interference questionnaire" relying on items formulated by Heckhausen, 1980, and Sarason, 1972). All scales employed showed satisfactory psychometric qualities (internal consistency generally above .80).

Ten days later intelligence was assessed by administering the two "general knowledge" subtests of a widely used German intelligence test (see Horn, 1969). Both subtests are good indicators of general ability because they correlate highly with the total IQ ($r =$ .75). In addition, for each subject the English grades of the two preceding semesters were determined and served as indicators of the present knowledge level in English. Here again a high score represents a low level.

The following hypotheses were formulated: First, for the good preparation condition, a positive relationship exists between the repression-sensitization disposition and performance level. Actual sensitive coping and reported cognitive interference are not significantly associated with performance. Second, for the bad preparation condition, a negative relationship exists between both actual sensitive coping and reported cognitive interference and performance. The repression-sensitization disposition is not significantly associated with performance.

These hypotheses were tested by means of product-moment correlation, multiple-regression analysis, and path analysis. The path analysis was based on the following model: Intelligence and the disposition repression-sensitization function as "exogene" variables. Intelligence determines knowledge level, and this, in turn, determines performance. Furthermore, knowledge level is also related to test anxiety (self-doubts or worrying): Poor grades lead to increased self-doubt or worry cognitions. Repression-sensitization disposition should also be associated with increased self-doubt that, in turn, leads to actual sensitive coping. This sensitive coping will be experienced as cognitive interference (probably as increased time pressure). For tasks with inadequate preparation conditions, this interference will be manifested in frequency of mistakes in classroom tests (performance). For a task with good preparation conditions, however, a direct negative path extends from the repression-sensitization disposition to rate of mistakes. State anxiety (self-perceived arousal) is generally dependent on the cognitive component of test anxiety and not related to performance.

Correlational Analysis. Of the intercorrelations in Table 1, we will consider only those for which theoretical expectations have been formulated. Table 1 reveals that repression-sensitization disposition is under no condition directly associated with performance ($r = -.06$ for the good and $r = -.02$ for the bad preparation condition). As predicted, actual sensitive coping is associated with frequency of mistakes ($r = .32$; $p < .05$) only in the bad preparation condition. For the good preparation condition, this correlation is markedly lower ($r = .20$; $p > .10$), although the difference between the two coefficients is not significant. There are almost no sizable correlations between self-reported cognitive interference and performance ($r = .20$ for the good, and $r = .24$ for the bad, preparation condition). Consistent with expectations, test anxiety is significantly associated with performance ($r = .29$; $p < .05$) only for the bad preparation condition. Under good preparation conditions, no relation between anxiety and performance can be observed ($r = .12$; $p > .10$).

Contrary to expectation, knowledge level is not directly associated with worry and self-doubt cognitions (test anxiety). Taking all ninety subjects together, however, this correlation becomes significant ($r = .20$; $p < .05$). Similarly, intelligence is negatively associated with test anxiety ($r = -.24$; $p < .05$). Students with bad grades or low IQs report more worry and self-doubt cognitions. When the questionnaire data are inspected, a high correlation between test anxiety and repression-sensitization disposition can be observed. Equally high are the correlations between test anxiety and cognitive interference and between actual sensitive coping and cognitive interference. Therefore, doubts seem to be justified as to

Table 1. Intercorrelations Among Variables Under Good and Bad Conditions of Preparation.

	1	2	3	4	5	6	7	8	N
Intelligence	—	-11	-22	-31*	-14	-28	-17	-08	42
Knowledge	-48**	—	-01	16	-02	07	22	51**	44
Repression-Sensitization Disposition	-18	-05	—	74**	63**	66**	57**	-06	45
Test Anxiety	-24	25	53**	—	53**	61***	60***	12	45
State Anxiety	-10	-06	62**	43***	—	57***	50***	01	45
Sensitive Coping	01	07	34*	37***	68**	—	79***	20	45
Cognitive Interference	-07	12	54**	62**	69***	75**	—	26	45
Rate of Mistakes	-28*	49**	-02	29*	12	32*	24	—	45
N	47	46	49	49	49	49	49	49	

Note: Intercorrelations above the diagonal are from the good preparation condition; below the diagonal are from the bad preparation condition. Decimals have been omitted.

* $P < .05$

** $P < .01$

the degree to which these indicators assess distinguishable constructs. Future studies will have to analyze the discriminant validity of these instruments.

One striking outcome is that repression-sensitization disposition and test anxiety are differentially correlated with actual sensitive coping, depending on the preparation condition. While in the good preparation condition both variables are highly associated with actual coping behavior ($r = .66$ and $.61$), markedly lower coefficients are found ($r = .34$ and $.37$) for the bad preparation condition. These differences are statistically significant ($p < .05$). Obviously, in an examination for which persons cannot prepare well, their coping behavior is largely determined by circumstances other than their acquired behavioral dispositions.

Finally, correlations between ability and performance variables will be considered. As expected, knowledge level and actual performance are highly associated ($r = .51$ and $.49$). Differential correlations can be observed between intelligence and performance. In the good preparation condition, intelligence has no influence on the performance level attained ($r = -.08$; $p > .10$). However, with tasks for which persons cannot prepare well, performance is more closely related to intelligence ($r = -.28$; $p < .05$). We assume that under good preparation conditions persons with lower ability can partly compensate for their handicap by increased effort. Finally, intelligence and knowledge level are significantly correlated ($N = 90$; $r = -.33$; $p < .01$).

Multiple-Regression Analysis. Since no direct relationship between repression-sensitization disposition and performance could be observed, we assumed that this disposition might exert an indirect influence on performance level. It could be that sensitive coping during preparation (as assessed by the RS disposition scale) generally facilitates good performance. However, since repression-sensitization disposition is also positively correlated with (performance-debilitating) sensitive coping during the exam (as assessed by the RS actual behavior scale), this positive effect might be destroyed again. In this case we would expect the criterion variable "rate of mistakes" to depend on several predictor variables. In order to test this assumption, a multiple-regression analysis with the predictor variables test anxiety (worry and self-doubt cognitions), intelligence, state anxiety, actual sensitive coping, cognitive interference, knowledge level (preceding grades), and repression-sensitization disposition was carried out for each preparation condition.

Results in general confirmed our hypotheses. For the good preparation condition, a multiple R of .65 ($F = 3.52$; $p < .01$) was obtained. Significant beta coefficients were found for knowledge level (.44; $F = 9.15$; $p < .01$) and repression-sensitization disposition ($-.54$; $F = 5.68$; $p < .05$). The remaining beta coefficients were insignificant. This result indicates that in the good preparation condition performance is mainly influenced by knowledge level and the *facilitating* effect of the repression-sensitization disposition. For the bad preparation condition, a multiple R of .62 ($F = 3.28$; $p < .01$) was obtained. Again, the best prediction was based on knowledge level (beta = .34; $F = 4.50$; $p < .05$). The postulated debilitating influence of actual sensitive coping, however, was only of marginal significance (beta = .34; $F = 2.26$; $p = .14$). The remaining coefficients were again insignificant.

Path Analysis. As a next step we inspected by means of path analysis the relationships within the predictor variables. Since some expectations but no definite, theoretically deduced hypotheses were formulated with regard to these relations, path analysis was used primarily as an instrument for generating hypotheses and only secondarily to test hypotheses.

Figure 1 shows the results of the path analyses for the two preparation conditions. The structures of the path diagrams essentially comply with the expectations formulated above. Since all residual correlations are below .30, these solutions represent good adaptations to the data. In both conditions a substantial part of the performance is determined by the knowledge level. As predicted, only for the classroom test with inadequate preparation does actual sensitive coping have a performance-debilitating effect. Surprisingly, worry and self-doubt cognitions do not influence performance directly but only via actual sensitive coping behavior.

Problem solving in the good preparation condition is not influenced by the cognitive component of test anxiety and actual sensitive coping. Instead, as expected, a performance-facilitating effect of the repression-sensitization disposition can be observed. This effect obviously originated in the preparation period. As postulated, state anxiety (self-perceived arousal) has in no condition

Figure 1. Path Diagram for the Two Preparation Conditions.

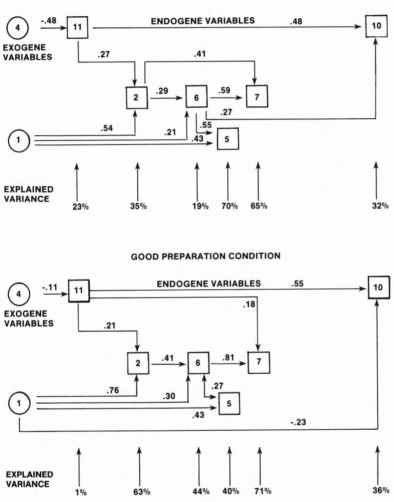

Note: Variables include (1) depression-sensitization disposition, (4) intelligence, (11) knowledge level, (2) test anxiety, (6) actual sensitive coping, (5) state anxiety, (7) cognitive interference, and (10) number of mistakes.

any effect on performance. It should be noted, however, that state anxiety is dependent on repression-sensitization (disposition as well as actual behavior) but not on the cognitive component of test anxiety.　Finally, the strong positive relations between repression-sensitization disposition and worry and self-doubt cognitions should be mentioned.

　　Our assumption that repression-sensitization can have both positive and negative effects on performance, depending on the degree to which a person can prepare for an exam, was supported. In both preparation conditions, a strong positive relationship between dispositional sensitive coping on the one hand, and worry, self-doubt, and actual sensitive coping, on the other, was found. However, only for the bad preparation condition could a performance-debilitating effect be observed.　Generally speaking, this negative influence of defensive motivation on performance level is in accordance with the "traditional" conception of the relation between anxiety and performance.　Our data, however, cast some doubt on this view.　Obviously, a performance-debilitating effect is restricted to problem solving under bad preparation conditions. Under good preparation conditions, worry and self-doubt cognitions, as well as sensitive coping, do not exert a negative influence on performance.　Instead, a positive direct relation between repression-sensitization disposition (sensitive coping behavior in a clearly defined preparation condition) and performance can be observed.

　　It should be mentioned, however, that this approach still contains some weaknesses.　Many of the arguments advanced rest on data gathered by questionnaires.　Although this data source is the one most commonly found in test anxiety research, doubts concerning the validity of these instruments are still justified.　One knows too little about what they really measure (as exemplified above with instruments assessing anxiety states).　Additionally, the high intercorrelations among these instruments indicate a common factor within the data variance.　It is our guess that this factor has something to do with the tendency to admit or deny personal inadequacies.　A second weakness is based on the comparatively low correlations between predictor variables (except for knowledge level) and criterion (performance).　Therefore, our interpretations can be considered only tentative.　Further investigations that move from field research to controlled laboratory studies will have to follow. However, other difficulties may arise in those studies: for example, efforts to produce ego threats may not be effective.　We therefore plan to embark upon a cycle that seems especially appropriate to the area of stress and anxiety research (Schönpflug, 1979). In short, we intend to move from concept and hypothesis formation through field research and laboratory study to the critique of concepts and hypotheses.

References

Averill, J. R. "Personal Control over Aversive Stimuli and Its Relationship to Stress." *Psychological Bulletin,* 1973, *80,* 286–303.

Baddeley, A. D., and Hitch, G. "Working Memory." In G. H. Bower (Ed.), *Recent Advances in Learning and Motivation.* Vol. 8. New York: Academic Press, 1974.

Bell, P. A., and Byrne, D. "Repression-Sensitization." In H. London and J. E. Exner (Eds.), *Dimensions of Personality.* New York: Wiley, 1978.

Bronzaft, A. L., and Stuart, I. R. "Test Anxiety, GSR, and Academic Achievement." *Perceptual and Motor Skills,* 1971, *33,* 535–538.

Brower, P. E., and Mueller, J. H. "Serial Position Effects in Immediate and Final Recall as a Function of Test Anxiety and Sex." *Bulletin of the Psychonomic Society,* 1978, *12,* 61–63.

Byrne, D. "Repression-Sensitization as a Dimension of Personality." In B. A. Maher (Ed.), *Progress in Experimental Personality Research.* Vol. 1. New York: Academic Press, 1964.

Cowen, E. L., and others. "The Relation of Anxiety in Schoolchildren to School Record, Achievement, and Behavioral Measures." *Child Development,* 1965, *36,* 685–695.

Craik, F. I. M., and Tulving, E. "Depth of Processing and the Retention of Words in Episodic Memory." *Journal of Experimental Psychology: General,* 1975, *1,* 268–294.

Cronbach, L. J., and Snow, R. E. *Aptitudes and Instructional Methods.* New York: Halsted, 1977.

Culler, R. E., and Holahan, C. J. "Test Anxiety and Academic Performance: The Effects of Study-Related Behaviors." *Journal of Educational Psychology,* 1980, *72,* 16–20.

Deffenbacher, J. L. "Relationship of Worry and Emotionality to

Performance on the Miller Analogies Test." *Journal of Educational Psychology*, 1977, *69*, 191–195.

Doctor, B., and Altman, F. "Worry and Emotionality as Components of Test Anxiety: Replication and Further Data." *Psychological Reports*, 1969, *24*, 563–568.

Dornic, S. "Mental Load, Effort, and Individual Differences." Report No. 509. Department of Psychology, University of Stockholm, 1977.

Dowaliby, F. J., and Schumer, H. "Teacher-Centered Versus Student-Centered Mode of College Classroom Instructions Related to Manifest Anxiety." *Journal of Educational Psychology*, 1973, *64*, 125–132.

Eysenck, M. W. "Anxiety, Learning, and Memory: A Reconceptualization." *Journal of Research in Personality*, 1979, *13*, 363–385.

Gaudry, E., and Spielberger, C. D. (Eds.). *Anxiety and Educational Achievement*. New York: Wiley, 1971.

Grimes, J. W., and Allinsmith, W. "Compulsivity, Anxiety, and School Achievement." *Merrill-Palmer Quarterly*, 1961, *7*, 247–271.

Harleston, B. W., Smith, G. M., and Arey, D. "Test Anxiety Level, Heart Rate, and Anagram Problem Solving." *Journal of Personality and Social Psychology*, 1965, *1*, 551–557.

Haywood, H. C., and Spielberger, C. D. "Palm Sweating as a Function of Individual Differences in Manifest Anxiety." *Journal of Personality and Social Psychology*, 1966, *3*, 103–105.

Heckhausen, H. "Achievement Motivation and Its Constructs: A Cognitive Model." *Motivation and Emotion*, 1977, *1*, 283–329.

Heckhausen, H. "Task-Irrelevant Cognitions During an Exam: Incidence and Effects." In H. W. Krohne and L. Laux (Eds.), *Achievement, Stress, and Anxiety*. Washington, D.C.: Hemisphere, 1980.

Heinrich, D. L., and Spielberger, C. D. "Anxiety and Complex Learning." In H. W. Krohne and L. Laux (Eds.), *Achievement, Stress, and Anxiety*. Washington, D.C.: Hemisphere, 1980.

Hodapp, V. "Angst und Schulleistung: Zur Frage der Richtung des Einflusses." In L. H. Eckensberger (Ed.), *Bericht über den 31. Kongress der Deutschen Gesellschaft für Psychologie in Mannheim 1978* (Band 2). Göttingen: Hogrefe, 1979.

Hodapp, V., Laux, L., and Spielberger, C. D. *Die deutsche Form des Test Anxiety Inventory.* Weinheim: Beltz, in press.

Holmes, D. S., and Houston, B. K. "Effectiveness of Situation Redefinition and Affective Isolation in Coping with Stress." *Journal of Personality and Social Psychology,* 1974, *29*, 212–218.

Holroyd, K. A., and others. "Performance, Cognition, and Physiological Responding in Test Anxiety." *Journal of Abnormal Psychology,* 1978, *87*, 442–451.

Horn, W. *Prüfsystem für Schul- und Bildungsberatung (PSB).* Göttingen: Hogrefe, 1969.

Houston, B. K. "Dispositional Anxiety and the Effectiveness of Cognitive Coping Strategies in Stressful Laboratory and Classroom Situations." In C. D. Spielberger and I. G. Sarason (Eds.), *Stress and Anxiety.* Vol. 4. New York: Halsted: 1977.

Houston, B. K. "Trait Anxiety and Cognitive Coping Behavior." In H. W. Krohne and L. Laux (Eds.), *Achievement, Stress, and Anxiety.* Washington, D.C.: Hemisphere, 1980.

Houston, B. K., and Hodges, W. F. "Situational Denial and Performance Under Stress." *Journal of Personality and Social Psychology,* 1970, *16*, 726–730.

Jacobs, B. "Angst in der Prüfung." *Arbeitsberichte aus der Fachrichtung Allgemeine Erziehungswissenschaft, Universität des Saarlandes,* no. 2, 1980.

Janis, J. L. *Psychological Stress.* New York: Wiley, 1958.

Kahneman, D. *Attention and Effort.* Englewood Cliffs, N.J.: Prentice-Hall, 1973.

Katkin, E. S. "Relationship Between Manifest Anxiety and Two Indices of Autonomic Response to Stress." *Journal of Personality and Social Psychology,* 1965, *2*, 324–333.

Kissel, S., and Littig, L. W. "Test Anxiety and Skin Conductance." *Journal of Abnormal and Social Psychology,* 1962, *65*, 276–278.

Krohne, H. W. *Angst und Angstverarbeitung.* Stuttgart: Kohlhammer, 1975.

Krohne, H. W. *Theorien zur Angst.* Stuttgart: Kohlhammer, 1976.

Krohne, H. W. "Individual Differences in Coping with Stress and Anxiety." In C. D. Spielberger and I. G. Sarason (Eds.), *Stress and Anxiety.* Vol. 5. New York: Halsted, 1978.

Krohne, H. W. "Angsttheorie: Vom Mechanistischen zum Kognitiven Ansatz." *Psychologische Rundschau*, 1980a, *31*, 12–29.

Krohne, H. W. "Prüfungsangst: Defensive Motivation in Selbstwert-Relevanten Situationen." *Unterrichtswissenschaft*, 1980b, *8*, 226–242.

Krohne, H. W. *Angstverarbeitungsskalen-R-S.* Weinheim: Beltz, in press.

Krohne, H. W., and Rogner, J. "Repression-Sensitization as a Central Construct in Coping Research." In H. W. Krohne and L. Laux (Eds.), *Achievement, Stress, and Anxiety.* Washington, D.C.: Hemisphere, 1980.

Krohne, H. W., Schaffner, P., and Spielberger, C. D. *Fragebogen zur Erfassung von Zustandsangst und Ängstlichkeit bei Kindern — STAI-K.* Weinheim: Beltz, in press.

Lazarus, R. S. *Psychological Stress and Coping Process.* New York: McGraw-Hill, 1966.

Liebert, R. M., and Morris, L. W. "Cognitive and Emotional Components of Test Anxiety: A Distinction and Some Initial Data." *Psychological Reports*, 1967, *20*, 975–978.

Lissmann, U. "Wechselwirkungen von Schülermerkmalen und Schulischen Leistungen." *Zeitschrift für Empirische Pädagogik*, 1977, *1*, 24–28.

McGuigan, F. J., Calvin, A. D., and Richardson, E. C. "Manifest Anxiety, Palmar Perspiration Index, and Stylus Maze Learning." *American Journal of Psychology*, 1959, *72*, 434–438.

Maltzman, J., and Wolff, C. "Preference for Immediate Versus Delayed Noxious Stimulation and the Concomitant GSR." *Journal of Experimental Psychology*, 1970, *83*, 76–79.

Mandler, G., and Sarason, S. B. "A Study of Anxiety and Learning." *Journal of Abnormal and Social Psychology*, 1952, *47*, 166–173.

Monat, A., Averill, J. R., and Lazarus, R. S. "Anticipatory Stress and Coping Reactions Under Various Conditions of Uncertainty." *Journal of Personality and Social Psychology*, 1972, *24*, 237–253.

Morris, L. W., and Liebert, R. M. "Effects of Anxiety on Timed and Untimed Intelligence Tests." *Journal of Consulting and Clinical Psychology*, 1969, *33*, 240–244.

Morris, L. W., and Liebert, R. M. "Relationships of Cognitive and Emotional Components of Test Anxiety to Physiological Arousal and Academic Performance." *Journal of Consulting and Clinical Psychology,* 1970, *35,* 332–337.

Neisser, U. *Cognition and Reality.* San Francisco: W. H. Freeman, 1976.

Niemelä, P. "Coping Pattern in Shock Anticipation and in Everyday Stress." *Scandinavian Journal of Psychology,* 1974, *15,* 268–272.

Paul, G. L., and Eriksen, C. W. "Effects of Test Anxiety on 'Real-Life' Examinations." *Journal of Personality,* 1964, *32,* 480–494.

Peterson, P. L. "Interactive Effects of Student Anxiety, Achievement Orientation, and Teacher Behavior on Student Achievement and Attitude." *Journal of Educational Psychology,* 1977, *69,* 779–792.

Prell, S. "Die Auswirkung von Prüfungsangst auf Verschiedene Formen der Lernzielkontrolle." *Psychologie in Erziehung und Unterricht,* 1973, *20,* 14–30.

Pribram, K. H., and McGuinness, D. "Arousal, Activation, and Effort in the Control of Attention." *Psychological Review,* 1975, *82,* 116–149.

Sarason, I. G. "Experimental Approaches to Test Anxiety: Attention and the Uses of Information." In C. D. Spielberger (Ed.), *Anxiety: Current Trends in Theory and Research.* Vol. 2. New York: Academic Press, 1972.

Sarason, I. G. "Anxiety and Self-Preoccupation." In I. G. Sarason and C. D. Spielberger (Eds.), *Stress and Anxiety.* Vol. 2. New York: Halsted, 1975.

Sarason, I. G. "The Test Anxiety Scale: Concept and Research." In C. D. Spielberger and I. G. Sarason (Eds.), *Stress and Anxiety.* Vol. 5. New York: Halsted, 1978.

Sarason, I. G. (Ed.). *Test Anxiety: Theory, Research, and Application.* Hillsdale, N.J.: Erlbaum, 1980.

Schönpflug, W. "Regulation und Fehlregulation im Verhalten." *Psychologische Beiträge,* 1979, *21,* 174–202.

Scott, S., and Kessler, M. "An Attempt to Relate Test Anxiety and Palmar Sweat Index." *Psychonomic Science,* 1969, *15,* 90–91.

Sieber, J. E., Kameya, L. I., and Paulson, F. L. "Effects of Memory Support on the Problem-Solving Ability of Test Anxious Children." *Journal of Educational Psychology*, 1970, *61*, 159–168.

Sieber, J. E., O'Neil, H. F., and Tobias, S. *"Anxiety, Learning, and Instruction."* Hillsdale, N.J.: Erlbaum, 1977.

Spence, J. T., and Spence, K. W. "The Motivational Components for Manifest Anxiety: Drive and Drive Stimuli." In C. D. Spielberger (Ed.), *Anxiety and Behavior*. New York: Academic Press, 1966.

Spielberger, C. D. "The Effects of Anxiety on Complex Learning and Academic Achievement." In C. D. Spielberger (Ed.), *Anxiety and Behavior*. New York: Academic Press, 1966a.

Spielberger, C. D. "Theory and Research on Anxiety." In C. D. Spielberger (Ed.), *Anxiety and Behavior*. New York: Academic Press, 1966b.

Spielberger, C. D. "Anxiety as an Emotional State." In C. D. Spielberger (Ed.), *Anxiety: Current Trends in Theory and Research.* Vol. 1. New York: Academic Press, 1972.

Spielberger, C. D. *Preliminary Test Manual for the State-Trait Anxiety Inventory for Children.* Palo Alto, Calif.: Consulting Psychologists, 1973.

Spielberger, C. D. *Test Anxiety Inventory (TAI).* Palo Alto, Calif.: Consulting Psychologists, 1980.

Vagt, G., and Kühn, B. "Zum Zusammenhang zwischen Ängstlichkeit und Schulleistung: Die Berücksichtigung des Ausmasses der Häuslichen Vorbereitung auf Schulische Prüfungssituationen." *Zeitschrift für Experimentelle und Angewandte Psychologie*, 1976, *23*, 163–173.

Wachtel, P. L. "Anxiety, Attention, and Coping with Threat." *Journal of Abnormal Psychology*, 1968, *73*, 137–143.

Wine, J. D. "Test Anxiety and Direction of Attention." *Psychological Bulletin*, 1971, *76*, 92–104.

Wine, J. D. "Evaluation Anxiety: A Cognitive Attentional Construct." In H. W. Krohne and L. Laux (Eds.), *Achievement, Stress, and Anxiety*. Washington, D.C.: Hemisphere, 1980.

9   Willy Lens

ℛ ℛ ℛ ℛ ℛ ℛ ℛ ℛ ℛ ℛ ℛ ℛ ℛ

Fear of Failure
and Performance
on Ability Tests

I do not intend to review the different and numerous conceptualizations of anxiety as a motivational concept or the research in which behavioral effects of different types of anxiety are studied. I will rather limit myself to discussing test anxiety as a fear of failure in the context of Atkinson's "expectance X value" theory of achievement motivation (Atkinson, 1957, 1964) and Atkinson and Birch's more general theory of motivation, the so-called dynamics of action theory (Atkinson and Birch, 1970, 1978). Second, I will review some research data showing how test anxiety or fear of failure may affect the level of test performance in opposite ways.

Achievement Motivation

The theory of achievement motivation assumes that all individuals can be characterized by a motive to achieve success and a motive to avoid failure. The motive to achieve success is defined as a general and relatively stable personality disposition to react with pride and satisfaction to success or accomplishment. Individual differences in the strength of this motive are usually measured by content analysis of Thematic Apperception Test (TAT) stories (McClelland and others, 1953; Atkinson, 1958). The motive to avoid failure is seen as a general and also relatively stable personality disposition to react with shame, embarrassment, and dissatisfaction to failure. Individual differences in the strength of this motive are usually measured with the Test Anxiety Questionnaire (Mandler and Sarason, 1952).

Each achievement situation, such as taking an ability test or a school examination, not only implies the promise of success but also the threat of failure. Therefore, achievement-oriented situations simultaneously arouse the achievement motive and the motive to avoid failure. The situationally aroused expectation that a certain act may be instrumental in obtaining a positively evaluated success arouses the achievement motive. But the expectation that the same act may be followed by a negative evaluation simultaneously arouses the motive to avoid failure.

The aroused achievement motive (Ts), or the tendency to succeed, is a multiplicative function of the achievement motive (Ms), the expectancy or probability of success (Ps), and the positive incentive value of that success (Is):

$$Ts = Ms \times Ps \times Is.$$

The positive incentive value of success is totally determined by the probability of success or the difficulty of the task: $Is = 1 - Ps$. The more difficult the task, the higher the incentive value of success. The total value of success in a certain task depends, however, not only on the difficulty of the task for the subject but also on the strength of his or her achievement motive. The total positive value of an anticipated success can be represented by the product of the motive to succeed and the incentive value of the success. The hungrier you are, the higher the rewarding value of the food object. The stronger the need to achieve success, the higher the rewarding value of success at a certain task. Rewriting the formula for the tendency to achieve success as the product of $Ps \times (Ms \times Is)$ clearly shows that theory of achievement motivation is an "expectancy $\times$ value" theory or, in the language of decision theory, a "probability $\times$ utility" model.

The aroused motive to avoid failure (Taf), or the tendency to avoid failure, is a multiplicative function of the strength of the motive to avoid failure (Maf), the expectancy or probability of failure (Pf), and the negative incentive value of failure ($-If$):

$$Taf = Maf \times Pf \times (-If).$$

The probability of failure is inversely related to the probability of success: $Pf = 1 - Ps$. The negative incentive value of failure equals the probability of success: $-If = -Ps$. The easier the task, or the higher the probability of success, the more negative the anticipated incentive value of failure is. Failure at an easy task is more embarrassing than failure at a more difficult one. Hence, the formula for the tendency to avoid failure can be rewritten as:

$$Taf = Maf \times (1 - Ps) \times (-Ps).$$

The tendency to achieve success is a positive, approach-oriented tendency that instigates and sustains action directed toward successful accomplishment. In his original interpretation of the motivational meaning of the tendency to avoid failure, Atkinson (1957) assumed that, in a constrained situation, an individual motivated by a strong tendency to avoid failure will do his best and will work hard in order to reach his goal, the avoidance of failure. He came to realize, however, that when he applied the logic of decision theory to his "expectancy × value" or "risk-taking model," the theory began to say something different (Atkinson, 1964, pp. 244–246). The theory, speaking for itself, opposed his commonsense assumption. The formula for the strength of the tendency to avoid failure will always result in a negative product because of the negative incentive value of the expected failure. In the theory of achievement motivation, the tendency to avoid failure or the aroused fear of failure is considered to be a negative, inhibitory, or avoidance type of motivation. It makes the individual avoid or inhibit actions that are expected to lead to failure. Conceptually, the motivation or tendency to avoid failure does not allow a prediction of what the individual will do. It only predicts what he or she will not do, namely, start a task in which failure is a possible outcome: "Motivation to avoid failure should always be conceived as inhibitory in character. It specifies what activities a person is not likely to undertake. This avoidant tendency always opposes, resists, or dampens the influence of motivation to achieve success and extrinsic positive motivational tendencies to undertake some tasks" (Atkinson, 1966, p. 19). The resultant achievement motivation that affects the choice and level of performance in achievement-oriented behavior is the algebraic sum of the positive tendency to succeed and the negative inhibitory tendency to avoid failure:

$$Tres. = Ts + (-Taf) = (Ms - Maf) Ps (1 - Ps).$$

Highly anxious individuals (their motive to avoid failure being stronger than their motive to achieve success) will always have a negative resultant achievement motivation that will inhibit all actions that may lead to failure. They will only engage in achievement-oriented behavior and take the risk of failure when extrinsic sources of positive motivation overcome the negative resultant achievement motivation. That is at least what the original theory of achievement motivation predicts. As we will see, however, this no longer holds true within the dynamics of action theory.

Action and Negative Action Tendencies

In the dynamics of action theory, which is more general and less stimulus-bound than other motivational theories, the original theory of achievement motivation becomes a theory about the determinants of instigating forces and inhibitory forces. The tendency to achieve success (T) is conceptualized as an instigating force (F) that arouses an action tendency. The strength of this action tendency is a function of the strength of its instigating force and of the duration of the exposure to it. Action tendencies are reduced in strength by being expressed in actions. The extent to which an action tendency is reduced by being expressed represents the consummatory force (C) of that action. At each moment in time, the strength of an action tendency equals the difference between its instigating force and the consummatory force of the action in which it is actually expressed:

$$T = F - C.$$

The negative tendency to avoid failure is now conceptualized as an inhibitory force (I). Exposure to such an inhibitory force arouses a negative action tendency (N), the strength of which is a function of the strength of the inhibitory force and of the duration of the exposure to it. A negative action tendency resists the positive action tendency to initiate or to continue an activity whose anticipated outcome may also be negative. It is expressed and consumed in resistance. The extent to which the negative action tendency is reduced as a consequence of its resisting the positive action tendency is the magnitude of the force of resistance (R). In the same way as the hunger drive is reduced by eating or the tendency to achieve success is reduced by obtaining success, the tendency to avoid failure is reduced by resisting achievement-oriented behavior.

The behavioral implications of an action tendency are opposite to those of its negative action tendency. The former tendency is expressed in action, the latter in resistance or in nonaction. The result of the conflict between a positive action tendency and its negative action tendency is a resultant action tendency. Even for highly anxious subjects, the strong negative action tendency can be consumed completely in resisting achievement-oriented behavior, so that the resultant action tendency after a certain period of time may become positive.

The inhibitory negative action tendency does not compete with the positive action tendency in the sense that the strongest one will affect behavior, but it conflicts with it and subtracts from it to yield a positive, negative, or zero resultant action tendency. When the resultant action tendency is negative or zero, the activity will not be initiated or continued. When it is positive, it competes with other positive resultant action tendencies, and at each moment in time the strongest one will be expressed in action. A change in the hierarchy of competing resultant action tendencies will cause a change in behavior. By considering behavioral changes in a continuous stream of behavior as the subject matter of motivational psychology, the dynamics of action theory shows how the initiation of an action at a certain moment in time — and its duration or persistence — not only depends on the strength of the resultant action tendency for that action but also on the number and strength of competing resultant action tendencies.

The motivation to achieve success, now treated as an instigating force, is the origin of a tendency to engage in an action that is expected to lead to success. The motivation to avoid failure, now treated as an inhibitory force, is the origin of a tendency not to engage in that same action because it may also lead to failure. Because all individuals are characterized by a motive to succeed and a motive to avoid failure, with the strength of these motives varying for each individual, every achievement situation creates an approach-avoidance type of conflict. The positive tendency to achieve success is in conflict with the negative inhibitory tendency not to engage in achievement-oriented behavior. A positive algebraic sum of the two tendencies or the positive resultant achievement tendency competes, in an approach-approach type of conflict, with alternative and incompatible tendencies to initiate action or persist in ongoing action.

Fear of Failure and Test Performance

The theory of achievement motivation and the dynamics of action theory both imply that, all other motivational sources being constant, individuals with a greater fear of failure or a greater degree of test anxiety will always be less strongly motivated to achieve success than subjects with less fear of failure. The stronger the fear of failure, the weaker the resultant achievement motivation. On the assumption that the level of performance is a multiplicative function of ability and motivation (Vroom, 1964, p. 203), it is generally hypothesized that the aroused fear of failure or tendency to avoid failure affects the level of performance in a negative way by decreasing the strength of the total positive motivation to achieve success. The level of performance is assumed to be positively related to the positive resultant achievement motive and to the positive need for achievement, but negatively to the strength of the fear of failure.

Three hypotheses about the behavioral effects of differences in relative strength of the need for achievement and test anxiety have been confirmed repeatedly in research undertaken to validate the theory of achievement motivation. Atkinson's theory predicts indeed that subjects with a strong motive or need to succeed and a weak motive to avoid failure (1) have greater preference for achievement tasks with an intermediate level of difficulty; (2) perform more and more efficiently in achievement-related tasks when these are presented as important ability tests, while subjects with a strong test anxiety suffer performance decrements; and (3) are less persistent in solving very difficult achievement tasks when they have the opportunity to undertake alternative achievement tasks.

Let me briefly summarize the results of two important studies that sustain the conceptualization of fear of failure as a negative, inhibitory motivator that affects achievement performance negatively. Atkinson and Litwin (1960) found that students with a high need for achievement and low test anxiety expressed a greater preference for intermediate risk, spent significantly more time working on a final exam, and obtained significantly higher final exam scores than a comparable group of students with a low need for achievement and high test anxiety. When the dependent measures were related to the two motives separately, the same picture emerged: In comparison with subjects with low anxiety, highly anxious subjects persisted significantly less in a final exam, obtained significantly lower grades, and had a much lower preference for intermediate risks. Subjects with a high need for achievement persisted longer and scored higher than subjects with a low need for achievement.

As predicted, Feather (1961) found that, when confronted with repeated failures, subjects with a high need for achievement and low test anxiety persisted more when the stated difficulty of the test was low and less when the stated difficulty was very high. As also predicted, he found the opposite for highly anxious subjects. Those subjects with a low need for achievement and high test anxiety persisted longer when the stated difficulty was very high and much less when it was rather low.

It has been well documented that test anxiety relates negatively to performance criteria, because it decreases the strength of the total motivation to achieve success. Some years ago, however, Atkinson and O'Connor formulated what they called "a novel hypothesis concerning test anxiety" (1966, p. 323). According to this hypothesis, test anxiety may have behavioral effects opposite to the ones we discussed. In some conditions, high test anxiety may positively affect (increase) the level of test performance.

There was already empirical evidence showing that the positive relationship between need for achievement or the resultant achievement motive and test performance is much lower when other (extrinsic) incentives to perform well are also offered. Atkinson and Reitman (1956) found that, in an achievement-oriented condition, subjects with a strong achievement motive attempted significantly more arithmetical problems and solved significantly more of them correctly than subjects with a low achievement motive. However, in a multi-incentive condition in which the achievement motive and the need for social approval were aroused and monetary incentives were offered, these performance differences between subjects high and low in achievement motive disappeared. In addition, subjects low in achievement motive performed much better in the multi-incentive condition than in the achievement-oriented condition. Subjects high in achievement motive performed much more poorly in the multi-incentive condition than in the condition with only the achievement incentives.

When additional incentives are offered to increase the strength of total motivation, high achievement-motivated subjects seem to suffer a performance decrement. Atkinson and O'Connor (1966, p. 319) refer to the old Yerkes-Dodson hypothesis (or law) to explain this decrement (Yerkes and Dodson, 1908). This hypothesis holds that the relationship between strength of motivation and level of test performance may be curvilinear (inverted U-shaped) rather than linear. When the strength of motivation is higher than an optimal level, the individual will be less efficient in his performance. It is also hypothesized that the optimal level of motivation will be lower the more difficult the task is. Various theoretical explanations have been formulated for this curvilinear relationship (Lewin, 1938; Easterbrook, 1959; Broen and Storms, 1961; Atkinson, 1978; Atkinson and Lens, 1980). For high achievement-motivated subjects, additional extrinsic incentives to perform well may increase the strength of their total motivation to do well beyond the optimal level.

Thus, Atkinson and O'Connor (1966) related achievement-oriented performance (risk preference, speed, and persistence) to resultant achievement motives and to extrinsic incentives (social approval). They also found "suggestive evidence of a performance decrement among those [subjects] Ss who were relatively strong in both achievement and affiliative motivation" (p. 321). The empirical evidence for a performance decrement when total motivation to achieve success was at more than optimal strength brought Atkinson and O'Connor to the conclusion that the negative behavioral effect of test anxiety or the negative relationship between test anxiety and test performance holds only when the total positive motivation is not too strong and the resultant total of motivation is thus lower than optimal. When the intensity of the total positive motivation (achievement motivation and extrinsic motivation) is well above the optimal level, the negative inhibitory tendency to avoid failure will weaken the resultant total motivation, will bring it closer to the optimal level, and hence will enhance the level of performance.

Table 1 with four hypothetical subjects illustrates the opposite behavioral effects that the inhibitory tendency to avoid failure can have on the level of test performance. The assumed relationship between strength of resultant motivation and level of performance is depicted in Figure 1. The exact form of the curve is not important so long as it is an inverted U-shaped curve.

For subjects A and B the strength of total positive motivation to achieve success equals +7, which is just below the optimal level of 8 (see Figure 1). For these subjects the strength of the tendency to

Table 1. The Opposite Behavioral Effects of the Tendency to Avoid Failure (Taf).

Subject	Ts	Motivational Tendencies Textr	Taf	Tres	Level of Performance
A	+2	+5	−4	+3	6
B	+2	+5	−1	+6	9
C	+9	+5	−4	+10	9
D	+9	+5	−1	+13	6

Note: Ts = tendency to succeed
Textr = extrinsic motivation
· Taf = tendency to avoid failure
Tres = resultant achievement motivation

Figure 1. Curvilinear Relationship Between Strength of Motivation and
Level of Performance.

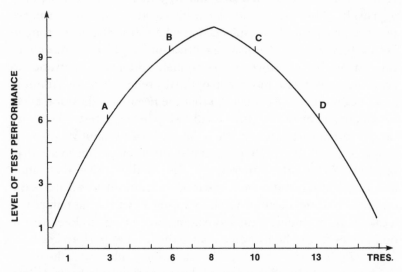

avoid failure relates negatively to the level of performance. The
highly anxious subject A (Ts < Taf) performs worse than the
nonanxious subject B. For both subjects the tendency to avoid
failure (*Taf*) makes the discrepancy between the optimal level of
motivation and the resultant motivation larger than it would have
been without anxiety. They perform more poorly than they would
have performed without anxiety.

     For subjects C and D the strength of the total positive motiva-
tion is 14 (9 + 5), which is far beyond the optimal level in Figure 1.
For these subjects the tendency to avoid failure relates positively to
the level of performance. It brings the strength of the resultant
motivation closer to the optimal level; hence, the level of performance will increase. The subject with the strongest fear of failure
(subject C) performs better than the subject with a weak fear of
failure (subject D).

     Empirical evidence for the positive behavorial effects of the
tendency to avoid failure is shown in Table 2. The three motivational conditions are ordered from left to right according to the
degree to which they are assumed to arouse motivation. This
ordering is confirmed by the subjects' post-test ratings of how hard

Table 2. Mean Correct Arithmetic Performance According to Strength of Achievement-Related Motives Under Various Conditions.

| *Motive Groups* | | | *Motivational Conditions* | |
n Ach	*Test Anxiety*	*Relaxed*	*Achievement*	*Multi-Incentive*
High	Low	53.0	78.8	55.3
High	High	55.1	66.0	58.7
Low	Low	56.4	71.3	71.5
Low	High	34.8	55.8	85.3
Test Anxiety				
High		48.33	53.92	70.31
Low		55.43	75.71	64.74

Source: Atkinson (1978, p. 130).

they had worked. The results in the first row (for the subjects with a high need for achievement and a low fear of failure) correspond with the hypothesis of a curvilinear relationship between strength of motivation and level of performance. These highly motivated subjects perform much lower in the multi-incentive condition than in the achievement condition that is assumed to arouse motivation to a lesser degree. The total motivation of these subjects in the highly arousing multi-incentive condition seems from the data to be beyond the optimal level. For the weakly motivated subjects (low need for achievement and high test anxiety), the level of performance increases from the relaxed condition to the multi-incentive condition.

The positive behavioral effects that the tendency to avoid failure may have are clearly shown within the multi-incentive condition. In this condition, which is the most motivation-arousing situation, subjects with a high fear of failure perform better than subjects with a low fear of failure (high-high versus high-low; low-high versus low-low). Subjects with a low achievement motive and strong test anxiety perform much better in this multi-incentive condition than subjects with a high achievement motive and low test anxiety. To quote Atkinson (1978): "The hypothesis that strong anxiety, in dampening motivation, should function to enhance performance efficiency when an individual might otherwise be 'overmotivated' is certainly supported by the trends of the differences between subgroups alike in n Achievement but different in anxiety in the multi-incentive condition when compared with their counterparts in the achievement (alone) condition" (pp. 130–131).

In a recent study, a colleague and I (Lens and De Volder, 1980) tested the curvilinear relationship between strength of achievement motivation and test performance. Instead of using simple arithmetical problems, we used Drenth's test for nonverbal abstraction (Drenth, 1965). This test is intended to measure higher levels of intelligence, whereas many other intelligence tests do not discriminate adequately among able subjects. Subjects were 229 first-year students in psychology or educational sciences at the University of Louvain. Strength of achievement motive was measured with the Mehrabian male and female scales of the tendency to achieve (Mehrabian, 1968, 1969). The distribution of all 229 achievement motive scores was divided into quarters (high, medium-high, medium-low, and low). Assuming as is often done in research on achievement motivation that about 25 percent of the college population has a stronger fear of failure than desire to achieve, we also considered the low-motive group to be negatively achievement motivated. Their actual scores on the Mehrabian scale were lower than −6.

Intelligence was measured in a neutral and in a high ego-involvement condition. In the neutral condition ($N = 79$) the test was introduced to the subjects as a new test that psychologists were developing and as one whose value was not yet known. These instructions were intended to prevent the achievement motive from being aroused too strongly. In the high ego-involvement condition ($N = 150$), however, the same test was introduced as a very valuable instrument for measuring higher levels of intelligence and as highly predictive of academic achievement. These instructions were intended to arouse the achievement-oriented motives strongly. The range of strength of achievement motivation was much broader in the high ego-involvement condition than in the neutral condition. The low-motive group (test anxiety stronger than the need for achievement) was more relaxed and less negatively achievement motivated, and hence the members had a stronger total positive motivation to achieve success in the neutral than in the high ego-in-

volvement condition. The positively achievement-motivated subjects (*n* Achievement stronger than test anxiety) were more strongly
motivated in the high ego-involvement condition than in the less
motive-arousing neutral condition, in which achievement-related
motives were not aroused by the instructions.

Table 3 shows the mean intelligence test scores for the eight
subgroups (four motive groups in two experimental conditions). As
expected, strength of motivation and intelligence test scores are
curvilinearly related in the high-ego involvement condition. The
linear trend component is not significant; the quadratic one is at the
.05 level. Members of the low-motive group, assumed to be negatively achievement motivated, perform better in the neutral condition than in the highego-involvement condition. In the neutral
condition their fear of failure is much less aroused than in the
highego-involvement condition, so that their total motivation to do
well is stronger in the former condition than in the latter one. At
the lower end of the motivational continuum, the aroused fear of
failure has a detrimental effect on test performance. At the higher
end of the continuum, the high-motive group scores lower in the
high ego-involvement condition than in the neutral condition. In
both conditions the most highly motivated group scores lower than
the medium-high group, again evidencing a performance decrement
because of too strong a level of motivation.

The expectation of a negative evaluation as the outcome of an
achievement-oriented task arouses a tendency to avoid such failure.
This tendency is a negative one and subtracts from the positive

**Table 3. Mean Intelligence Test Scores of Four Motive Groups in a
Neutral and in a High Ego-Involvement Condition.**

| | Condition | |
Motive Group	Neutral	High Ego-Involvement
High	25.29	23.95
Medium-High	27.45	27.19
Medium-Low	24.42	24.21
Low	26.79	23.63

Source: Lens and De Volder (1980, p. 54).

tendency to achieve success. The stronger the fear of failure, the weaker the overall motivation to succeed will be.

The behavioral effects of this inhibitory tendency to avoid failure, may, however, be positive as well as negative. In conditions where the level of performance is an increasing function of the strength of motivation, the tendency to avoid failure has a negative effect on performance. In contrast, when the level of performance is a decreasing function of the strength of motivation, the tendency to avoid failure has a positive effect on the level of performance by bringing the total motivation closer to the optimal level.

Empirical research in this field should now concentrate on the exact form of this relationship for different types of achievement tasks. More specifically, when the relationship is curvilinear, we should try to determine where on the motivational continuum the most optimal level is situated for those different types of tasks. Linear product-moment correlations should not be applied blindly in the process of relating test scores to motivational measures. Whether test anxiety or fear of failure does indeed have a negative effect on the level of test performance is an empirical question and depends on the exact form of the relationship between strength of motivation and level of performance on that test, as well as on the overall level of the positive motivation to succeed.

References

Atkinson, J. W. "Motivational Determinants of Risk-Taking Behavior." *Psychological Review*, 1957, *64*, 359–372.

Atkinson, J. W. (Ed.). *Motives in Fantasy, Action, and Society*. New York: D. Van Nostrand, 1958.

Atkinson, J. W. *An Introduction to Motivation*. New York: D. Van Nostrand, 1964.

Atkinson, J. W. "Motivational Determinants of Risk-Taking Behavior." In J. W. Atkinson and N. T. Feather (Eds.), *A Theory of Achievement Motivation*. New York: Wiley, 1966.

Atkinson, J. W. "Strength of Motivation and Efficiency of Performance." In J. W. Atkinson and J. O. Raynor (Eds.), *Personality, Motivation, and Achievement*. New York: Halsted, 1978.

Atkinson, J. W., and Birch, D. *The Dynamics of Action*. New York: Wiley, 1970.

Atkinson, J. W., and Birch, D. "The Dynamics of Achievement-Oriented Activity." In J. W. Atkinson and J. O. Raynor (Eds.), *Personality, Motivation, and Achievement*. New York: Halsted, 1978.

Atkinson, J.W., and Lens, W. "Fähigkeit und Motivation als Determinanten Momentaner und Kumulativer Leistung." In H. Heckhausen (Ed.), *Fähigkeit und Motivation in Erwartungswidriger Schulleistung*. Göttingen: Hogrefe, 1980.

Atkinson, J. W., and Litwin, G. H. "Achievement Motive and Test Anxiety Conceived as Motive to Approach Success and Motive to Avoid Failure." *Journal of Abnormal and Social Psychology*, 1960, *60*, 52–63.

Atkinson, J. W., and O'Connor, P. "Neglected Factors in Studies of Achievement-Oriented Performance: Social Approval as Incentive and Performance Decrement." In J. W. Atkinson and N. T. Feather (Eds.), *A Theory of Achievement Motivation*. New York: Wiley, 1966.

Atkinson, J. W., and Reitman, W. R. "Performance as a Function of Motive Strength and Expectancy of Goal Attainment." *Journal of Abnormal and Social Psychology*, 1956, *53*, 361–366.

Broen, W. E., and Storms, L. H. "A Reaction Potential Ceiling and Response Decrements in Complex Situations." *Psychological Review*, 1961, *68*, 405–415.

Drenth, P. J. D. *Test voor Niet-Verbale Abstractie Handleiding*. Amsterdam: Swets & Zeitlinger, 1965.

Easterbrook, J. A. "The Effect of Emotion on Cue Utilization and the Organization of Behavior." *Psychological Review*, 1959, *66*, 183–201.

Feather, N. T. "The Relationship of Persistence at a Task to Expectation of Success and Achievement-Related Motives." *Journal of Abnormal and Social Psychology*, 1961, *63*, 552–561.

Lens, W., and De Volder, M. "Achievement Motivation and Intelligence Test Scores: A Test of the Yerkes-Dodson Hypothesis." *Psychologica Belgica*, 1980, *20*, 49–59.

Lewin, K. *The Conceptual Representation and the Measurement of Psychological Forces*. Durham, N.C.: Duke University Press, 1938.

McClelland, D. C., and others. *The Achievement Motive.* New York: Appleton-Century-Crofts, 1953.

Mandler, G., and Sarason, S. B. "A Study of Anxiety and Learning." *Journal of Abnormal and Social Psychology,* 1952, *47,* 166–173.

Mehrabian, A. "Male and Female Scales of the Tendency to Achieve." *Educational and Psychological Measurement,* 1968, *28,* 493–502.

Mehrabian, A. "Measures of Achieving Tendency." *Educational and Psychological Measurement,* 1969, *29,* 445–451.

Smith, C. P. "Situational Determinants of the Expression of Achievement Motivation in Thematic Apperception." Unpublished doctoral dissertation, University of Michigan, 1961.

Vroom, V. H. *Work and Motivation.* New York: Wiley, 1964.

Yerkes, R. M., and Dodson, J. D. "The Relationship of Strength of Stimulus to Rapidity of Habit Formation." *Journal of Comparative and Neurological Psychology,* 1908, *18,* 459–482.

Part Four

ℜ ℜ ℜ ℜ ℜ ℜ ℜ ℜ ℜ ℜ ℜ ℜ ℜ

Latent Trait Theories and Applications

The three chapters in this section on latent trait analysis go well beyond its routine application to item analysis and scaling. Erling Andersen begins the discussion in Chapter Ten with a treatment of the Rasch model as an example of a general method of analyzing data. In a nontechnical way, he demonstrates the appropriate arrangement of data, goes on to discuss the development of parameters, and shows how the data may be tested for goodness of fit to the model. This test is not seen as the end of the process, but as a basis for searching for correctable deviations. If the model does in fact fit the data, one can estimate the individual parameter for the ability of a person and establish appropriate confidence limits for that estimate. It may be of more interest, however, to estimate the distribution of ability in the population, particularly if a comparison of two or more distributions is the concern. Examples of this approach, as well as of the methods to be used, are given, and the advantages of using the estimated distributions over the actual distributions are discussed. Extensions are also suggested for use with questionnaires, with more than one latent variable, and with vector-valued latent variables.

In Chapter Eleven, Charles Lewis concentrates on the difference between making inferences about individual abilities and making inferences about item characteristics. In the latter case, there are usually reasonably large numbers of individuals available as a basis for estimating item difficulties. Most work has been done with these estimates for the purpose of improved test development. As the interest shifts to individual ability estimates, however, a new set of statistical considerations appears because of the limited number of items typically available for making individual estimates. While the restricted item response model is satisfactory for evaluating items, it may be unrealistic or misleading for studying individuals. To deal with this problem, a nonparametric item response model with two full Bayesian analyses is introduced. It defines an ordinal ability scale in terms of the character of the items estimated to be answered correctly with a chance of at least .5. The procedure takes into consideration the pattern of actual responses, not just the number correct as in the Rasch model. A number of individual examples make clear the differences in the two approaches.

In the final chapter, Wilhelm Kempf takes testing and measurement to task for depending on statistical rather than psychological theory. He castigates classical test theory for having led to this state of affairs, speaking of its undefined terms and "mathematically convenient but psychologically unfounded assumptions." His major concerns are with that theory's dependence on the concept of randomness and the obvious difficulties created by successive independent repetitions of the same test by any individual. He finds similar difficulties with the use of latent trait concepts but does see a way to handle these difficulties through latent class analysis, with the Rasch model providing answers statistically. In this manner, in terms of ratios of correct answers, he finds psychological meaning to be allied to statistical analysis. An example is provided in the stepwise accumulation of knowledge and hypotheses about children's learning as they observe and manipulate weights on a balance beam. Here, in common with Lewis's treatment, the analysis provides information about the pattern of responses, and it seeks meaning in the deviations from regularity. Kempf concludes that latent trait models do have application in educational research but "must not be applied routinely. Statistical theories of test scores cannot substitute for psychological theorizing and our need for a clearly defined psychological terminology."

10 Erling B. Andersen

ജ ജ ജ ജ ജ ജ ജ ജ ജ ജ ജ ജ ജ

Analyzing Data Using the Rasch Model

In this chapter I will survey some of the statistical methods that arise in connection with the Rasch model. I will do so by making reference as often as possible to tables and graphs that display real data rather than rely on formulas and mathematics. Some formulas and a few Greek letters will be needed, but they are well-known and easily understood quantities. For any success in analyzing data, it is important to arrive at satisfactory answers to the following questions:

1. What kind of data are we dealing with?
2. What models are relevant for the problem?
3. How can data be analyzed to throw maximum light on the problem?
4. Can we use the results?

In this chapter I will deal primarily with the first three questions. It is likely that the reader will then be able to give his or her own answer to the last question. Although many of the reflections in the present chapter are of a general character, I have chosen to concentrate on the Rasch model and its applications. Among the many reasons for doing so is the very important one that the Rasch model is illustrative of how basic psychological theory and modern statistical theory can work hand in hand.

Data Forms

The data to be considered here are all basically of the form shown in Table 1. I call this *data in raw form;* that is, data as they are available in our computer. Such data are derived as the answers to k items of a given battery of test items. We score an item with a 1 if we get a correct or positive answer and with a 0 if we get an incorrect or negative answer. For each person a simple calculation gives the raw score, which is simply the sum of 1's. This raw score is a first rough measure of how able or positive a given person is.

The data of Table 1 can be rearranged in two different ways. First, we may summarize the data by collecting all individuals with exactly the same response pattern. Thus person number 1 and person number 6 of Table 1 will be put together. In Tables 2 and 3 are shown two examples of such data displays. Table 2 shows the possible response patterns for four items of a questionnaire on role conflict by Stouffer and Toby (1951). A positive or 1 answer indicates a universalist attitude on the part of an individual confronted with a situation of role conflict. A 0 answer indicates a particularist attitude. We will return to this data set later in the chapter.

As another example of this way of summarizing the data, Table 3 shows the observed number of persons for each response

Table 1. Data in Raw Form.

Person Number	*Item Number*								Raw Score
	1	*2*	*3*	*4*	*5*	*6*	*7*	*8*	
1	1	0	1	0	1	0	0	0	3
2	1	1	1	0	1	0	1	0	5
3	0	1	0	1	0	0	0	0	2
4	1	0	1	1	1	1	0	0	5
5	1	1	1	1	1	1	1	1	8
6	1	0	1	0	1	0	0	0	3
7	0	0	1	0	0	0	0	0	1

Table 2. Number of Persons for Each Response Pattern on Four Items of the Stouffer-Toby Data.

Response Pattern				Number of Persons
1	1	1	1	42
1	1	1	0	23
1	1	0	1	6
1	1	0	0	25
1	0	1	1	6
1	0	1	0	24
1	0	0	1	7
1	0	0	0	38
0	1	1	1	1
0	1	1	0	4
0	1	0	1	1
0	1	0	0	6
0	0	1	1	2
0	0	1	0	9
0	0	0	1	2
0	0	0	0	20
Total				216

pattern on two subsets of five items each of the Law School Admission Test (LSAT). Here a 1 answer corresponds to a correct answer. The data were first given by Bock and Lieberman (1970). These two sets of data will also be analyzed later.

Second, we can group the data according to score group; that is, we can group all persons with raw score r into score group G_r. For each of the $k + 1$ possible score groups, we count the number of 1 answers on each item. In Table 4 this way of summarizing the data is shown for the Stouffer-Toby data of Table 2. The thirty-six persons of score group 3 are thus the twenty-three persons with response pattern (1110), the six persons with pattern (1101), the six persons with pattern (1011), and, finally, the one individual with response pattern (0111). The sum 35 under $j = 1$ is obtained by adding $23 + 6 + 6$, since only the person with pattern (0111) does not have item 1 correct.

As we shall see later, the data may be summarized even further once it is determined that the Rasch model describes them adequately. Under the Rasch model, the number of individuals n_r in score group r, together with the item totals s_j, are sufficient for the

Table 3. Number of Persons for Each Response Pattern on Two Subsets of Items from the Law School Admission Test (LSAT).

Response Pattern					Number of Persons	
					Section 6	Section 7
0	0	0	0	0	3	12
0	0	0	0	1	6	19
0	0	0	1	0	2	1
0	0	0	1	1	11	7
0	0	1	0	0	1	3
0	0	1	0	1	1	19
0	0	1	1	0	3	3
0	0	1	1	1	4	17
0	1	0	0	0	1	10
0	1	0	0	1	8	5
0	1	0	1	0	0	3
0	1	0	1	1	16	7
0	1	1	0	0	0	7
0	1	1	0	1	3	23
0	1	1	1	0	2	8
0	1	1	1	1	15	28
1	0	0	0	0	10	7
1	0	0	0	1	29	39
1	0	0	1	0	14	11
1	0	0	1	1	81	34
1	0	1	0	0	3	14
1	0	1	0	1	28	51
1	0	1	1	0	15	15
1	0	1	1	1	80	90
1	1	0	0	0	16	6
1	1	0	0	1	56	25
1	1	0	1	0	21	7
1	1	0	1	1	173	35
1	1	1	0	0	11	18
1	1	1	0	1	61	136
1	1	1	1	0	28	32
1	1	1	1	1	298	308
Total					1000	1000

estimation of the individual parameters and item parameters of the model. The term *sufficient*, basic to statistical theory, means that when we want to estimate — or otherwise investigate — the parameters, we can restrict attention to the sufficient quantities.

Table 4. Item Sums Within Score Groups for the Stouffer-Toby Data.

Score Group	Score r	Number of Persons in G_r	Item Totals $j=1$	2	3	4
G_0	0	20	0	0	0	0
G_1	1	55	38	6	9	2
G_2	2	63	56	30	30	10
G_3	3	36	35	30	30	13
G_4	4	42	42	42	42	42
	Total	216	171	108	111	67

In order to estimate the parameters of a Rasch model, let us use as an example the Stouffer-Toby data as shown in Table 5. As another example, we will consider data from the Scholastic Aptitude test (SAT)—data first analyzed by Lord (1968). Table 6 is taken from Andersen (1973a), who analyzed these same data by means of a Rasch model.

The Rasch Model

We shall not go too deeply into the mathematics of the Rasch model but rather outline the basic elements of the model and of the statistical analysis based on it. The Rasch model is a very simple form of an item characteristic curve. As is well known, the item characteristic curve (ICC-curve) is the probability of a 1 answer on item j, given the individual parameter Θ. We shall denote this function $p_j(\Theta)$. Figure 1 shows this kind of ICC-curve. The

Table 5. Score Group Totals and Item Totals for the Stouffer-Toby Data.

Score Group r	n_r	Item j	s_j
0	20	1	171
1	55	2	108
2	63	3	111
3	36	4	67
4	42		

Table 6. Score Group Totals and Item Totals
for the Scholastic Aptitude Test (SAT).

Score Group		Item	
r	n_r	j	s_j
0	18	1	140
1	25	2	223
2	25	3	239
3	41	4	315
4	46	5	541
5	57	6	537
6	56	7	390
7	53	8	419
8	55	9	668
9	69	10	691
10	95	11	77
11	93	12	206
12	95	13	268
13	81	14	425
14	82	15	696
15	58	16	713
16	33	17	685
17	11	18	720
18	4	19	784
19	3	20	726
20	0		

mathematical form is given by

$$p_j(\Theta) = e^{\theta - \alpha_j}/(1 + e^{\theta - \alpha_j}),$$

where α_j is the Θ point for which $p_j(\Theta) = .5$. We may also write $p_j(\Theta)$ as

$$p_j(\Theta) = \Psi(\Theta - \alpha_j), \tag{1}$$

where $\Psi(x) = e^x/(1 + e^x)$ is the so-called logistic growth curve. We note that the ICC-curve depends only on the distance between Θ and α_j, which means that the item parameter α_j is only defined relative to the individual parameter Θ.

Given that Θ is an individual parameter (that is, each person

Figure 1. The ICC-Curve for a Rasch Model.

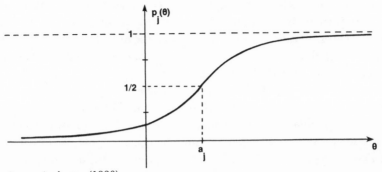

Source: Anderson (1980).

has a true parameter value at a specific point on the Θ axis), the interpretation of the item parameter is straightforward. The value of α_j makes a point on the Θ axis that separates individuals who are most likely to get a correct or 1 answer from those who are most likely to get a wrong or 0 answer. The higher the value of α_j, the fewer the people who will be likely to answer correctly. This property can be interpreted in the same way as *item difficulty* when we are dealing with ability tests. If we deal with attitude tests, where a 1 answer indicates a positive attitude, α_j should be interpreted as the general tendency of the item to provoke negative answers, since the higher the value of α_j, the fewer the individuals who will be likely to give positive answers.

Since, in contrast, p_j (Θ) increases with Θ, the individual parameter may be described as individual *ability* for ability tests and as *degree of positiveness* in the case of an attitude test. In the classical work by Lord (1952) on ICC-curves, the function p_j (Θ) was chosen as

$$p_j(\Theta) = \Phi((\Theta - \alpha_j)\beta_j), \tag{2}$$

where Φ is the cumulative distribution function of the standard normal distribution. Θ and α_j have the same interpretation as in (1), while β_j is the so-called item-discriminating power, which determines the slope of the ICC-curve at $\Theta = \alpha_j$. For the Rasch model β_j-1 for all items.

The two alternative functions Ψ and Φ do not (after a suitable scaling on the Θ axis) differ very much. Hence we might choose between them from the point of view of statistical properties. Here the Rasch model with the logistic ICC-curve seems to be superior to the ICC-curve based on Φ. The statistical analysis consists of two steps: (1) estimation of the parameters of the model and (2) a check of the model, that is, applying a goodness of fit test for the ability of the model to describe the given data.

As mentioned earlier, one important property of the Rasch model is that the item totals and the raw scores are sufficient statistics for the parameters. This means that in order to estimate the unknown values of the item parameters $\alpha_1, \ldots, \alpha_k$, we only have to know the item totals $s_1, \ldots, s_k$, together with the model structure. Another way to express this is that the estimates for $\alpha_1, \ldots, \alpha_k$ are simple transformations of $s_1, \ldots, s_k$ that, for example, preserve the order of the s_j's.

In the same way the raw score r is a sufficient statistic for the Θ

Table 7. Sufficient Statistics and Parameter Estimates for the Scholastic Aptitude Test (SAT).

Score r	Estimate $\hat{\Theta}_r$	Item j	Item Total s_j	Estimate $\hat{\alpha}_j$
0	$-\infty$	1	140	$+2.01$
1	-3.57	2	223	$+1.37$
2	-2.77	3	239	$+1.26$
3	-2.26	4	315	$+0.81$
4	-1.85	5	541	-0.38
5	-1.50	6	537	-0.36
6	-1.19	7	390	$+0.41$
7	-0.89	8	419	$+0.25$
8	-0.61	9	668	-1.09
9	-0.33	10	691	-1.23
10	-0.05	11	77	$+2.73$
11	$+0.24$	12	206	$+1.48$
12	$+0.52$	13	268	$+1.08$
13	$+0.82$	14	425	$+0.22$
14	$+1.14$	15	696	-1.26
15	$+1.48$	16	713	-1.37
16	$+1.85$	17	685	-1.19
17	$+2.29$	18	720	-1.42
18	$+2.85$	19	784	-1.88
19	$+3.70$	20	726	-1.46
20	$+\infty$			

parameter of those individuals who fall in score group G_r. This means that all individuals with score r get the same estimate $\hat{\Theta}$. It also means that the $\hat{\Theta}$'s for different score groups are ordered according to the value of r.

As an illustration, Table 7 shows the estimates of the α's and the Θ's for the SAT data of Table 6. The estimation methods used are conditional maximum likelihood estimation for the α_j's and direct maximum likelihood estimation (given the values of the $\hat{\alpha}_j$'s) for the $\hat{\Theta}$'s. More details on these methods can be found in Andersen (1980). For the Stouffer-Toby data, the estimates are shown in Table 8.

The goodness of fit test for the model derives from Andersen (1973a). It is based on the fact that the raw score r is sufficient for the estimation of Θ for individuals in score group G_r. The statistical meaning of sufficiency is that the value of a sufficient statistic exhausts the information contained in the data about the parameter in question. Translated to the present situation, this means that when we know the raw score of an individual, there is nothing more to be gained from the data about the value of his parameter Θ. The distribution of the responses over the items for individuals all belonging to the same score group should accordingly carry no information about Θ that is not already available in the value of r. The distribution of item totals within the score group as shown in Table 4 can thus only tell us something about the values of the item parameters. In a sense, this again means that we can get independent estimates of the α_j's from the different score groups. The idea of the goodness of fit test is, therefore, to estimate the item parameters from the item totals in each score group and compare each of these

Table 8. Sufficient Statistics and Parameter Estimates
for the Stouffer-Toby Data.

Score r	Estimate $\hat{\Theta}_r$	Item j	Item Total s_j	Estimate $\hat{\alpha}_j$
0	$-\infty$	1	171	-1.187
1	-1.375	2	108	$+0.148$
2	$+0.030$	3	111	$+0.092$
3	$+1.385$	4	67	$+0.947$
4	$+\infty$			

sets to the overall estimates obtained from the overall item totals. We shall denote the item parameter estimates obtained from the item totals in score group G_r,

$$s_1^{(r)}, \ldots , s_k^{(r)},$$

by

$$\hat{\alpha}_1^{(r)}, \ldots , \hat{\alpha}_k^{(r)}. \tag{3}$$

These estimates are obtained by exactly the same algorithm as the overall estimates. We only have to imagine that the whole sample belongs to score group G_r.

The score group estimates (3) can be compared to the overall estimates in two ways. We can plot the $\hat{\alpha}_j^{(r)}$'s against the $\hat{\alpha}_j$'s for each score value r. We should then find points that cluster at random

Table 9. Item Totals and Item Parameter Estimates for the Law School Admission Test (LSAT), Section 6.

Item Totals	Item Number				
	3	2	4	5	1
$r = 0$	0	0	0	0	0
1	1	1	2	6	10
2	7	24	28	49	62
3	63	109	139	188	212
4	184	277	296	329	342
5	298	298	298	298	298
Total	553	709	763	870	924

Item Parameter Estimates	Item Number				
	3	2	4	5	1
$r = 1$	+0.938	+0.938	+0.204	−0.834	−1.345
2	+1.504	+0.247	+0.069	−0.666	−1.214
3	+1.218	+0.543	+0.184	−0.616	−1.329
4	+1.216	+0.445	+0.174	−0.605	−1.229
Overall	+1.236	+0.475	+0.168	−0.623	−1.256

around straight lines with slopes 1 passing through the origin. Or we can apply a goodness of fit test derived as a likelihood ratio test based on the conditional likelihoods assigned to score groups. The test quantity, called z, is asymptotically χ^2-distributed with a number of degrees of freedom equal to $(g - 1)(k - 1)$, where k is the number of items and g is the number of score groups for which we have score group item parameter estimates of the form (3).

As an example, we shall analyze the two subsections of the LSAT (see the basic data in Table 3). In order to illustrate the structure of the data when a Rasch model fits — or does not fit — the data, the items have been rearranged according to the value of the overall item totals. Table 9 shows the item totals for each of the six score groups, the overall item totals, the score group item parameter estimates, and the overall estimates for the LSAT, section 6. In Table 10, the corresponding figures are shown for the LSAT, section 7.

Table 10. Item Totals and Item Parameter Estimates for the Law School Admission Test (LSAT), Section 7.

Item Totals	Item Number				
	4	*2*	*3*	*5*	*1*
$r = 0$	0	0	0	0	0
1	10	1	3	7	19
2	24	21	43	70	70
3	88	88	132	157	150
4	185	231	286	289	293
5	308	308	308	308	308
Total	615	649	772	831	840

Item Parameter Estimates	Item Number				
	4	*2*	*3*	*5*	*1*
$r = 1$	−0.644	+1.658	+0.560	−0.288	−1.286
2	+0.665	+0.811	−0.011	−0.732	−0.732
3	+0.570	+0.570	−0.104	−0.595	−0.440
4	+0.960	+0.547	−0.398	−0.488	−0.621
Overall	+0.758	+0.583	−0.134	−0.566	−0.641

The plots of $\hat{\alpha}_j^{(r)}$ against $\hat{\alpha}_j$ are shown in Figures 2 and 3. It is rather obvious that we have the prescribed structure in the data from section 6, but not in the data from section 7. The goodness of fit test statistics confirm this. For section 6, we get

$$z = 3.1, \qquad df = 12$$

and for section 7, we get

$$z = 35.9, \qquad df = 12.$$

Compared with the percentiles of a χ^2 distribution, $z = 3.1$ is not

Figure 2. Score Group Estimates Against Overall Estimates of Item Parameters for the Law School Admission Test (LSAT), Section 6.

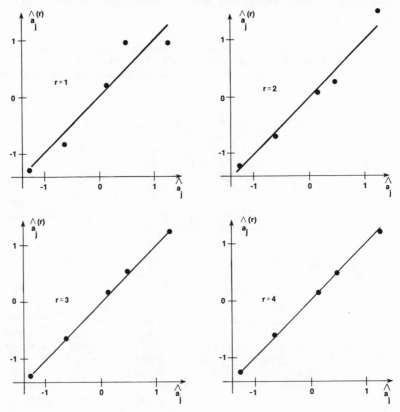

Figure 3. Score Group Estimates Against Overall Estimates of Item
Parameters for the Law School Admission Test (LSAT), Section 7.

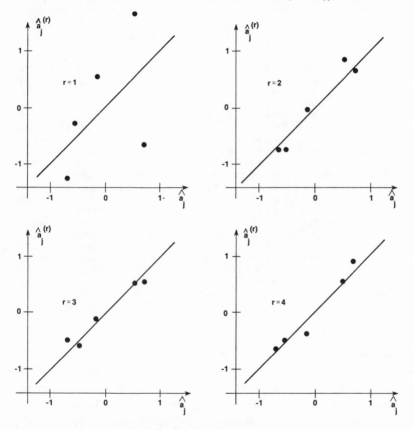

significant, and $z = 35.9$ is highly significant. The deviations from
the model for section 7 seem in particular to be connected with the
low-score groups, indicating that individuals with low Θ values do
not conform to the model, while individuals with higher Θ values
seem to do so.

The data for the twenty items of the SAT were analyzed by
Lord (1968), who used a model with item difficulties as well as
item-discriminating powers and guessing parameters. In the Rasch
model there is no guessing parameter, and all item-discriminating
powers are equal. We should not, therefore, expect the Rasch
model to fit the data. In Table 11 the score group estimates of item

Table 11. Score Group Item Parameter Estimates and Overall Estimates
for the Scholastic Aptitude Test (SAT).

Item Number	0-9	10-11	Score Group 12	13-14	15-20	Overall
1	+2.59	+1.91	+1.93	+1.81	+1.83	+2.01
2	+0.76	+1.29	+1.68	+1.59	+1.23	+1.37
3	+1.24	+1.23	+1.22	+1.10	+1.20	+1.26
4	+1.01	+0.80	+0.64	+0.67	+0.43	+0.81
5	-0.66	-0.31	-0.40	-0.21	-0.47	-0.38
6	-0.40	-0.48	-0.51	-0.61	-0.22	-0.36
7	+0.29	+0.56	+0.37	+0.17	+0.20	+0.41
8	-0.50	+0.37	+0.72	+0.53	+0.70	+0.25
9	-1.07	-1.55	-1.52	-1.42	-0.78	-1.09
10	-1.16	-2.10	-1.90	-1.20	-1.20	-1.23
11	+3.99	+3.08	+2.53	+2.47	+2.41	+2.73
12	+2.26	+1.74	+1.46	+1.43	+0.43	+1.48
13	+1.75	+1.48	+0.80	+0.83	+0.05	+1.08
14	+0.35	+0.17	-0.08	-0.14	+0.28	+0.22
15	-1.59	-1.05	-1.23	-1.01	-0.90	-1.26
16	-1.64	-1.40	-1.23	-1.20	-0.66	-1.37
17	-1.56	-1.20	-0.73	-0.85	-0.56	-1.19
18	-1.70	-1.40	-1.23	-1.07	-1.04	-1.42
19	-2.20	-1.82	-1.52	-1.20	-1.62	-1.88
20	-1.74	-1.30	-0.99	-1.70	-1.20	-1.46

parameters and the overall estimates are shown for five score groups. When we have many items, we usually group the individuals into larger score groups, in such a way that a score group contains individuals with scores in a given interval. The test remains valid, and we can still compare the estimates graphically. For the SAT data the following score groups were chosen:

Group	Score Range
1	0-9
2	10-11
3	12
4	13-14
5	15-20

Figure 4 shows the plottings of score group estimates against overall estimates for the five score groups. We notice the apparent

Figure 4. Score Group Estimates Against Overall Estimates of Item Parameters for the Scholastic Aptitude Test (SAT).

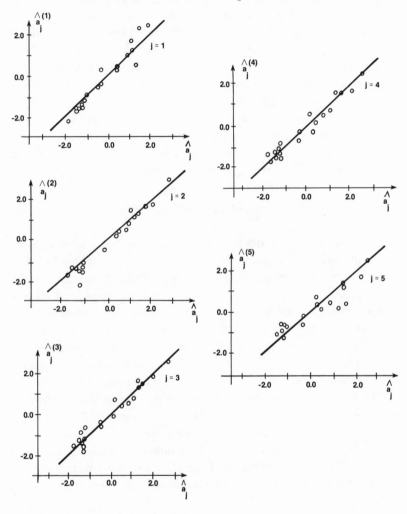

deviations from the model. For the low-score groups we have a clear clustering around lines with slopes larger than 1, while for the high-score groups the points cluster around lines with slopes less than 1. The goodness of fit test statistic becomes

$$z = 266.4, \qquad df = 76,$$

which is highly significant. The earlier findings of Lord are thus confirmed. In Andersen (1973a), a rough argument showed that the deviations in Figure 4 indicated varying discriminating powers. One of the things to look for during the check of the model is deviations from the model that are subject to correction. If the model thus gives a good fit except for a few badly behaving items, one may exclude these items from the test. In the case of the LSAT, section 7, we saw that there were problems in particular for individuals with low scores. This may lead to the conclusion that we can apply the test when individuals have reasonably high scores but that the test is not reliable for low-score values. This would, for example, be the case if there is guessing involved.

Analysis of Latent Distributions

If the Rasch model fits our data, the raw score is, as we have seen, the sufficient estimate for the individual parameter Θ. The study of Θ is usually the real aim of testing a population of individuals by a battery of items. There are two types of problems we can consider in this respect. On the one hand, we may be interested in estimating Θ for a given individual. If this is the case, we can estimate Θ from the individual's score r and, if it is required, give confidence limits for the estimate. Table 7 shows the estimates for the individuals on the SAT. A look at the Stouffer-Toby data of Table 8 reveals, however, that with some items, the Θ estimate provides only a very rough idea of the true value of Θ for a given individual, although this is the best we can do.

We may, on the other hand, be more interested in the distribution of Θ in the population. Figure 5 shows the two elements of our problem. We have the observed distribution $f(r)$ of the scores, where

$$f(r) = n_r/n. \qquad (4)$$

And we have the density $\varphi(\Theta)$ of Θ in the population. Since the values of r are sufficient estimates of the unknown Θ's, $f(r)$ gives a picture of how Θ varies in the population. The density $\varphi(\Theta)$ of Θ in the population can be hypothesized to exist, but it cannot be ob-

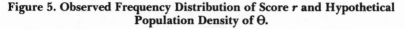

Figure 5. Observed Frequency Distribution of Score *r* and Hypothetical Population Density of Θ.

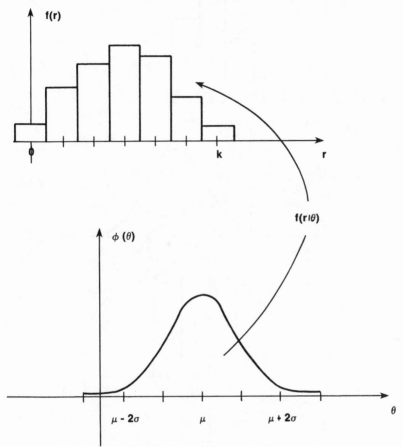

served. The question is whether we can make inferences concerning $\varphi(\Theta)$ based on $f(r)$. Here the Rasch model is the instrument of choice because it gives us a model for the distribution of r given the value of Θ. The distribution of r given Θ can be expressed through

$$\pi(r|\Theta) = P(\text{score } r|\text{given } \Theta).$$

In Figure 6 the distributions $\pi(r|\Theta)$ given three typical values of Θ are shown together with $\varphi(\Theta)$, here chosen as a normal density.

Figure 6. Marginal Frequency Distribution of Score r, Population Density of Θ, and Three Selected Conditional Frequency Distributions $\pi(r|\Theta)$.

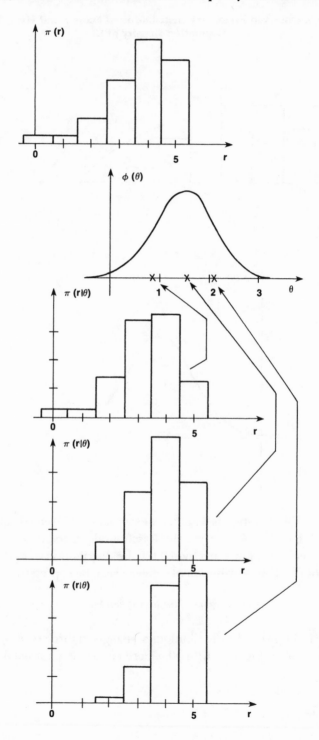

The figure also shows the marginal distribution of $\pi(r)$, which we get by weighting the $\pi(r|\Theta)$'s together and using $\varphi(\Theta)$ as a weight function. $\pi(r) = P(\text{score } r)$ is thus a *marginal* probability. We shall not go into the mathematics of how to combine the population density $\varphi(\Theta)$, the score frequency $f(r|\Theta)$ given Θ, and the observed score frequency $f(r)$. It suffices to note that we have a typical Bayesian setup except that $\varphi(\Theta)$ is not a subjective prior but rather an existing probability density, which we cannot observe.

In other connections Θ is known as a *latent variable*, as opposed to the score, which is a *manifest variable*. Hence, we will refer to $\varphi(\Theta)$ as a *latent population density*.

Suppose now that $\varphi(\Theta)$ is a normal distribution with mean μ and variance σ^2; that is,

$$\Theta \sim N(\mu, \sigma^2). \tag{5}$$

Assume further that the individuals answer the items independently and that the Rasch model holds. It can then be shown that we have the following mathematical expressions. (Details can be found in Andersen and Madsen, 1977, or Andersen, 1980.) We get

$$\pi(r|\Theta) = c(r; \alpha_1, \ldots, \alpha_k) e^{r\theta} / \prod_{j=1}^{k} (1 + e^{\theta - \alpha_j}), \tag{6}$$

where $c(r; \alpha_1, \ldots, \alpha_k)$ is a certain function of r and the α's, that is independent of Θ and hence does not influence statistical inference about Θ.

If we write φ as $\varphi(\Theta|\mu, \sigma^2)$ to stress the dependency upon μ and σ^2, we further get

$$\pi(r) = c(r; \alpha_1, \ldots, \alpha_k) \cdot \int e^{r\theta} \left[\prod_{j=1}^{k} (1 + e^{\theta - \alpha_j}) \right]^{-1} \varphi(\Theta|\mu, \sigma^2) d\Theta. \tag{7}$$

Given the values of $\pi(o), \ldots, \pi(k)$ by this formula, we derive the probability distribution of the observed score distribution. It can be seen that the vector $(n_o, \ldots, n_k)$ follows a multinominal distribution with cell probabilities $(\pi(o), \ldots, \pi(k))$, which is often written

$$(n_o, \ldots, n_k) \sim M(n; \pi(o), \ldots, \pi(k)). \tag{8}$$

The mathematical or the statistical argument applied to get from (5) to (8) can be expressed in nonmathematical terms as follows: *If* we have a model (5) for the variation of the latent variable Θ in the population and *if* we have checked that a given model (6) can describe the distribution of the scores *given* the value of the latent variable, *then* the marginal distribution of the score (7) can be derived, and the observed score distribution $f(r)$ is related to the theoretical score distribution $\pi(r)$ by (8) and the fact (4) that

$$f(r) = n_r/n \approx \pi(r).$$

As we can see, the statistical model (8) for the observed score distribution is complicated in the mathematical sense, since it involves integrals of the form (7). It turns out, however, that by means of modern computer techniques the involved numerical problems can be solved rather easily. Hence we can do two things based on (8):

1. We can estimate μ and σ^2, which are the only unknown parameters, if the α's are estimated by the methods in the preceding section.
2. We can check the model by an ordinary χ^2 goodness of fit test.

The expected value of n_r is by (8)

$$E[n_r] = n\pi(r),$$

where we may write $\pi(r)$ as $\pi(r|\mu,\sigma^2)$ to express the dependency of μ and σ^2 through (7). An ordinary χ^2 test would take the form

$$q = \sum_{r=o}^{k} (n_r - n\pi(r|\hat{\mu},\hat{\sigma}^2))^2/(n\pi(r|\hat{\mu},\hat{\sigma}^2)),$$

where $\hat{\mu}$ and $\hat{\sigma}^2$ are the values estimated under (1). For the actual tests in the example below, we have used the approximately equivalent form

$$z = 2 \sum_{r=o}^{k} n_r[ln(n_r) - ln(n\pi(r|\hat{\mu},\hat{\sigma}^2))]. \tag{9}$$

Both test quantities are approximately χ^2 distributed with k-2 degrees of freedom if we observe the usual requirement of $n\pi(r|\hat{\mu},\hat{\sigma}^2) > 5$ for all r. We accept the normal distribution as a description of the latent population density if

$$z < \chi^2_{0.95} (k-2).$$

The number of degrees of freedom is reduced if we have to group some scores together in order to have expected numbers larger than 5.

We shall now show how this procedure works for two of the previously treated examples. For the Stouffer-Toby data of Table 4, we get the estimates

$$(\hat{\mu},\hat{\sigma}^2) = (0.20, 2.26).$$

The expected numbers $n\pi(r|\hat{\mu},\hat{\sigma}^2)$ computed with these values of μ and σ^2 from (7) are shown in Table 12. When we compute the test statistic (9) from the numbers in Table 12, we get

$$z = 10.3, \qquad df = 2.$$

The number of degrees of freedom is computed as $df = 4 - 2$, since $k = 4$. We have $\chi^2_{0.95} (2) = 5.99$, so that there is a lack of fit by a normal latent density. As we can see, the lack of fit is mainly for the score $r = 4$, which seems to indicate that there is an overrepresentation of positive answers. Maybe individuals in doubt tend to use the universalistic alternative.

For the LSAT data of Table 9, we find the score distribution shown in Table 13. The estimates of μ and σ^2 became

Table 12. Observed and Expected Numbers in Each Score Group
for the Stouffer-Toby Data.

$r =$	0	1	2	3	4
n_r	20	55	63	36	42
$n\pi(r)$	24.7	47.8	55.3	52.9	35.3

**Table 13. Observed and Expected Numbers in Each Score Group
for the Law School Admission Test (LSAT), Section 6.**

$r =$	0	1	2	3	4	5
n_r	3	20	85	237	257	298
$n\pi(r)$	23.3		88.6	227.3	264.9	295.9

$(\hat{\mu},\hat{\sigma}^2) = (+1.48, 0.57)$. For these data we get

$$z = 0.75, \qquad df = 2,$$

so that we have a very good fit. (Note that we can fit very skewed score distributions.)

As another example, consider a Danish questionnaire used to measure psychic vulnerability. The scores indicating high or low vulnerability were obtained as the number of yes answers to questions such as "Do you often suffer from headaches?" and "Do you often suffer from stomach pain?" Table 14 shows the score distribution for six such items. The estimates for μ and σ^2 were computed to produce

$$(\hat{\mu},\hat{\sigma}^2) = (-2.81, 4.33).$$

Again we see that the skewness is reflected in a value $\hat{\mu}$ substantially different from 0. The goodness of fit test gave

$$z = 4.5, \qquad df = 2,$$

with the result that in this case we have a good fit.

In itself it is of minor interest to fit a latent distribution to a

**Table 14. Observed and Expected Numbers in Each Score Group
for a Test on Psychic Vulnerability.**

$r =$	0	1	2	3	4	5	6
n_r	46	18	5	9	1	3	1
$n\pi(r)$	46.3	16.3	8.5	5.2		6.7	

given score distribution. An estimated latent density may, however, be an important instrument for solving various problems. One such problem is treated in the next section.

Comparison of Latent Distributions

We shall now show how we can use the methods described in the previous section to compare two or more latent distributions. In Figure 7 an attempt is made to visualize how the comparison of two latent distributions is made directly between the fitted normal latent densities rather than between the two observed score distributions.

The procedure is as follows: We estimate $\hat{\mu}_1$ and $\hat{\sigma}_1^2$ from the observed score distribution in Population 1 and $\hat{\mu}_2$ and $\hat{\sigma}_2^2$ from the observed score distribution in Population 2. At this stage the model can be checked independently for each population. It may then be assumed that $\sigma_1^2 = \sigma_2^2$, and the common value σ^2 can be estimated from the joint distribution of scores in both populations. If we denote the estimates under the hypothesis

$$H_1: \sigma_1^2 = \sigma_2^2 = \sigma^2$$

Figure 7. Comparison of Two Latent Distributions.

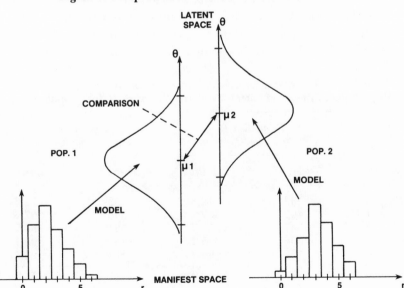

by μ_1, μ_2, $\hat\sigma^2$, we can compare the observed and the expected numbers in the score groups by a χ^2 test, where we use $(\hat\mu_1, \hat\sigma^2)$ as estimates in Population I and $(\hat\mu_2, \hat\sigma^2)$ as estimates in Population II. If we still have a good fit, we can accept H_1.

We can repeat these steps with common estimates $(\hat\mu, \hat\sigma^2)$ for both populations. In this way we can check that H_1, as well as

$$H_2: \mu_1 = \mu_2,$$

holds. Tables 15 and 16 show these various steps. The data are from Solomon (1961) and concern attitudes toward science. High scores indicate positive attitudes. The population of 2,982 individuals was divided into two groups, one characterized by low IQ and one by high IQ. The tests of Table 16 are all approximate χ^2 distributed test quantities of the general form

$$z = 2 \, \Sigma \text{ observed } \{ln \text{ (observed)} - ln \text{ (expected)}\}.$$

Thus the simultaneous test quantity $z = 36.5$ for the final model with latent population densities and common mean and variance is given by

$$z = 2\{82(ln(82) - ln(72.8)) + \ldots + 122(ln(122) - ln(94.7))\}.$$

From Table 16 we see that the model of a normal latent distribution can be accepted. But both an assumption of equal variances and an assumption of equal means will have to be rejected. Thus, it seems that students with lower IQs have signifi-

Table 15. Observed and Expected Numbers in Score Groups Under the Hypotheses of the Same Latent Mean and Variance in Both Populations.

Score	Population 1: Low IQ		Population 2: High IQ	
	Observed	Expected	Observed	Expected
$r = 0$	82	72.8	53	72.8
1	402	367.7	345	367.7
2	547	560.7	521	560.7
3	398	395.1	450	395.1
4	62	94.7	122	94.7
Total	1491	1491.0	1491	1491.0

Table 16. Summary of Test Statistics for Various Hypotheses Using the Solomon Data.

Hypothesis	Population 1: Low IQ $\hat{\mu}_1$	$\hat{\sigma}_1{}^2$	Population 2: High IQ $\hat{\mu}_2$	$\hat{\sigma}_2{}^2$	Test Statistic	Degrees of Freedom
Normal latent distribution	−0.08	0.29	+0.24	0.52	8.4	4
Common variance: $\sigma_1{}^2 = \sigma_2{}^2$	−0.08	0.46	+0.24	0.46	5.6	1
Common mean: $\mu_1 = \mu_2$	+0.08	0.47	+0.08	0.47	22.5	1
Normal distribution with common μ and σ^2					36.5	6

cantly more negative attitudes toward science than do those with high IQs.

In order to illustrate the method for four populations, we have chosen the test for psychic vulnerability mentioned in connection with Table 14. The data in Table 17 are from an investigation

Table 17. Observed and Expected Scores for a Test on Psychic Vulnerability.

Score Group	Men Age < 50 Obs.	Exp.	Men Age > 50 Obs.	Exp.	Women Age < 50 Obs.	Exp.	Women Age > 50 Obs.	Exp.
$r = 0$	531	535.3	227	221.3	447	436.3	151	138.6
1	235	242.1	128	139.7	218	234.1	108	121.8
2	112	112.8	86	85.1	129	125.1	91	92.4
3	53	54.1	55	62.6	64	76.7	66	70.6
4	36	24.9	39	37.1	44	37.5	56	57.6
5	15	14.8	27	19.5	25	19.7	47	39.7
6	14	10.2	14	11.2	14	13.3	30	23.2
7	9	6.4	14	8.1	15	10.2	13	13.5
8	1	5.5	4	6.6	6	6.9	12	9.4
9–12	0		6	8.8	4	6.2	9	16.2
Total	1006	1006.1	600	600.0	966	966.0	583	583.0

Table 18. Estimates for μ and σ^2 in the Four Populations
Under Various Hypotheses — Vulnerability Data.

Estimates Under		Men		Women	
		<50	>50	<50	>50
H_0	$\hat{\mu}$	−3.42	−2.65	−3.04	−2.00
	$\hat{\sigma}^2$	2.10	2.26	2.17	2.01
H_1	$\hat{\mu}$	−3.41	−2.63	−3.03	−2.02
	$\hat{\sigma}^2$	2.12	2.12	2.12	2.12
H_2	$\hat{\sigma}$	−2.91	−2.91	−2.91	−2.91
	$\hat{\sigma}^2$	2.27	2.27	2.27	2.27

with a total sample of some 3,155 individuals who were interviewed in Denmark in May and October of 1974. For this investigation a set of twelve items from the battery of vulnerability questions was found to fit the Rasch model. In Table 17 the observed numbers are shown for the sample after it has been divided into four groups according to sex and age. The table also shows the expected numbers under the hypothesis of a normal latent distribution.

In Table 18 we have summarized the estimates under the various hypotheses. The hypotheses are

H_0: Normal latent densities
H_1: Equal variances: $\sigma_j^2 = \sigma^2, j = 1, \ldots, 4.$
H_2: Equal means: $\mu_j = \mu, j = 1, \ldots, 4.$

In Table 19 the test statistics are summarized. As we can see, the hypothesis of normal latent densities can be accepted, as can the hypothesis of equal variances. But the hypothesis of equal means is clearly rejected. The situation is illustrated by Figures 8 and 9, in

Table 19. Test Statistics for the Three Hypotheses
H_0, H_1, and H_2 — Vulnerability Data.

Hypothesis	Test Statistic	Degrees of Freedom
H_0	44.9	28
H_1	0.2	3
H_2	252.6	3
Total model	297.7	34

Figure 8. Observed Score Distributions for the Four Subpopulations — Vulnerability Data.

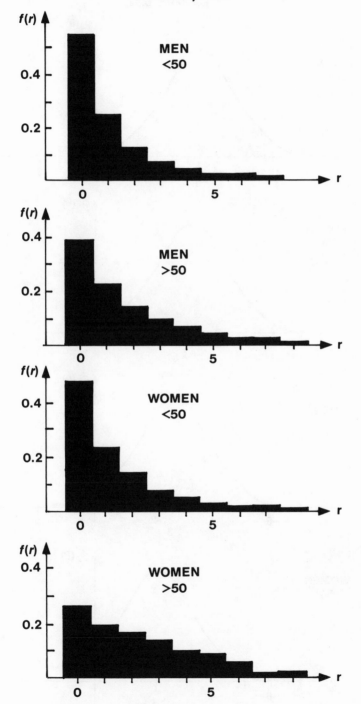

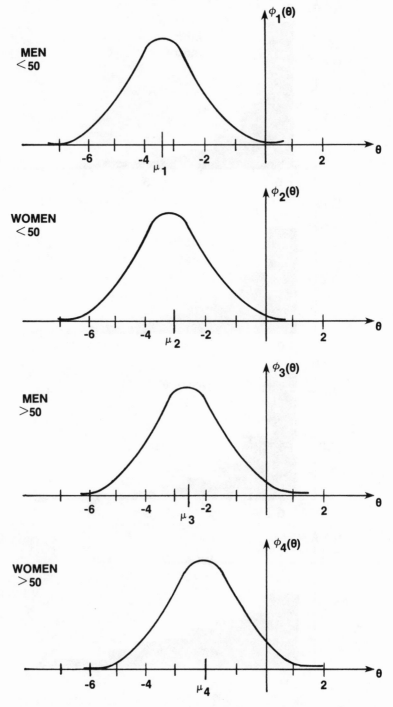

which we have graphed the observed score distributions for the four subpopulations and the corresponding latent densities. The densities in Figure 9 are drawn with the same estimated variance $\hat{\sigma}^2 = 2.27$ and with the estimated mean values $(-3.41, -2.63, -3.03, -2.02)$ under H_2.

It is obvious from Figures 8 and 9 that it is much easier to see the systematic differences between the four subpopulations in latent space than in the observed score distributions. (Parameters are estimated under an assumption of common variance.)

Possible Extensions

There are various ways in which the theory and methods of the previous sections can be extended. The Rasch model for questionnaires with more than two answer categories has been treated by Rasch (1961), Bock (1972), Andersen (1973b, 1980), and Fischer (1974). If we assume a one-dimensional latent variable, it is relatively straightforward to extend the methods of the previous section to this case. Details on the estimation of item parameters and a check of the model can be found in Andersen (1980) or Fischer (1974). The m-category model is somewhat more complicated than the dichotomous case, and we would violate the reasonable limits of this chapter if we gave more details.

An extension in another direction is to consider models with more than one latent variable. If we assume that the latent variable is a vector, we have a whole range of new models. Of special interest are cases where the different latent variables are correlated. Thus if $\Theta = (\Theta_1, \ldots, \Theta_q)$, we can assume that $(\Theta_1, \ldots, \Theta_q)$ follows a multidimensional normal distribution with mean $(\mu_1, \ldots, \mu_q)$ and covariance matrix $\underset{\sim}{\Sigma}$ of order $q \times q$. The means $\mu_1, \ldots, \mu_q$ and the diagonal of $\underset{\sim}{\Sigma}$, being the variances of $\Theta_1, \ldots, \Theta_q$, can be estimated from the marginal densities of the Θ's, and this does not give rise to substantially new problems. The problem is to estimate the off-diagonal elements or, equivalently, the correlations between the Θ's. Simplifications are possible by assuming a factor model structure for $\underset{\sim}{\Sigma}$ or other simple structures for $\underset{\sim}{\Sigma}$.

So far very little work has been done on models with vector-valued latent variables. A parallel problem, where the normal ogive rather than the Rasch model is used for the item characteristic curve, has been treated by Christofferson (1975) and Muthèn (1978). Bartholomew (1980) also discusses models with vector-valued latent variables.

The most typical problem of this sort is the longitudinal model, where the same individuals are tested on several occasions. Let $t_1, \ldots, t_q$ be the time points where the repeated testing takes place. We can then let $\Theta_1, \ldots, \Theta_q$ be the values of the latent parameters at the q time points. On the one hand, it is not reasonable to assume that the Θ's are independent, which would mean that latent variables of the individuals at the different points in time are totally unrelated. It is, on the other hand, reasonable to assume that some changes in value do occur, with the result that the Θ's are to some extent dependent. One assumption would be that the correlations between Θ's depend on time. If the t's are equidistant with $t_j = t_1 + j\Delta t$, we could then assume that

$$\Theta_j = p\Theta_{j-1} + e_j, \tag{10}$$

where the e_j's are mutually independent and independent of the Θ_j's. The correlation between Θ_j and Θ_{j-1} would then be p, the correlation between Θ_j and Θ_{j-2} would be p^2, and so on. A model with the structure (10) is called an *autoregressive model*.

The remarks in this section are intended only as an indication of the rich and virgin fields that remain open for research.

References

Andersen, E. B. "A Goodness of Fit Test for the Rasch Model." *Psychometrika*, 1973a, *38*, 123–140.

Andersen, E. B. "Conditional Inference and Multiple-Choice Questionnaires." *British Journal of Mathematical and Statistical Psychology*, 1973b, *26*, 31–44.

Andersen, E. B. *Discrete Statistical Models with Social Science Applications.* Amsterdam: North Holland Publishing, 1980.

Andersen, E. B., and Madsen, M. "Estimating the Parameters of the Latent Population Distribution." *Psychometrika*, 1977, *42*, 357–374.

Bartholemew, D. J. "Factor Analysis for Categorical Data." *Journal of the Royal Statistical Society*, (Series B) 1980, *42*, 293–321.

Bock, R. D. "Estimating the Item Parameters and Latent Ability When Responses Are Scored in Two or More Nominal Categories." *Psychometrika*, 1972, *37*, 29–51.

Bock, R. D., and Lieberman, M. "Fitting a Response Model for *n* Dichotomously Scored Items." *Psychometrika*, 1970, *35*, 179–197.

Christofferson, A. "Factor Analysis of Dichotomized Variables." *Psychometrika*, 1975, *40*, 5–32.

Fischer, G. H. *Einführing in die Theorie Psychologischer Tests.* Bern: Huber, 1974.

Lord, F. M. "A Theory of Test Scores." *Psychometric Monograph*, No. 7, 1952.

Lord, F. M. "An Analysis of the Verbal Scholastic Aptitude Test Using Birnbaum's Three-Parameter Logistic Model." *Educational and Psychological Measurement*, 1968, *28*, 989–1020.

Muthèn, B. "Contributions to Factor Analysis of Dichotomous Variables." *Psychometrika*, 1978, *43*, 551–560.

Rasch, G. "On General Laws and the Meaning of Measurement in Psychology." *Proceedings of Fourth Berkeley Symposium on Mathematical Statistics and Probability*, 1961, *5*, 321–333.

Solomon, H. "Classification Procedures Based on Dichotomous Response Vectors." In H. Solomon (Ed.), *Studies in Item Analysis and Prediction.* Stanford, Calif.: Stanford University Press, 1961.

Stouffer, S. A., and Toby, J. "Role Conflict and Personality." *American Journal of Sociology*, 1951, *56*, 395–406.

11

Charles Lewis

৩২ ৩২ ৩২ ৩২ ৩২ ৩২ ৩২ ৩২ ৩২ ৩২ ৩২ ৩২ ৩২

Bayesian Inference for Latent Abilities

Although the latent abilities of individuals and the difficulties of items play more or less equivalent roles in item response (or latent trait) theories, the relative attention given to them has been far from equivalent. The emphasis—quite appropriately for the stage of test development—has been on inferences regarding the item characteristics. Once satisfactory knowledge has been gained regarding items, however, interest should turn to inferences for individual abilities, that is, to the purpose for which the items were presumably designed. It should be recognized that a new set of statistical considerations arises here—considerations quite different from those that are relevant for test development.

When inferences are made about abilities, it does not seem appropriate to rely on methods (such as maximum likelihood) that have only asymptotic justification. In the development of a test, responses from a large number of individuals are usually available. The completed test is, however, seldom of more than moderate length. Consequently, the amount of information available regarding the ability of any one individual is limited. A second consideration regards the form of the item characteristic curves. When items are selected and modified for a test, it is very helpful to adopt a restricted item response model as a yardstick against which the items may be evaluated. When the responses of a single individual are considered, however, such a model is apt to be unrealistic and, possibly, misleading. Finally, given the limited and imperfect nature of the information available from the responses of an individual, any prior information that is available regarding the ability of either the individual being tested or similar individuals should probably not be ignored when inferences are made regarding that ability.

After a brief historical review of ability estimation in the context of item response theories, a new approach to the problem will be outlined that addresses the concerns described above. It provides exact, small-sample results, employs a "nonparametric" item response model, and gives a full Bayesian analysis that allows flexible use of prior information. Within the model, an ordinal definition of ability — relative to item difficulties — is proposed. A posterior probability distribution for ability is obtained, and this distribution combines prior and sample information in an intuitively sensible way. This posterior distribution may be used directly, either to make decisions regarding the individual or to provide point and interval estimates of the individual's ability.

Alternative Approaches

Approaches to the estimation of abilities within the context of item response theory may be roughly divided into three major categories: (1) those that treat abilities as "fixed" parameters, (2) those that consider abilities to be a random sample from some population ("empirical" Bayesian), and (3) those that allow prior information about abilities to enter systematically into the estimation process ("subjective" Bayesian).

Most of the early work in item response theory, as summarized in Lord and Novick (1968) and Fischer (1974), falls into the first category. Abilities are estimated either jointly with item characteristics or under the assumption that these characteristics are known exactly. An important variation, but still within the fixed abilities category, is the work on sequential or adaptive testing (discussed in Lord, 1974). Here again item characteristics are assumed to be known, but the sequential nature of the process has an automatic, self-correcting quality, making it less sensitive to violations of assumptions. Recently, some attention has been given to robust estimation of fixed abilities in the standard testing situation (Wright and Stone, 1979; Wainer and Wright, 1980). This work lacks any well-developed theoretical basis, but it reflects some of the concerns expressed in the previous section and is appealing from a practical point of view.

Turning now to the second category, it is worth noting that approaches in which ability is treated as a random variable have something in common with the treatment of true scores in "classical" test theory. For example, the work on estimating true score for binomial error models summarized in Lord and Novick (1968) may be applied to item response models in the special case of equivalent items.

More recently, Andersen and Madsen (1977) and Sanathanan and Blumenthal (1978) have developed estimates for the mean and variance of the population from which the abilities are sampled rather than for the abilities themselves. This last step has, however, been taken by de Gruijter (1980), who considers expressions for the mean and variance of the conditional distribution of ability, given true scores. These are analogues (within the Rasch model) of the Kelley true score regression formulas of classical test theory. Moreover, they are in the spirit of the James-Stein approach to multiple estimation (Efron and Morris, 1975) and represent the best sampling theory technology currently available for estimating individual abilities.

Finally, there has been only a limited amount of work in item response theory that incorporates prior information via Bayes' Theorem when inferences are made about abilities. Moreover, the technical difficulties are such that results to date typically suffer from serious restrictions. Thus, Birnbaum (1969) derives posterior distributions for abilities in the two-parameter logistic model, but only for the case of equivalent items. Freeman (1970), working in the context of bioassay, develops a full Bayesian treatment of sequential testing for a special case that is equivalent to working with the Rasch model and having items with at most three distinct (and known) levels of difficulty. Owen (1975) gives a sequential procedure that is only partially Bayesian, approximating the true posterior for ability by a normal density at each stage. He does, however, work with a three-parameter (normal ogive) model and items that are available with a wide variety of (known) difficulty, discrimination, and guessing parameter values.

Although not developed in the context of item response theory, work on the estimation of proportions by Leonard (1972), Novick, Lewis, and Jackson (1973), and Lewis, Wang, and Novick (1975) gives modern Bayesian analyses for the case of equivalent items. Leonard, in fact, works directly with the logistic Rasch scaling of abilities. In these papers, the proportions (abilities) are assumed to be exchangeable across groups (persons), following the general theory of Lindley and Smith (1972). The results are related to those of de Gruijter (1980) but are now interpreted in (subjective) Bayesian terms.

A Nonparametric Approach

Mokken (1971) proposed a nonparametric item response model in which item characteristic curves were assumed only to be monotone increasing and nonintersecting. The procedures he developed, however, are primarily directed at test construction (identifying items that satisfy the model) rather than at ability estimation.

There is related Bayesian and non-Bayesian work (summarized in Barlow and others, 1972) in nonparametric bioassay that uses the techniques of isotonic regression to estimate quantal response functions. Bayesian developments dealing with "smoothed" isotonic regression include those of Kraft and van Eeden (1964), Ramsey (1972), and the recent work of Stewart (1979).

Lewis (1970) gives a nonparametric definition of the term *threshold* in a psychophysical application of the isotonic model, and develops a simple procedure for the construction of confidence intervals in the case of one binary response per stimulus level. It is this definition that will be adopted here for abilities, with a Bayesian approach to inference replacing the sampling theory treatment of the earlier work.

Begin by supposing that there are k mutually exclusive classes of dichotomous items under consideration and that items within each class are, for all practical purposes, equivalent. As a common special case, of course, each class might contain only one item.

Sometimes it may be useful to include one or more (hypothetical) empty classes. In any event, these classes effectively define the ability scale of interest in the sense that no inferences are made regarding performance on items not included in one of the classes.

Next, restrict attention to a single individual for whom inferences are to be made regarding his or her ability on the scale defined by the items. For this individual, denote the probability of a correct answer on any item in class i by π_i. The first critical assumption is that it is possible to order the item classes for this individual so that

$$1 > \pi_1 > \pi_2 > \ldots > \pi_k > 0. \tag{1}$$

The information required to do this would, in practice, presumably be obtained at the stage of test development. If this earlier work had been carried out by using the Rasch model, for instance, the items might be ordered according to their estimated difficulties (and items with approximately the same difficulty might be collected in a single class).

This assumption makes possible the following definition of the individual's ability on the scale defined by the item classes: If Θ is used to denote this ability, let

$$\Theta = \begin{cases} 0 \text{ if } \pi_1 < \tfrac{1}{2} \\ i \text{ if } \pi_i \geq \tfrac{1}{2} > \pi_{i+1}, i = 1(1)k - 1, \text{ and} \\ k \text{ if } \pi_k \geq \tfrac{1}{2}. \end{cases} \tag{2}$$

To verbalize this definition, the individual's ability is defined as the number of (classes of) items that he or she can answer correctly with a chance of at least $\tfrac{1}{2}$. Note that this is a purely ordinal definition. No underlying continuous scale of ability is assumed to exist. Different ability levels have meaning only in relation to the character of the items in the classes used to define the scale.

Suppose for a moment that the Rasch model was an appropriate description of the process that generated the responses to the set of items. Then, on the logistic Rasch scale of ability, all individuals having ability below the difficulty of the easiest item would be assigned to an ability level of zero by definition (2). Those with Rasch abilities falling between the difficulties of the two easiest items (or item classes) would be assigned to level one, and so on. Finally, individuals with ability greater than or equal to the difficulty of the hardest item would be placed at level k. Thus (2) might be thought of as defining a monotone-increasing transformation for logistic Rasch abilities in the special case where the Rasch model applies. The transformation is, of course, "many-to-one," and the amount of information lost by applying it in this case will depend on the number and spacing of the item classes used to define the scale.

Statistical Analysis

Continuing with the definitions and assumptions necessary to develop the approach described in the previous section, let y_i equal the number of correct responses out of a total of n_i responses of the given individual to the items in class i. The special case in which one or more n_i equals zero should not be neglected. It may arise when class i is purely hypothetical (contains no items), when no items in class i were presented to this particular individual, or when he or she did not respond (for whatever reason) to the items in this class that were presented. (In the last case, unanswered items might also be scored as incorrect, but this is a question for those wishing to interpret the test results to decide.)

The second critical assumption made in this approach (ordering the π_i was the first) is that the Σn_i responses of the individual to the items are conditionally independent, given $\{\pi_i\}$. To put this another way, all dependencies among the responses of the individual are due to the probabilities of correct responses to these items. This is a standard assumption in item response theory — for an exception, see Kempf (1976) — and analogous to the uncorrelated errors assumption of classical test theory.

The conditional independence requirement implies a likelihood given by

$$\prod_{i=1}^{k} \pi_i^{y_i} (1 - \pi_i)^{n_i - y_i}, \tag{3}$$

which is only defined for values of the π_i that satisfy the order restriction (1). Maximum likelihood estimates for $\{\pi_i\}$ are given by applying isotonic regression to the (y_i, n_i) pairs, as described in Barlow and others (1972). A corresponding estimate for the ability Θ could be obtained by applying definition (2) to the estimated π_i

values. But if two or more of these were exactly $\frac{1}{2}$ (a definite possibility with isotonic regression), it would not be clear what estimate to use for Θ, because the conditions in (2) are based on the assumption that no more than one π_i may be exactly equal to $\frac{1}{2}$. In any event, it is not at all clear what properties such an estimator for Θ would have, except in the unlikely case where Σn_i is large relative to the number of item classes k.

To make inferences about Θ from a Bayesian point of view, a prior distribution is required that summarizes all information available other than that contained in the response data. Although this information is likely to be most directly relevant for the ability Θ, the formalities of Bayesian inference require that it be expressed in terms of the original parameters of the item response model, namely $\{\pi_i\}$.

For mathematical convenience, and because it seems to provide a flexible family, the prior densities considered here will be restricted to the form

$$C_0 \prod_{i=1}^{k} \pi_i^{\alpha_i - 1} (1 - \pi_i)^{\beta_i - 1}, \tag{4}$$

defined only for $\{\pi_i\}$ satisfying the order restriction (1). Here C_0 is a constant chosen on the assumption that the result of integrating (4) over the region described by (1) is unity. The (α_i, β_i) pairs are hyperparameters that should be chosen to reflect prior information.

Because (4) has a form that is a "natural conjugate" to the likelihood (3), the α_i and β_i can be directly interpreted as numbers of *hypothetical* correct and incorrect responses, respectively, given by the individual in question to items in class i. This notion of relating prior information to the results of a hypothetical study is a common one in Bayesian inference. (See, for other examples, Novick and Jackson, 1974.) In particular, the size of $\alpha_i + \beta_i$ relative to n_i gives an indication of the relative roles that prior and sample information will play in the final inferences. This may be seen by examining the form of the posterior density of $\{\pi_i\}$, which is proportional to the product of likelihood (3) and prior (4):

$$C_1 \prod_{i=1}^{k} \pi_i^{y_i + \alpha_i - 1} (1 - \pi_i)^{n_i - y_i + \beta_i - 1}. \tag{5}$$

While (5) is the direct result of applying Bayesian techniques to the item response model under consideration, it may not be clear what it has to do with the stated goal of the analysis: making inferences about Θ. Specifically, interest will typically be directed toward the posterior distribution for Θ, given the responses of an individual to the items. Incidentally, when a prior density is chosen for $\{\pi_i\}$, it will usually be of interest to examine the consequences that any choice has with respect to the prior for Θ.

In either case, the definition of Θ in (2) implies the following relationships:

$$\text{Prob}(\Theta = 0) = \text{Prob}(\pi_1 < \tfrac{1}{2}),$$
$$\text{Prob}(\Theta = i) = \text{Prob}(\pi_i \geq \tfrac{1}{2} \text{ and } \pi_{i+1} < \tfrac{1}{2}), \text{ for } i = 1(1)k - 1, \text{ and}$$
$$\text{Prob}(\Theta = k) = \text{Prob}(\pi_k \geq \tfrac{1}{2}). \tag{6}$$

The required probabilities for the π_i may be obtained by integration of the densities (4) or (5) over the appropriate regions. This integration must, in general, be carried out with the help of the computer; but, as is shown in the Appendix to this chapter, it is a relatively simple computational problem whose complexity increases only linearly with the number of item classes being used.

Properties of Priors

There are a few situations for which analytic integration of the prior density (4) is feasible, and the results are sufficiently surprising to justify some attention. Consider, for instance, the case in which all $\alpha_i = \beta_i = 1$. This generates via (4) a uniform distribution for $\{\pi_i\}$ over the region defined by the order restriction (1). Although this seems to indicate relatively little prior knowledge regarding the π_i, it can be shown (see Appendix) that such a choice implies the following distribution for Θ:

$$\text{Prob}(\Theta = i) = \frac{k!}{i!(k - i)!}(\tfrac{1}{2})^k, \text{ for } i = 0(1)k. \tag{7}$$

The distribution (7) is immediately recognizable as binomial, with parameters k and $\tfrac{1}{2}$, and seems to express fairly definite prior knowledge about Θ.

Table 1. Prior and Posterior Probability Distributions
for Ability (Θ) of an Individual with All Items Correct
on a (Hypothetical) Test of Five Items.

	Prior	*Posterior*		
Θ	*1,2,3*	*1*	*2*	*3*
0	—	—	—	—
1	.2	.1	—	—
2	.3	.2	.1	—
3	.3	.3	.3	—
4	.2	.3	.4	.3
5	—	.1	.2	.7

Note: Prior 1 has $\alpha_i = \beta_i = 5$; prior 2 has $\alpha_i = \beta_i = 1$; prior 3 has $\alpha_i = \beta_i = 0$. Probabilities are rounded to the nearest tenth and those less than .05 are replaced by a —, all for ease of reading.

Moreover, it is shown in the Appendix that setting all $\alpha_i = \beta_i = a$ in (4), for any positive value a, also implies the prior (7) for Θ. Thus a whole class of priors for $\{\pi_i\}$ gives rise to a simple prior for Θ. How then do these priors for $\{\pi_i\}$ actually differ? Simply stated, changing a modifies the weight given to (7) in determining the posterior distribution of Θ. This is illustrated, for a very simple hypothetical example, in Table 1.

Specifically, consider a 5-item test for which the binomial distribution given in (7) is judged to be roughly appropriate as a prior for Θ. This is displayed numerically as the leftmost distribution in the table. It may be produced by setting all α_i and β_i to any positive constant value. To show the effect of varying this constant, Table 1 also displays some posteriors for an individual who answers all five items correctly. Posterior 1 in the table is produced by choosing the prior constant equal to 5. It shows only a mild shift from the prior in the direction of the test result. Posterior 2 arises from a prior constant equal to 1 (that is, a uniform density for $\{\pi_i\}$). Here the data have produced a marked modification of the prior probabilities. Finally, posterior 3 is the result of working with a prior constant equal to zero.* It clearly reflects the information provided by the responses and bears little resemblance to the binomial prior.

This example gives some idea of the flexibility and range of choice available in priors of the form (4), the more so if it is realized that any of the three posteriors in Table 1 might also be considered as a possible prior in another situation. This last observation follows from the fact that the posterior (5) has exactly the same form as the prior (4). To summarize, if the parameters α_i and β_i are suitably chosen, a wide variety of priors for Θ may be obtained. Moreover, these priors may be given varying weights relative to the item responses of an individual. Finding a suitable set of α_i and β_i will typically be a question of trial and error. An interactive program called ABILITY has been written to facilitate the process of searching for appropriate priors, as well as analyzing test results. It allows the user to supply a tentative choice of α_i and β_i, computes and displays the resulting prior for Θ, and repeats this process until the user indicates that he or she is satisfied with the result. In the same way, the user may combine various priors with possible item responses and see the effect on the posterior, as in Table 1. (ABILITY is written in BASIC and is available from the author on request.)

In common with the entire process of test development, choosing a prior distribution for the ability of an individual has a basically subjective character. The subjective choices should, however, be at least broadly defensible, with regard to both their origins and their consequences. Indeed, one of the advantages of adopting

---

* Formally, setting all α_i and β_i equal to zero in the prior (4) would cause problems with integrability. The logits of the π_i, namely

$$\log_e\!\left(\frac{\pi_i}{1 - \pi_i}\right),$$

would then be uniformly distributed over the region of k-dimensional space that satisfies the order constraint corresponding to (1). In fact, all results reported in this chapter are obtained by restricting the logits to the interval $(-10, 10)$ or, equivalently, the π_i to $(.000045, .999955)$. This has little effect on precision for cases where α_i and β_i are positive, and it guarantees finite integrals when some or all of the α_i and β_i are zero.

a formal Bayesian framework is that it makes subjective decisions and their implications explicit and, thus, open to examination and discussion.

Examples of Analysis

As a means of better understanding the possibilities for working with the approach outlined in the previous sections, let us examine some concrete illustrations based on actual response records.   Wright and Stone (1979) provide detailed information regarding the results of administering a simple nonverbal ability test (the Knox Cube Test) to a group of schoolchildren.   Specifically, the table on page 33 of their book gives a binary response matrix for thirty-four individuals to fourteen items.   To apply the present approach to these data requires a rank ordering of the difficulties of the items.   While a rough ordering is possible on theoretical grounds, it was decided to base the analyses here on the ordering implied by Wright and Stone's analysis of the data on the basis of the Rasch model.   The estimated item difficulties (taken from the table

Table 2. Ability Levels (Θ) Related to Estimated Difficulties of Fourteen Items on the Knox Cube Test.

Θ	Item Class	Item Number	Item Difficulty[a]
0	1	4	−4.2
1	2	5,7	−3.6
2	3	6,9	−3.2
3	4	8	−2.2
4	5	10	−1.5
5	6	11	.8
6	7	13	1.9
7	8	12	2.1
8	9	14	3.2
9	10	15,16,17	4.6
10			

[a] These are logistic Rasch difficulties, estimated using unconditional maximum likelihood from the responses of thirty-four subjects.

Note: In addition to the information used in this table, Wright and Stone (1979, p. 60) supply a description and further references to the test and method of analysis.

on page 60 of their book) are reproduced here in Table 2, together with the corresponding item classes and ability levels. Note that, although there are fourteen items, there are only ten distinct item classes implied by the estimated item difficulties.

It is important to stress that the adoption of the ordering in Table 2 was done purely for simplicity of illustration. In practice, the ordering should be determined from *previous* administrations of the test. Moreover, it should be based on a sufficiently large sample so that its accuracy is not open to serious question. In the present case, with only thirty-four individuals, the exact ordering is, in fact, rather doubtful. Deletion of two, possibly irregular, response records modifies it somewhat (Wright and Stone, 1979, p. 82), as does the analysis of data collected from a second group (p. 92). Thus the analyses that follow should be thought of as appropriate only for responses to items whose difficulties were *truly* ordered according to Table 2.

In the choice of prior for the analyses, the desire for simplicity of illustration again played a decisive role. Specifically, all α_i and β_i were set equal to zero in (4) for all analyses in an attempt to reflect rather vague prior knowledge regarding individuals' performance. As discussed in the previous section, this generated a binomial prior (7) for Θ, with $k = 10$, a distribution that is illustrated in Figure 1. Note that an ability level of 5 is the mean (median, mode) for this prior and that Θ is thought to be at least 2, but no greater than 8, with a probability of about .98.

As a first illustration, it may be interesting to see what happens with individuals whose responses are, in a sense, maximally consistent with prior expectations. Referring again to Table 2, we see that such an individual might correctly answer all seven items in the first five item classes correctly and all the remaining items incorrectly. In fact, there were seven such response records in the present set (Wright and Stone, 1979, p. 33). The posterior distribution for the ability of any of these seven individuals is given in Figure 2. For ease of interpretation, the response record is indicated below the ability scale by means of plus and minus signs.

In comparing the prior and posterior of Figure 1 and Figure 2, we find that the latter is relatively highly concentrated around the modal value of 5. Thus, the posterior probability that $\Theta = 5$ is .64.

Figure 1. Prior Distribution for the Ability Θ Used in Analyses of Wright and Stone's Data.

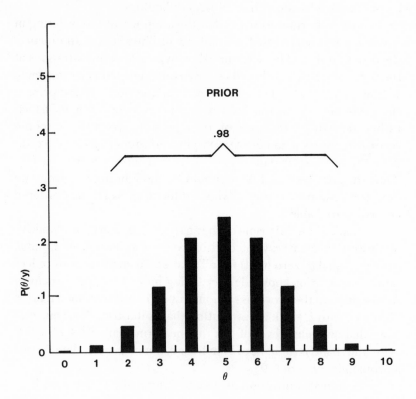

Moreover, as indicated on Figure 2, the chance that Θ is at least 4 and no greater than 6 is about .96, given these responses. To summarize, confirmation of a relatively vague prior with maximally consistent responses results in a peaked posterior, an outcome that reflects considerable certainty as to the individual's true ability level.

How much is this conclusion changed if the individual gives responses that are maximally consistent with an ability level other than that expected a priori? There were two individuals in Wright

Figure 2. Posterior Distribution for the Ability Θ of an Individual with Seven out of Fourteen Items Correct.

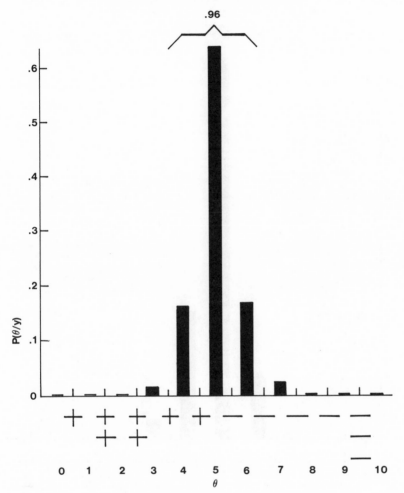

and Stone's group who answered correctly all six items in the first four classes and responded incorrectly to the rest. They might be thought to represent a minor deviation from expectations. There was also one individual who answered all nine items in the first seven classes correctly and the rest incorrectly. This response record might be considered a moderate deviation. The posterior distribu-

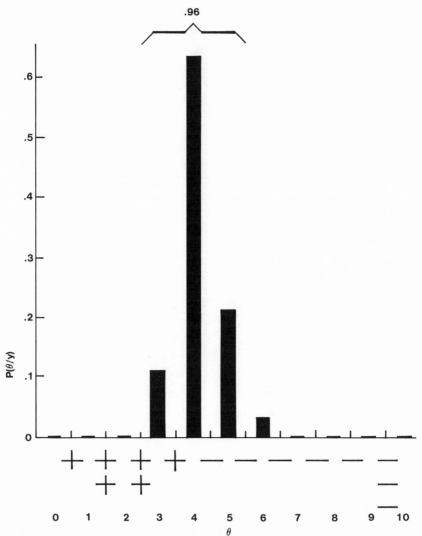

Figure 3. Posterior Distribution for the Ability Θ of an Individual with a Perfect Response Pattern and Six out of Fourteen Items Correct.

tions for these two situations are given in Figures 3 and 4. The modes of these two distributions faithfully reflect the information provided by the responses. Judging by the indicated 95- or 96-percent intervals, they are essentially as "peaked" as the posterior in Figure 2. The form of the prior is reflected, if at all, in the

skewnesses of the two distributions.   In each case, the heavier tail lies
on the side of the prior expectation ($\Theta = 5$).

All the response records analyzed so far are examples of what
Wright and Stone (1979, p. 171) call "plodding," that is, they are
perfectly consistent responses from which the best guess for an
individual's ability is unambiguous.   Almost half (sixteen out of
thirty-four) of the records in their data set are of this type.   The next
most common pattern of responses (six out of thirty-four) involves a

**Figure 4. Posterior Distribution for the Ability Θ of an Individual with a
Perfect Response Pattern and Nine out of Fourteen Items Correct.**

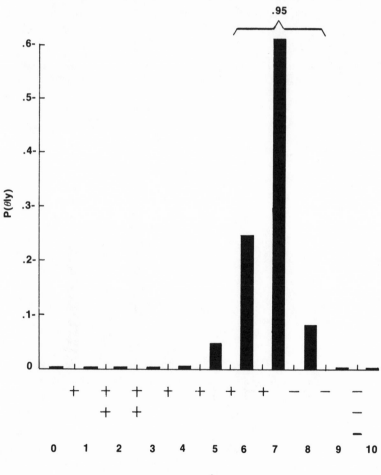

single reversal of correct and incorrect. An individual with such a pattern correctly answers all the easier items up to some point, gets the next item wrong and the item after that right, and answers all the remaining (more difficult) items incorrectly.

The posterior distribution illustrated in Figure 5 is the result of analyzing a response record with one reversal. As indicated by the plus and minus signs in the figure, this individual answered all eight items in the first six item classes correctly, the item in the seventh class incorrectly, the item in the eighth class correctly, and all four items in the ninth and tenth classes incorrectly. Intuitively, one would say that the most likely values for Θ are 6, 7, and 8. Note in Figure 5 that these are also the values receiving the highest posterior probability. The fact that $\Theta = 6$ is the mode of the

Figure 5. Posterior Distribution for the Ability Θ of an Individual with Nine out of Fourteen Items Correct and a Pattern with a Single Reversal.

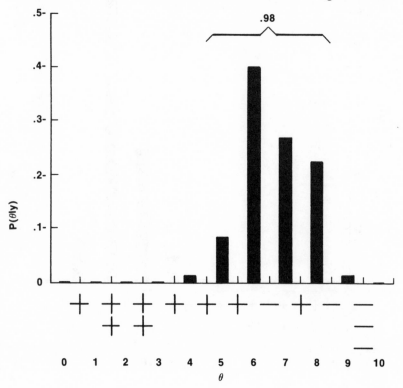

posterior and that $\Theta = 5$ has greater probability than $\Theta = 9$, is primarily a reflection of the prior (Figure 1).

When this posterior is compared with the one in Figure 4, which was based on a "perfect" pattern with the same number of items correct, it becomes clear that the increased ambiguity of the responses for Figure 5 has been translated into a greater spread in the distribution and into greater reliance on the prior.

These two trends are also apparent when a more ambiguous set of responses (still with nine items correct) is analyzed. The posterior distribution (Figure 6) for this case of a "double reversal" assigns most (97 percent) of the probability to the five values of

Figure 6. Posterior Distribution for the Ability Θ of an Individual with Nine out of Fourteen Items Correct and a Pattern with a Double Reversal.

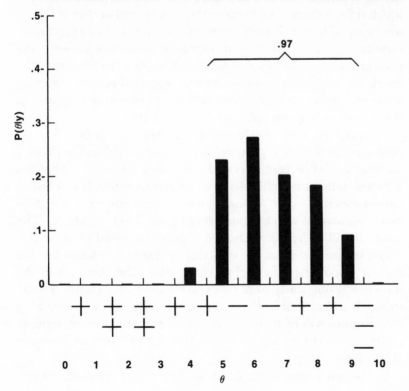

Θ (5-9) that seem intuitively most plausible. The distribution is flatter than that of Figure 5, and, while Θ = 6 is still the mode, the role of the prior has become clearer in the sense that Θ = 5 is now the second most likely value.

All the response records analyzed so far may be placed in the category of "reasonable" patterns, given the model. What happens in the case of somewhat less reasonable patterns? Consider, for instance, the subject in Wright and Stone's sample who answered all six questions in the easiest four item classes correctly, the next three items (classes) incorrectly, the item in the eighth class correctly, and the remaining four items (in the two most difficult classes) incorrectly. It is tempting to estimate this individual's ability level as 4 and to consider the correct response to the item in class eight as a lucky guess.

The posterior distribution of ability associated with this response record is pictured in Figure 7. Note the mode at Θ = 4, which reflects the natural break in the pattern, rather than at Θ = 5, which would have reflected the number of item classes with correct responses. This illustrates an important difference between the present approach and that of the Rasch model. In the latter, the number of correct responses is the only information used in making inferences about an individual's ability. In the present approach, the pattern of responses plays an important role.

Looking more closely at Figure 7, one can observe that the posterior distribution it portrays has a definite positive skew: With a mode at 4, a 94-percent interval for Θ goes from 3 to 6. That this skewness reflects not only the prior expectation that Θ = 5 but — more important — the "unusual" correct response for the eighth-item class may be seen by comparing Figure 7 with Figure 3. The latter, it will be recalled, showed a posterior based on a perfect response pattern, identical with that in Figure 7 except for the correct response in the eighth class. Here the skewness in the posterior is due solely to prior expectations and is clearly less extreme than that seen in Figure 7. A second observation resulting from comparison of these two figures is that the perfect response pattern gives rise to less variability in the posterior than does the "lucky guess" pattern.

In conclusion, then, applying the present approach to the

Figure 7. Posterior Distribution for the Ability Θ of an Individual with Seven out of Fourteen Items Correct and a Pattern with One Apparently Unusual Response.

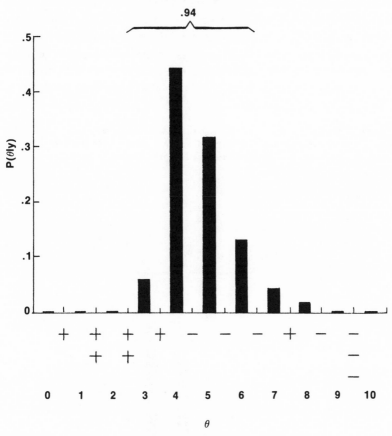

responses in Figure 7 identifies a most likely value (posterior mode) for ability—a value that ignores the one unusual response. This response is not, however, ignored when it comes to both the skewness and spread of the resulting posterior. Instead, it produces what might be referred to as "directed uncertainty" regarding the true value of Θ. All in all, this would seem to be a reasonable way of dealing with such a response pattern. Most interesting is that such a result is produced within the framework of a formal model rather than as the result of an ad hoc procedure.

Wright and Stone (1979, p. 81) identify the individual with code number 29 as having the most irregular response pattern (assessed relative to the Rasch model) of anyone in their sample. It may be instructive to apply the present approach to this individual's responses as well. They are indicated (in the usual manner) at the bottom of Figure 8 and clearly represent the most complex pattern considered so far. Nevertheless, if one had to provide an estimate — on intuitive grounds alone — for the ability level of person 29, a

Figure 8. Posterior Distribution for the Ability Θ of an Individual with Seven out of Fourteen Items Correct and a Pattern with Several Apparently Unusual Responses.

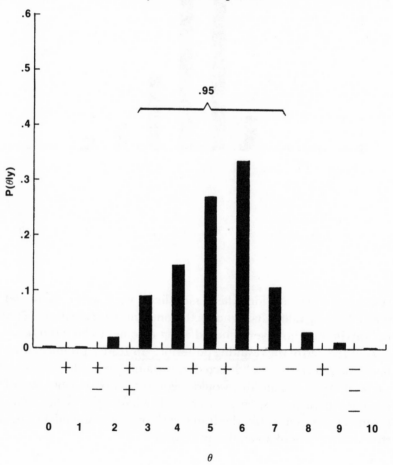

value of 6 would be a reasonable contender. There is, at least, a natural break from correct to incorrect responses occurring between item classes six and seven. Having provided such an estimate, one would of course continue to be uneasy about the incorrect responses in classes two and four, as well as the correct response in class nine.

Turning to the posterior distribution for person 29's ability, illustrated in Figure 8, we can observe at least two things. First, the most likely value for Θ is 6. Second, *both* tails of the distribution are relatively long. The analysis represented in Figure 7 produced one long tail as a consequence of what was, apparently, one unusual response. The analysis of Figure 6 produced a relatively flat distribution with short tails, based on no unusual responses but considerable uncertainty as to the exact location of Θ. Now, with apparently unusual responses on *both* sides of a natural estimate for Θ, two long tails would seem to provide a satisfactory representation of the resulting uncertainty.

The negative skewness of the distribution in Figure 8 (not so dramatic as the positive skew in Figure 7) may be thought of as reflecting the fact that there were two incorrect responses to apparently easy items and only one correct response to an apparently difficult item. It also must reflect, to some extent, the influence of prior expectations. In any event, the flexibility of the distributions worked with in the present approach, as well as their sensitivity to details of individual response patterns, is amply illustrated by these analyses of the Wright and Stone data.

Appendix

This appendix is devoted to showing how the integration necessary to obtain prior and posterior distributions for the ability Θ may be carried out on (4) and (5), the prior and posterior densities, respectively, for $\{\pi_i\}$. To begin, the problem may be generalized by considering a joint density for $\{\pi_i\}$ that satisfies the order restriction (1) with the form

$$C \prod_{i=1}^{k} g_i(\pi_i), \qquad (8)$$

for a set $\{g_i\}$ of positive integrable functions defined on the interval $(0,1)$.

Two additional sets of functions based on $\{g_i\}$ are also needed in this development. Let

$$f_0(u) = 1, \text{ for } 0 < u < 1.$$

Then, for $i = 1(1)k$, let

$$f_i(u) = \int_u^1 f_{i-1}(t)g_i(t)dt, \text{ for } 0 < u < 1. \tag{9}$$

Also, let

$$h_{k+1}(u) = 1, \text{ for } 0 < u < 1,$$

and, for $i = k(-1)1$, let

$$h_i(u) = \int_0^u g_i(t)h_{i+1}(t)dt, \text{ for } 0 < u < 1. \tag{10}$$

These sequences provide two paths for successive integration of the joint density (8). Since the total integral of the density over the region given by (1) must equal unity,

$$f_k(0) = h_1(1) = 1/C. \tag{11}$$

Although it is not of direct interest in the present development, it may be noted that the marginal density for any π_i based on the joint density (8) is given by

$$Cf_{i-1}(\pi_i)g_i(\pi_i)h_{i+1}(\pi_i).$$

Turning to the probability distribution of Θ, we find that the expressions in (6) imply

$$\text{Prob}(\Theta = i) = Cf_i(\tfrac{1}{2})h_{i+1}(\tfrac{1}{2}), \text{ for } i = 0(1)k. \tag{12}$$

Here integration has first been carried out with respect to all π_j for $j < i$ or $j > i + 1$. This results in the bivariate density for π_i and π_{i+1} (unless $i = 0$ or $i = k$). Finally, integration is carried out with respect to π_i on the interval $(\frac{1}{2},1)$, and with respect to π_{i+1} on the interval $(0,\frac{1}{2})$. This gives

$$\text{Prob}(\pi_i \geq \tfrac{1}{2} \text{ and } \pi_{i+1} < \tfrac{1}{2}),$$

which, by (6), is the desired probability that Θ equals i. (Obvious modifications of the above argument are necessary for i equal to zero or k.)

As an illustration, consider a test with $k = 4$ items. The joint density (8) for $\{\pi_i\}$ may be written out as

$$P(\pi_1,\pi_2,\pi_3,\pi_4) = Cg_1(\pi_1)g_2(\pi_2)g_3(\pi_3)g_4(\pi_4),$$

for
$$1 > \pi_1 > \pi_2 > \pi_3 > \pi_4 > 0. \tag{13}$$

Obtaining, for instance, the probability that Θ equals 2 may be represented as

$$\text{Prob}(\theta=2) = C \overbrace{\left(\int_{\frac{1}{2}}^{1} \overbrace{\left(\int_{\pi_2}^{1} g_1(\pi_1)d\pi_1 \right)}^{f_1(\pi_2)} g_2(\pi_2)d\pi_2 \right)}^{f_2(\frac{1}{2})} \cdot$$

$$\underbrace{\left(\int_{0}^{\frac{1}{2}} g_3(\pi_3) \underbrace{\left(\int_{0}^{\pi_3} g_4(\pi_4)d\pi_4 \right)}_{h_4(\pi_3)} d\pi_3 \right)}_{h_3(\frac{1}{2})}$$

$$= Cf_2(\tfrac{1}{2})h_3(\tfrac{1}{2}) \tag{14}$$

In general, the integrations in (9) and (10) are most conveniently carried out by numerical means rather than analytically. It is important to note that the amount of computational effort required is a *linear* function of the number of variables (k), rather than exponential, as is often the case with multiple numerical integration. This is a direct result of the product structure of the joint density (8), and implies that it is computationally feasible to analyze responses for relatively long tests.

Now consider a special case where analytic integration of the joint density $\{\pi_i\}$ is straightforward. It may be described in terms of the general density (8) by setting all $g_i(\pi_i) = 1$ for all π_i in the interval (0,1). Alternatively, it may be given in terms of the prior (4) by taking all $\alpha_i = \beta_i = 1$. In any event, the result is a uniform joint density for $\{\pi_i\}$ in the region given by (1).

For this case, from (9) to (10),

$$f_i(u) = (1 - u)^i/(i!) \quad \text{and}$$
$$h_{i+1}(u) = u^{k-i}/(k-i)!, \quad \text{for } i = 1(1)k$$
$$\text{and } 0 < u < 1.$$

Thus, from (11), the constant in (8) necessary to produce an integral of unity is given by

$$C = 1/f_k(0) = 1/h_1(1) = k!,$$

and, using the result (12), the distribution of Θ is

$$\text{Prob}(\Theta = i) = \frac{k!}{i!(k-i)!}(\tfrac{1}{2})^k, \text{ for } i = 1(1)k \qquad (15)$$

(also given as [7] in the main text).

Thus, it has been shown that a uniform distribution for $\{\pi_i\}$ implies a binomial distribution, with parameters k and $\tfrac{1}{2}$, for Θ. (It may be noted that this parallels a result in the theory of order statistics regarding confidence intervals for quantiles. See, for instance, Wilks, 1962, pp. 330–331.) For illustration, consider the above in the case of the test mentioned earlier with $k = 4$ items. The joint density (13) becomes

for
$$p(\pi_1,\pi_2,\pi_3,\pi_4) = 24,$$
$$1 > \pi_1 > \pi_2 > \pi_3 > \pi_4 > 0.$$

Performing the integrations indicated in (14) with $g_i(\pi_i) = 1$ gives

$$f_1(\pi_2) = \int_{\pi_2}^1 d\pi_1 = 1 - \pi_2,$$

$$f_2(\tfrac{1}{2}) = \int_{\tfrac{1}{2}}^1 (1 - \pi_2)d\pi_2 = -\tfrac{1}{2}(1 - \pi_2)^2|_{\tfrac{1}{2}}^1 = (\tfrac{1}{2})^2/2$$

$$h_4(\pi_3) = \int_0^3 d\pi_4 = \pi_3, \text{ and}$$

$$h_3(\tfrac{1}{2}) = \int_0^{\tfrac{1}{2}} \pi_3 d\pi_3 = \tfrac{1}{2}\pi_3^2|_0^{\tfrac{1}{2}} = (\tfrac{1}{2})^2/2.$$

Thus, from the last line of (14),

$$\text{Prob}(\Theta = 2) = \frac{24[(\tfrac{1}{2})^2/2][(\tfrac{1}{2})^2/2]}{2 \cdot 2}$$
$$= \frac{24}{2 \cdot 2} (\tfrac{1}{2})^4 = .375,$$

which agrees with (15) when $i = 2$ and $k = 4$.

Continuing with the theoretical development, the result (15) can be generalized to the case where the prior (4) is used with all $\alpha_i = \beta_i = a$, for any positive constant a. Alternatively, take

$$g_i(\pi_i) = [\pi_i(1 - \pi_i)]^{a-1}, \text{ for } i = 1(1)k,$$

in the general form (8). To see this, define a strictly increasing transformation $\phi(\pi)$ so that

$$\phi(0) = 0,$$
$$\phi(1) = 1, \text{ and}$$
$$\frac{d\phi}{d\pi} = b[\pi(1 - \pi)]^{a-1} \text{ for some } b > 0.$$

From symmetry considerations,

$$\phi(\tfrac{1}{2}) = \tfrac{1}{2}. \tag{16}$$

Letting

$$\phi_i = \phi(\pi_i), \text{ for } i = 1(1)k,$$

and transforming the prior (4) to a prior for $\{\phi_i\}$, the definition of $\phi(\cdot)$ implies that the result will be a uniform density over the region

$$1 > \phi_1 > \ldots > \phi_k > 0.$$

Moreover, because of the relation (16), the definition of Θ given in (2) may be restated, replacing each π_i by the corresponding ϕ_i. Consequently, all the assumptions and definitions made in terms of $\{\pi_i\}$ that were used to derive (15) can now be replaced by equivalent ones using $\{\phi_i\}$. This implies that, whenever the prior for $\{\pi_i\}$ has the form (4) with all $\alpha_i = \beta_i = a > 0$, then Θ has a binomial distribution with parameters k and $\tfrac{1}{2}$.

References

Andersen, E. B., and Madsen, M. "Estimating the Parameters of the Latent Population Distribution." *Psychometrika*, 1977, *42*, 357–374.

Barlow, R. E., and others. *Statistical Inference Under Order Restrictions.* New York: Wiley, 1972.

Birnbaum, A. "Statistical Theory for Logistic Mental Test Models with a Prior Distribution of Ability." *Journal of Mathematical Psychology*, 1969, *6*, 258–276.

de Gruijter, D. N. M. "Empirical Bayes Estimation in the Rasch Model: A Simulation." Paper presented at the European meeting of the Psychometric Society, Groningen, The Netherlands, June 19–21, 1980.

Efron, B., and Morris, C. "Data Analysis Using Stein's Estimator and its Generalizations." *Journal of the American Statistical Association*, 1975, *70*, 311–319.

Fischer, G. H. *Einführung in die Theorie Psychologischer Tests.* Bern: Huber, 1974.

Freeman, P. R. "Optimal Bayesian Sequential Estimation of the Median Effective Dose." *Biometrika*, 1970, *57*, 79–89.

Kempf, W. F. "Dynamic Models for the Measurement of 'Traits' in Social Behavior." In W. F. Kempf and B. H. Repp (Eds.), *Some Mathematical Models for Social Psychology.* Bern: Huber, 1976.

Kraft, C. H., and van Eeden, C. "Bayesian Bioassay." *Annals of Mathematical Statistics*, 1964, *35*, 886–890.

Leonard, T. "Bayesian Methods for Binomial Data." *Biometrika*, 1972, *59*, 581–589.

Lewis, C. *The Countback Method for Analyzing Sensitivity Data.* Research Bulletin 70-30. Princeton, N.J.: Educational Testing Service, 1970.

Lewis, C., Wang, M., and Novick, M. R. "Marginal Distributions for the Estimation of Proportions in *m* Groups." *Psychometrika*, 1975, *40*, 63–75.

Lindley, D. V., and Smith, A. F. M. "Bayes Estimates for the Linear Model." *Journal of the Royal Statistical Society* (Series B), 1972, *34*, 1–41.

Lord, F. M. "Individualized Testing and Item Characteristic Curve

Theory." In R. C. Atkinson and others (Eds.), *Contemporary Developments in Mathematical Psychology.* Vol. 2. San Francisco: W. H. Freeman, 1974.

Lord, F. M., and Novick, M. R. *Statistical Theories of Mental Test Scores.* Reading, Mass.: Addison-Wesley, 1968.

Mokken, R. J. *A Theory and Procedure of Scale Analysis with Applications in Political Research.* The Hague: Mouton, 1971.

Novick, M. R., and Jackson, P. H. *Statistical Methods for Educational and Psychological Research.* New York: McGraw-Hill, 1974.

Novick, M. R., Lewis, C., and Jackson, P. H. "The Estimation of Proportions in *m* Groups." *Psychometrika,* 1973, *38,* 19–46.

Owen, R. J. "A Bayesian Sequential Procedure for Quantal Response in the Context of Adaptive Mental Testing." *Journal of the American Statistical Association,* 1975, *70,* 351–356.

Ramsey, F. L. "A Bayesian Approach to Bioassay." *Biometrics,* 1972, *28,* 841–858.

Sanathanan, L., and Blumenthal, S. "The Logistic Model and Estimation of Latent Structure." *Journal of the American Statistical Association,* 1978, *73,* 794–799.

Stewart, L. "Multiparameter Univariate Bayesian Analysis." *Journal of the American Statistical Association,* 1979, *74,* 684–693.

Wainer, H., and Wright, B. D. "Robust Estimation of Ability in the Rasch Model." *Psychometrika,* 1980, *45,* 373–391.

Wilks, S. S. *Mathematical Statistics.* New York: Wiley, 1962.

Wright, B. D., and Stone, M. H. *Best Test Design.* Chicago: Mesa Press, 1979.

12 Wilhelm Kempf

ꙮ ꙮ ꙮ ꙮ ꙮ ꙮ ꙮ ꙮ ꙮ ꙮ ꙮ ꙮ ꙮ

Some Theoretical Concerns about Applying Latent Trait Models in Educational Testing

If there is one crucial problem with the application of so-called psychological test theories in education (or in any other context), it is that both test developers and test users just don't know what they are doing. Let me give you two examples:

First, we have been testing intelligence for three quarters of a century now, but there are virtually no test psychologists who can tell what intelligence is or what they are talking about when they use the word *intelligence*. Still, each of us has a more or less vague feeling that this or that achievement is a mark of intelligence. Although such a feeling does not provide us with any sound terminological basis for constructing a psychological theory of intelligence or for its assessment, it does keep us going. Why not just compare subjects with respect to a more or less arbitrarily chosen sample of achievements?

Second, when we test someone we know quite well, his or her achievement in the test situation is often not what we would have expected. Since we won't give up our expectations so easily, we say, "No, this is not his 'real achievement.'" Or, taking account of the fact that we have condensed the achievement into a single number, called a *score*, we say, "The test score is not in accordance with his 'true score.'" In any argument based on methodology, of course, our opponent would reply, "How can you defend this assertion, and, anyway, what do you mean by a 'true score'?" However, there was no such opponent in the early days of psychological test theory, and thus nobody forced us to come up with a clearly defined terminology.

We then proceeded to argue as follows: If a subject (v) has a score (x_{vt}) on a test (t) that is not in accordance with his true score (τ_{vt}), then there must be a difference between the two

$$f_{vt} = x_{vt} - \tau_{vt} \tag{1}$$

that we can call the *error of measurement*. But this amounted to the most ingenious fraud ever invented in order to provide a new discipline — test psychology — with high scientific honor.

Seemingly tautological and thus not disputable, equation (1) is neither a definition of the error of measurement nor a mathematical equation that allows for computing the error from given data. It would be so if and only if the concept of *true score* were defined in advance. Nonetheless it has the form of a mathematical equation and thus was highly instrumental in giving test psychology a scientific image: What could better satisfy scientific standards than the mathematical formulation of a theory? And even more: Did we not call the term on the left-hand side of the equation the *error of measurement*? And did this not imply that our tests were measuring instruments?

From here on, the door was closed for constructing a *psychological* test theory, but it was opened wide for constructing *statistical* theories of psychological test scores. There were several paths that could then have been followed, but the most naive one became the most popular; it led to classical test theory, and, beyond that, to the theory of generalizability and the method of factor analysis. The landmarks along the way were: (1) to keep the crucial terms of the theory undefined ("true score," "measurement") and (2) to compensate for the lack of definitions by a habit of inventing mathematically convenient but psychologically unfounded assumptions. These assumptions were often untestable (like the so-called axioms of classical test theory), or never tested in practice and not likely to withstand a critical test (like the assumption of the parallelism of tests), or, even worse, in contradiction to well-known statistical laws (like the assumption of homoscedasticity of error scores) if we take into account how psychological test scores are composed. Finally, some of these assumptions were simply not in accordance with psychological intuition.

An Attempt at Reformulation

Among the few attempts to put classical test theory on a sound methodological basis there is the reformulation by Novick (1966). As it turns out, however, this is the attempt of a statistician, not of a psychologist. A psychologist might ask, "How can the concept of true score be defined so that it will coincide with psychological intuition, that is, will explicate our implicit usage of the phrase *real achievement?*" But Novick posed the question, "How can the concept of true score be defined in order to transform the so-called axioms of classical test theory into mathematically derivable sentences?"

Novick's answer to the question was to state that to each subject v and to each test t there corresponds a random variable X_{vt} with finite expectation $E(X_{vt})$ and variance $\sigma^2(X_{vt})$. (Since any random variable defined on a finite interval has finite moments of every [positive] order and since test scores usually are constructed as the sum [or finite weighted sum] of finite scored responses to a finite number of test items, the latter is not really an assumption but noted just for the sake of completeness.) The true score of subject v on test t is then defined as the expected value of the observed score; that is

$$\tau_{vt} = E(X_{vt}). \tag{2}$$

Although Novick's definition is a suitable basis on which to found the axioms of classical test theory, there are at least two good reasons why we cannot agree with it: First, Novick's definition does not coincide with psychological intuition. This will become clear, as soon as we explicate our everyday usage of the term *true achievement.* Second, Novick's definition cannot be understood. To state that to each subject and to each test there corresponds a random variable implies that a subject's test score is the result of the application of a random generator or, at least, that it can be treated *as if* it were. This is not the case, since any random generator must satisfy the principle of repeatability; that is, after each application the random generator must be in the same state as before. Only if the principle of repeatability is satisfied can the concept of probability be defined so that the law of large numbers will hold and probability can be interpreted as the limiting value of relative frequency in an increasing number of experiments (that is, applications of a random generator).* As all of us know, psychological tests cannot be administered to the same subject an arbitrary number of times. Any subject may learn or remember something while working on a test that will influence performance when the test is administered the next time. If this were not the case, we would not need to construct special statistical theories of psychological test scores but could just administer the test repeatedly and apply the usual statistics. The only way around this would be to brainwash our subjects after each test administration. However, this would very quickly land us in the realm of science fiction.

---

* It is often claimed that probability can be defined "implicitly" by stating the axioms of probability theory. As it turns out, this is not the case, since the relations stated in the axioms hold for any relative frequencies as well. Thus, the so-called axiomatic definition cannot make clear what the difference between a frequency distribution and a probability distribution is. For the sake of mathematical reasoning the axioms of probability theory may suffice. They do not suffice, however, for transforming the application of probability predicates on psychological (or any other) events into meaningful sentences. It is also claimed that probability can be defined as the subjective chance of an event. As it turns out, such a definition would leave the axioms of probability theory without foundation and thus cannot help us understand the meaning of the computations based on these axioms. In other words, an intuitive definition of probability cannot make clear what mathematical probability theory and its application have to do with probability.

Latent Trait Theory

But if we decide to forget about classical test theory, what is the alternative? At first glance, the situation with latent trait theory seems to be even worse. The basic concept of latent trait theory as defined by Lazarsfeld (1950) is the item characteristic function. It states that to each subject (v) and to each test item (i) there corresponds a random variable (A_{vi}) with a characteristic probability function:

$$P(a_{vi}) = f_i(a_{vi}, \xi_v), \tag{3}$$

where ξ_v is a vector of parameters that measure the latent abilities of the subject that are involved in his or her response to the item. Implicit to this definition is the assumption of "local independence," which states that a subject's response to an item does not depend on his or her responses to prior items. Although local independence is an essential assumption of most latent trait models, it is not a necessary assumption but can be replaced by specified forms of what I call *local serial dependence* (Kempf, 1977), in which case the concept of item characteristic functions has to be replaced by the concept of conditional item characteristic functions:

$$P(a_{vi}|a_{v1}, \ldots, a_{vi-1}) = f_i(a_{vi}, \xi_v|a_{v1}, \ldots, a_{vi-1}).$$

As we can see from Lazarsfeld's definition, the concepts of randomness and probability are once again applied to nonrepeatable events, and — as it has turned out in the context of the Birnbaum (1968) model — this lack of repeatability not only hinders us in understanding the meaning of the probability predicate $P(a_{vi})$ but also involves us in serious statistical problems. (The Birnbaum model is taken as an example only. The same criticism holds for the whole class of latent trait models that do not allow for conditional inference.)

The Birnbaum model was constructed for the analysis of binary items with

$$a_{vi} = \begin{cases} 1 \text{ if S } v \text{ gives a 'correct' response to item } i \\ 0 \text{ if S } v \text{ gives a 'false' response to item } i. \end{cases} \tag{4}$$

It is defined by the item characteristic function

$$f_i(a_{vi}, \xi_v) = \exp(a_{vi}\alpha_i(\xi_v - \sigma_i))/(1 + \exp(\alpha_i(\xi_v - \sigma_i))) \qquad (5)$$

where σ_i is an item-difficulty parameter and α_i is an item discrimination parameter. ξ_v is the subject's ability parameter (a scalar, not a vector). As Figure 1 and Figure 2 show, the probability of a correct response $a_{vi} = 1$ is a strictly increasing function of the subject's ability parameter and a strictly decreasing function of the item difficulty parameter. The higher the item discrimination power is, the steeper the ascent of the function.

For any practical application of the model it is crucial to be able to estimate its parameters. Here the statistical problems begin because the well-known methods of parameter estimation (such as the maximum likelihood method) break down. They do not produce consistent estimators (see Neyman and Scott, 1948) because the number of parameters to be estimated does not converge toward a fixed number while the number of observations increases to infinity. This is just another way to state that the repeatability criterion for random generators is violated. Is there a way out of these problems? Can repeatability be established? There are two ways out: a simple one that gives up the concept of latent trait, and an ingenious one that has provided the basis for highly important developments within mathematical statistics.

The simple way out was chosen by Lazarsfeld and led to latent class analysis, which is based on the assumption that each subject belongs to one of a finite number of classes $L = 1, \ldots, M$ and that

$$P(a_{vi}|v \epsilon L) = \pi_{Li}{}^{a_{vi}}(1 - \pi_{Li})^{1 - a_{vi}} \text{ for all } i = 1, k \text{ and } L = 1, M \qquad (6)$$

where a_{vi} are binary responses as defined in (4), and π_{Li} denotes the probability of a response $a_{vi} = 1$ for a randomly chosen subject from class L. The method of latent class analysis then allows for estimation of the parameters π_{Li} and for assigning each subject v to the class that he or she most probably belongs to.

Since latent class analysis is rarely applied within the context of educational testing, let me give an example from clinical psychology: Suppose there are certain clinical syndromes (for example,

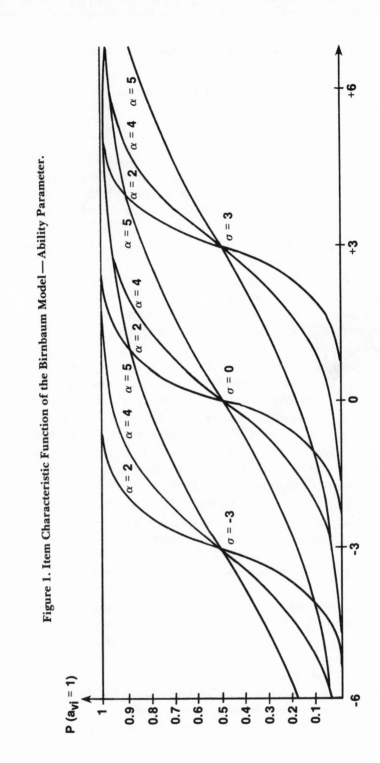

Figure 1. Item Characteristic Function of the Birnbaum Model — Ability Parameter.

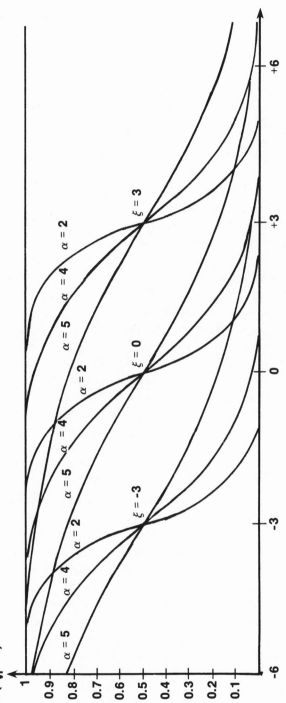

Figure 2. Item Characteristic Function of the Birnbaum Model — Item Difficulty Parameter.

forms of depression) that are made up of certain symptoms (for example, lowered psychomotor functioning, inhibited thinking, anxious-distressed-complaining mood, melancholy, and hypochondria). Then each syndrome (each *class* of depressive patients) will be defined by a typical, "ideal" pattern of syndromes (items). Such an ideal pattern will be made up of some symptoms shown by all patients, some symptoms shown by none, and some symptoms shown by some of the patients but not by others. Now, in reality not all the patients will show such an ideal pattern of symptoms; instead, many will show one or the other of the symptoms that do not belong to the syndrome of their illness and/or will not show certain symptoms that do belong. In such a situation the question arises: To which syndrome should the patient be assigned? A simple and straightforward solution would be to choose that syndrome for which the number of deviations from the ideal is a minimum. So far we do not need any special statistical theory.

The situation becomes more complicated, however, if we do not yet have a theory that tells us what the ideal syndromes look like and if we are still in the process of constructing such a theory. Then it is essential to have some experience with respect to which symptoms typically go together and which do not. This is the situation where latent class analysis applies: as a heuristic method for structuring data in order to get empirically based hypotheses about possible syndromes. These hypotheses can then be used as starting points for theoretical reasoning that in turn will result in the construction of ideal classes.

The second and more complex way to reestablish repeatability was chosen by Rasch (1960, 1965) and is closely related to the concept of measurement, where measurement is defined as a mapping of objects into the set of real numbers so that there is a one-to-one correspondence between certain empirically stated relations and corresponding numerical relations. From this definition it becomes clear that the empirical basis of measurement is the comparison of objects. Now, let us have a set of random generators R_{vi} ($v = 1,2, \ldots$; $i = 1,2, \ldots$), each of which defines a random variable A_{vi} with the probability function

$$P(a_{vi}) = f_i(a_{vi}, \xi_v). \tag{7}$$

Let us further suppose that we want to compare these random generators with respect to the parameters ξ_v so that none of the random generators may be applied repeatedly. Then we might ask what form the probability function must take for there to exist a conditional distribution for which the repeatability criterion holds and on which the (empirical) comparison of the random generators can be based.

As Rasch has shown, such a conditional distribution exists in the case of binary items if and only if the probability function has the form

$$f_i(a_{vi}, \xi_v) = \exp(a_{vi}(\xi_v - \sigma_i)) / (1 + \exp(\xi_v - \sigma_i)). \tag{8}$$

If (8) holds, then the conditional probabilities of the vector variables

$$P(a_{1i}, \ldots, a_{ni}) \mid \sum_{v=1}^{n} a_{vi} = r_i) = f_r((a_{1i}, \ldots, a_{ni}), (\xi_1, \ldots, \xi_n)) \tag{9}$$

are independent of the parameters σ_i; that is, they are the same for all $i = 1, 2, \ldots$ and thus pertain to repeatable events.

So far, the statistical problems have been solved: The empirical comparison of subjects can be based on the conditional probability distribution in (9). But what about the problem of psychological meaning? Here it is obvious that the existence of repeatable conditional events cannot establish the psychological meaning of the item characteristic function, which still pertains to unrepeatable events. Thus the item characteristic function has the status of an auxiliary construction that allows for the generation of repeatable and thus meaningful conditional events. For the comparison of any two subjects v and w, for instance, we get the conditional distribution

$$P(a_{vi}, a_{wi}) = (1,0) \mid a_{vi} + a_{wi} = 1) = \frac{\exp(\xi_v)}{\exp(\xi_v) + \exp(\xi_w)}. \tag{10}$$

Hence, if k items are administered to the subjects and if m of these items are solved by exactly one of the two subjects, then the number of items m_v solved by subject v but not by subject w will follow a binomial distribution with

$$P(m_v|m) = \binom{m}{m_v}\left(\frac{\theta_v}{\theta_v + \theta_w}\right)^{m_v}\left(\frac{\theta_w}{\theta_v + \theta_w}\right)^{m-m_v} \text{ with } \theta_v = \exp(\xi_v)$$

$$\text{and } \theta_w = \exp(\xi_w) \qquad (11)$$

so that the ratio $\theta_v/(\theta_v + \theta_w)$ can be estimated by the relative frequency m_v/m. Similarly, the ratio $\theta_w/(\theta_v + \theta_w)$ can be estimated by the relative frequency m_w/m so that

$$\frac{\theta_v}{\theta_w} \approx \frac{m_v}{m_w}. \qquad (12)$$

This gives us a straightforward interpretation for the comparison of subjects as carried out by the Rasch model: The ratio of any two antilog ability parameters θ_v/θ_w is an idealization of the ratio based on the numbers of items solved by one of the two subjects but not by the other.

Educational Testing

So far the problems of psychological meaning also seem to be in process of solution. To apply the Rasch model implies that for any two subjects v and w and for any sample of test items $i = 1, \ldots, k$, there will be a more or less stable ratio m_v/m_w and that subjects will be compared with respect to this ratio. But in educational testing is this the kind of comparison that we are really interested in? Are we really interested in finding out that there are x times as many items that subject v can solve but subject w cannot solve as there are items that subject w can solve but that subject v cannot solve? And what are the educational goals for which such knowledge could be useful? To quote Bob Dylan, "The answer is blowin' in the wind." But let me offer one example from educational testing that might be typical of many others.

Suppose we try to teach students a certain body of knowledge. Then it may be essential to find out what the students already know (or believe) in advance and what prior opinions we can build upon. Consider children's understanding of a two-arm balance, for instance, as shown in Figure 3. Here, according to studies by Siegler

Figure 3. The Balance Scale—"Which Side Will Go Down When the Blocks Are Moved?"

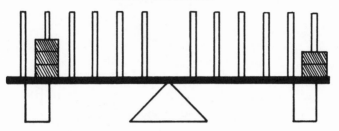

(1976), Klahr (1978), and May (1979), the typical development of children's understanding can be understood as a stepwise accumulation of knowledge and hypotheses.

Thus, on the lowest level, children know only that the weights are relevant for balance. Their balance scale predictions based on this knowledge may be described by a flow diagram as shown in Figure 4. Later on children come to realize that the scale is in balance with the same weights on both sides only if the distances are equal too and that otherwise the side with the greater distance will go down (see Figure 5). On level 3 children have realized that the distances are relevant when different weights are put on the two sides, but they don't yet know what will happen when the greater weight is not on the same side as the greater distance; that is, when there is a "conflict" between weights and distances (see Figure 6). On level 4 children come up with the hypothesis that in case of

Figure 4. Flow Diagram of Balance Scale Predictions of a Level-1 Child.

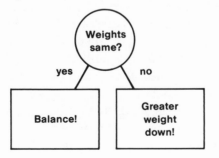

Figure 5. Flow Diagram of Balance Scale Predictions of a Level-2 Child.

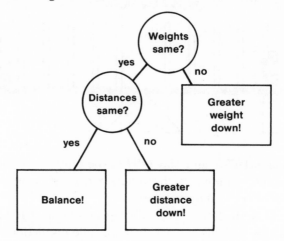

conflict between weights and distances the behavior of the balance will depend on whether there is a greater difference between the weights or between the distances (see Figure 7). On level 5 children will come to realize that it is not the differences but the ratios of weights and of differences that are relevant in case of conflict (see Figure 8).

If we now want to assess a student's prior opinions or knowledge by means of a test, we can do so because there is an analytical connection between a subject's opinion and his or her actions. Given his or her goals and his or her view of the situation, a subject will do exactly what he or she believes to be appropriate in that situation (see Kempf, 1978). In other words, if a subject follows the test administrator's instruction and if he or she does not misjudge the task (for example, he or she does not make a mistake in counting weights and measuring distances), then we can predict the response to the item if we know what the level of knowledge is. This allows us to distinguish several types of items and to contruct ideal response patterns as shown in Table 1.

In order to assess a subject's knowledge, we thus have to compare the pattern of his or her responses with the ideal response patterns and to decide which of these patterns it is in accordance

Figure 6. Flow Diagram of Balance Scale Predictions of a Level-3 Child.

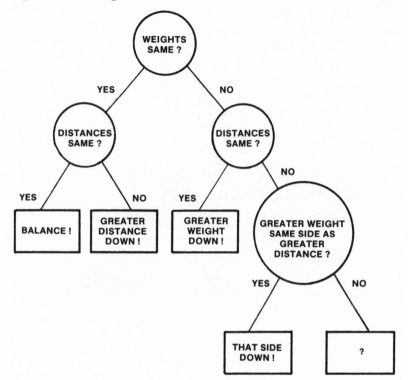

with. This means that we need a *qualitative* analysis of a subject's knowledge, not a *quantitative* measurement. With the construction of scores, such as the number of correct responses, the relevant information in the data may get lost. In our example, for instance, the number of correct responses could not discriminate between levels 2 through 4 (see Table 1).

Now, in reality the response patterns usually will deviate more or less from the ideal patterns. As the empirical experience available has shown, however, in a well-designed study the percentage of responses deviating from the ideal will not be more than 6 or 7 percent even with a paper and pencil test. Nonetheless, there arises the question of what to do with subjects whose response patterns are not identical to any of the ideal patterns. Would it be helpful in such a situation to apply the Rasch model and to describe the subjects'

Figure 7. Flow Diagram of Balance Scale Predictions of a Level-4 Child.

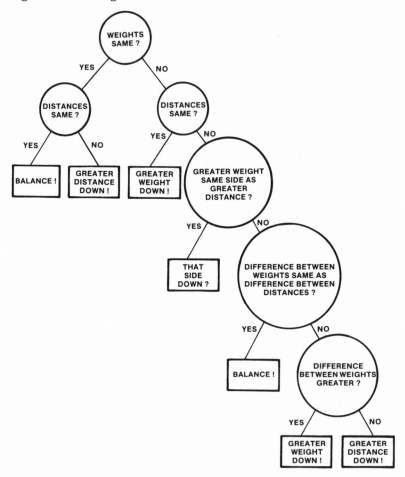

knowledge by means of their ability parameters as estimated from the model? Obviously it will not. Since a subject's score is a sufficient statistic for his or her ability parameter in the Rasch model, and since the parameter estimates are nothing more than a strictly increasing transformation of the scores, the ability parameter estimates cannot describe relevant information in the data; for example, a level 2 child and a level 3 child, both of whom give 6 percent

Figure 8. Flow Diagram of Balance Scale Predictions of a Level-5 Child.

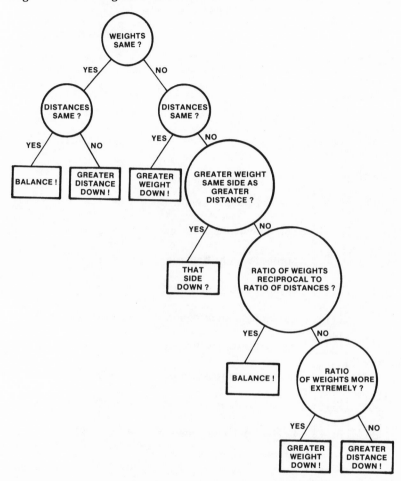

atypical responses. The expected score will still remain the same for both children.

So what do we do with a subject whose response pattern is not identical with any of the ideal patterns? The only reasonable approach is to search for reasons for such a deviation. There might be children, for instance, whose knowledge is entirely different from any of the typical levels previously described and who will therefore

Table 1. Type of Items and Ideal Response Patterns in a Balance Scale Test.

Type of Item		Level of Knowledge					
		1	2	3	4	5	atypical
	Balance	+	+	+	+	+	+
	Weight	+	+	+	+	+	−
	Distance	−	+	+	+	+	+
	Harmony	+	+	+	+	+	+
	Conflict-weight/weight	+	+	?	+	+	−
	Conflict-weight/distance	+	+	?	−	+	−
	Conflict-weight/balance	+	+	?	−	+	−
	Conflict-distance/weight	−	−	?	−	+	+
	Conflict-distance/distance	−	−	?	+	+	+
	Conflict-distance/balance	−	−	?	−	+	+
	Conflict-balance/weight	−	−	?	−	+	−
	Conflict-balance/distance	−	−	?	−	+	−
	Conflict-balance/balance	−	−	?	+	+	−
Expected score if test contains h items of each type and if random guessing is assumed in case of "?":		6	7	7	7	13	6 xh

have an entirely different ideal response pattern. In this situation we have to reconstruct the argument that may lead to the observed response pattern. If, for instance, we observe an atypical response pattern as shown in the last column of Table 1, this response pattern could be explained by stating that the child knows only that the distances are relevant for balance (see Figure 9).

**Figure 9. Flow Diagram of Balance Scale
Predictions of an Atypical Child.**

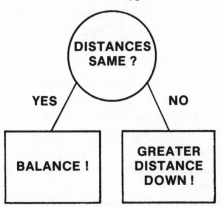

But what shall we do if we cannot reconstruct the knowledge so that the observed response pattern can be explained completely? Here we might be forced to retreat to the assumption of random errors and assign the subject to that class for which the number of deviations from the corresponding ideal response pattern is a minimum. Doing this also makes it clear what we mean when we talk of a subject's "true achievement": The term refers to nothing more than the ideal response pattern a subject would show if his or her knowledge really were what we suspect it to be.

In considering the application of latent trait models in an educational context and the question of which issues should be further developed from an applied point of view, my response was to give an example from educational psychology. The fact that latent trait models do not apply in this example does not necessarily mean that there is no field of application for them in educational research. But it does mean that latent trait models must not be applied routinely. Statistical theories of psychological test scores cannot substitute for psychological theorizing and for a clearly defined psychological terminology. And these are the issues that should be further developed: psychological terminology and psychological theorizing.

References

Birnbaum, A. "Some Latent Trait Models and Their Use in Inferring an Examinee's Ability." In F. M. Lord and M. R. Novick (Eds.), *Statistical Theories of Mental Test Scores.* Reading, Mass.: Addison-Wesley, 1968.

Kempf, W. "Dynamic Models for the Measurement of 'Traits' in Social Behavior." In W. Kempf and B. Repp (Eds.), *Mathematical Models for Social Psychology.* New York: Wiley, 1977.

Kempf, W. 'Rule Learning as a Methodological Principle." In J. M. Scandura and C. J. Brainerd (Eds.), *Structural / Process Models of Complex Human Behavior.* Alphen aan den Rijn: Sijthof and Noordhoff, 1978.

Klahr, D. "Information-Processing Models of Cognitive Development." In J. M. Scandura and C. J. Brainerd (Eds.), *Structural / Process Models of Complex Human Behavior.* Alphen aan den Rijn: Sijthoff and Noordhoff, 1978.

Lazarsfeld, P. F. "Logical and Mathematical Foundations of Latent Structure Analysis." In S. A. Stouffer and others (Eds.), *Studies in Psychology in World War II.* Vol. 4 : *Measurement and Prediction.* Princeton, N.J.: Princeton University Press, 1950.

May, R. "Wie Entwickelt sich das Verständnis von Proportionalität." Psychologische Diplomarbeit, Universität Konstanz, 1979.

Neyman, J., and Scott, E. L. "Consistent Estimates Based on Partially Consistent Observations." *Econometrika,* 1948, *16*(1), 1–32.

Novick, M. R. "The Axioms and Principal Results of Classical Test Theory." *Journal of Mathematical Psychology,* 1966, *3,* 1–18.

Rasch, G. *Probabilistic Models for Some Intelligence and Attainment Tests.* Copenhagen: Danish Institute of Educational Research, 1960.

Rasch, G. "Kolloquium über Messmodelle." Unpublished paper, 1965.

Siegler, R. S. "Three Aspects of Cognitive Development." *Cognitive Psychology,* 1976, *8,* 481–520.

Name Index

ஐ ஐ ஐ ஐ ஐ ஐ ஐ ஐ ஐ ஐ ஐ ஐ ஐ

A

Adams, F. P., 1
Adler, C., 21, 27
Aiken, L. R., 114, 126
Allinsmith, W., 156, 170
Alpert, R., 136, 148
Altman, F., 151, 152, 153, 154, 155, 170
Anastasi, A., 2, 5–28
Andersen, E. B., 191, 193–223, 226, 250
Anderson, S. B., ix-xii, 1–3, 57–60, 129–131, 136, 148, 191–192
Andrew, B. J., 62, 71, 85
Angoff, W. H., xii, 41, 42, 69–70, 71, 83, 86, 95
Arey, D., 154, 170
Atkinson, J. W., 2, 29–44, 93, 130, 175, 176, 177–178, 180–181, 182–183, 185–186, 188–189
Averill, J. R., 159, 160, 169, 172

B

Babad, E. Y., 21, 23
Baddeley, A. D., 155, 169
Bandura, A., 143, 148
Barker, R. G., 43
Barlow, R. E., 227, 229, 250
Bartholomew, D. J., 222, 223
Bayley, N., 13, 23
Beaman, A. L., 123, 126
Bell, P. A., 159, 169
Berger, B., 19, 23
Berger, P. L., 19, 23
Berk, R. A., 75, 83, 86
Berry, J. W., 18, 23–24
Binet, A., 8, 21, 22, 24, 36
Birch, D., 32, 35, 38, 39, 42–43, 175, 189
Birch, H. G., 35, 43
Birnbaum, A., 226, 250, 256–259, 270
Block, J. H., 67, 76, 79, 81, 83, 86

271

Bloom, B. S., 21, 24, 67, 86
Blumenthal, S., 226, 251
Bock, R. D., 195, 221, 223
Bolvin, J. O., 67, 88
Boring, E. G., 2, 3, 5–6, 24
Brennan, R. L., 62, 71, 72, 86
Brigham, C. C., 10, 24
Brink, W. P. van den, 124, 126
Broadhurst, P. L., 35, 43
Broder, L., 21, 24
Brody, N., 13, 26
Broen, W. E., 182, 189
Bronzaft, A. L., 154, 169
Brower, P. E., 158, 169
Brown, B., 21, 24
Buck, L. S., 95, 106
Budoff, M., 21, 23, 24
Burt, C., 46, 50, 55
Burton, N. W., 68, 86
Byrne, D., 159, 169

C

Calvin, A. D., 154, 172
Campbell, D. T., 10, 24, 51, 55
Carroll, J. B., 12, 15, 24
Cartwright, D., 33, 43
Cathcart, J. A., 103, 106
Cattell, R. B., 45, 46, 47, 49, 55
Charlesworth, W. R., 20, 24
Chein, I., 8, 24
Christofferson, A., 222, 223
Conaway, L. E., 65, 83, 86
Coombs, C. H., 124, 125, 126
Corman, L., 21, 24
Cowen, E. L., 153, 169
Craik, F. I. M., 158, 169
Crano, W. P., 51, 55
Crombag, H. F. M., xii, 119, 126
Cronbach, L. J., 9, 25, 29, 43, 65,
    67, 78, 86–87, 153, 169
Crutchfield, R. S., 21, 27
Culler, R. E., 156, 158, 169

D

Dansereau, D. F., 53, 55
Davis, E. L., 97, 107
Davis, F. B., 79, 87
Dawes, R. M., 124, 125, 126
Day, M. C., 21, 25
de Corte, G., xii
Deffenbacher, J. L., 152, 153,
    169–170
de Groot, A. D., 32, 43, 54, 56
de Gruitjer, D. N. M., 226, 227, 250
de Villiers, P. A., 38, 43
De Volder, M., 186, 187n, 189
Diamond, J. J., 79, 87
Doctor, B., 151, 152, 153, 154, 155,
    170
Dodson, J. D., 35, 44, 131, 182, 190
Donlon, T. F., 10, 25
Dornic, S., 158, 170
Dowaliby, F. J., 155–156, 170
Drenth, P. J. D., 186, 189
Duffy, E., 35, 43
Dylan, B., 262

E

Easterbrook, J. A., 182, 189
Ebel, R. L., 71, 72, 87, 95
Efron, B., 226, 250
Eignor, D. R., 61, 62, 65, 68, 75, 78,
    79, 83, 87
Ekstrom, R. B., 15, 25
Elshout, J. J., 2–3, 45–56
Eriksen, C. W., 153, 173
Erikson, E. H., 13, 25
Estes, W. K., 17, 25
Eysenck, H. J., 35, 43–44
Eysenck, M. W., 155, 156, 157, 170

F

Feather, N. T., 43, 181, 189
Ferguson, G. A., 12, 25

Ferrara, P., 72, 89
Festinger, L., 33, 43
Feuerstein, R., 10, 21, 22, 25
Fischer, G. H., 221, 223, 225, 250
Fiske, D. W., 10, 24
Flamer, G. B., 12, 26
Flavell, J. H., 12, 22, 25
Fleishman, E. A., 12, 25
Ford, M. P., 12, 25
Fraser, S. C., 123, 127
Freeman, P. R., 226, 250
French, J. W., 15, 25
Frost, N., 15–16, 26

G

Gagné, R., 52, 56
Galton, F., 46
Gaudry, E., 150, 170
Gilmartin, K. J., 53, 55, 56
Ginsburg, H., 12, 25
Glaser, R., 10, 21, 25, 27, 64, 67, 87
Glass, G. V., 61, 62–64, 66, 68,
  71–72, 76, 79, 84, 87, 120, 127
Gleser, G. C., 65, 78, 87
Glick, J., 19, 26
Goodnow, J. J., 13, 18, 26
Gottfried, A. W., 13, 26
Graff, G., 103, 106
Green, D. R., 12, 26
Grimes, J. W., 156, 170
Gruyter, D. de, 121, 127
Gullion, C. M., 72, 89, 96, 106

H

Haber, R. N., 136, 148
Hambleton, R. K., 61, 62, 63, 64,
  65, 68, 75, 78, 79, 83, 87–88
Harleston, B. W., 154, 170
Havighurst, R. J., 13–14, 26
Haywood, H. C., 154, 170
Hebb, D. O., 2, 35, 44, 46, 56
Hecht, J. T., 62, 71, 85
Heckhausen, H., 153, 162, 170

Heinrich, D. L., 150, 170
Helmick, J. S., ix-xii, 1–3, 57–60,
  129–131, 191–192
Hernnstein, R. J., 38, 43
Hill, K. T., 147, 148
Hitch, G., 155, 169
Hodapp, V., 153, 161, 171
Hodges, W. F., 160, 171
Hofstee, W. K. B., 58, 59, 60,
  109–127
Hogarty, P. S., 13, 27
Holahan, C. J., 156, 158, 169
Holmes, D. S., 160, 171
Holroyd, K. A., 152, 154, 171
Horn, J. L., 11, 13, 26
Horn, W., 162, 171
Houston, B. K., 160, 171
Huff, S., 100, 106
Hull, C. L., 33, 35, 44
Humphreys, L. G., 114, 127
Hunt, E., 15–16, 26, 47, 53, 56
Hunt, J. M., 12, 21, 26
Hurlburt, N., 13, 27
Husek, T. R., 64, 89
Huynh, H., 79, 80, 81, 83, 88

J

Jackson, P. H., 227, 230, 251
Jacobs, B., 156, 171
Jacobs, P. I., 21, 26
Jeager, R. M., 61, 62, 65, 68, 72,
  78, 83, 88, 95, 106
Janis, J. L., 160, 171
Jongman, R. W., 54, 55, 56

K

Kahneman, D., 153, 157, 171
Kameya, L. I., 158, 173
Kaplan, R. M., 142, 148
Katkin, E. S., 154, 171
Kaufman, A. S., 13, 26
Kaufman, N. L., 13, 26
Kellner, H., 19, 23

Kempf, W. F., 192, 229, 250, 252–270
Kenny, I., 51, 55
Kessler, M., 154, 173
Kissel, S., 154, 171
Klahr, D., 16, 26–27, 263, 270
Kleinke, D. J., 62, 71, 72, 88
Kling, S., 62, 71, 90
Koffler, S. L., 62, 71, 88
Korbee, C. J. M., 122, 123, 127
Kraft, C. H., 227, 250
Kreitzberg, C., xii
Kriewall, T. E., 79, 88
Krohne, H. W., 129, 130, 150–174
Krueger, K., 95, 106
Kühn, B., 156, 174

L

Laux, L., 161, 170
Lawsche, C. H., 96, 106
Lazarsfeld, P. F., 256, 257, 270
Lazarus, R. S., 159, 160, 172
Lens, W., 32, 38, 39, 41, 43, 129, 130–131, 175–190
Leonard, T., 227, 250
Lerner, B., 106, 107
Lewin, K., 29–30, 31, 33, 35, 44, 182, 189
Lewis, C., 80, 83, 89, 191–192, 224–251
Lewis, M., 13, 27
Lieberman, M., 195, 223
Liebert, R. M., 136, 148, 151, 152, 153, 172–173
Lindley, D. V., 80, 83, 89, 227, 250
Lindvall, C. M., 67, 88
Linn, R. L., 68, 88
Lissmann, U., 153, 172
Littig, L. W., 154, 171
Litwin, G. H., 181, 189
Livingston, S. A., 73, 79, 80, 83, 88–89, 90, 96, 98, 107
Loacher, G., 99, 107
Lockwood, R. E., 62, 71, 72, 86, 96, 97, 107

Lord, F. M., xii, 197, 199, 205, 208, 223, 225, 226, 250–251
Lunneborg, C., 15–16, 26

M

McCall, R. B., 13, 27
McClelland, D. C., 35, 44, 176, 190
McCordick, S. M., 142, 148
McGuigan, F. J., 154, 172
McGuinness, D., 153, 173
McGurk, H., 13, 27
Madaus, G. F., 68, 89
Madsen, M., 211, 222–223, 226, 250
Maltzman, J., 160, 172
Mandler, G., 136, 148, 154, 172, 176, 190
Maslow, A. P., 58, 60, 91–108
Matarazzo, J. D., 8, 27
May, R., 263, 270
Meehl, P. E., 9, 25
Mehrabian, A., 186, 190
Mellenberg, G. J., 80, 83, 90, 120, 127
Menges, R. J., 98, 107
Mentkowski, M., 99, 107
Meskauskas, J. A., 61, 89
Messick, S., 1, 3
Miller, J. W., 107
Millman, J., 61, 64, 66, 79, 89
Mills, O., 107
Mokken, R. J., 227, 251
Monat, A., 160, 172
Moorman, B., xii
Morris, C., 226, 250
Morris, L. W., 136, 148, 151, 152, 153, 172–173
Mueller, J. H., 158, 169
Muthèn, B., 222, 223

N

Naerssen, R. F. van, 114, 121–122, 124, 127

Nairn, A., 57n
Nedelsky, L., 70–71, 72, 89, 95
Neisser, U., 17, 18, 19, 27, 154, 173
Newell, A., 53, 55, 56
Neyman, J., 257, 270
Niemalä, P., 160, 173
Nottelmann, E. D., 147, 148
Novick, M. R., 78, 80, 83, 87, 89, 225, 226, 227, 230, 250, 251, 254–255, 270

O

O'Connor, P., 182–183, 189
Olson, D. R., 19–20, 27
Olton, R. M., 21, 27
O'Malley, P. M., 32, 38, 39, 41, 43
O'Neil, H. F., 150, 174
Opper, S., 12, 25
Orlans, H., 60, 100, 102, 107
Owen, R. J., 226, 251

P

Paradise, N., 52, 56
Parker, R. K., 21, 25
Paul, G. L., 153, 173
Paulson, F. L., 158, 173
Peleg, R., 21, 27
Peterson, P. L., 156, 173
Piaget, J., 10, 12–13, 16
Popham, W. J., 63, 64, 84, 89
Powell, S., 61, 62, 65, 68, 83, 87
Prell, S., 157, 173
Pribram, K. H., 153, 173
Price, L. A., 15, 25

R

Ramsey, F. L., 227, 251
Rasch, G., 221, 223, 260, 261, 270
Raynor, J. O., 32, 43
Reitman, W. R., 182, 189
Resnick, L. B., 15, 21, 27

Richardson, E. C., 154, 172
Rock, D. A., 95, 96, 97, 107
Rogner, J., 159, 172

S

Sanathanan, L., 226, 251
Sarason, I. G., 92–93, 129–130, 133–146, 150, 151, 153, 154, 162, 173
Sarason, S. B., 136, 148, 149, 154, 172, 176, 190
Sauser, W. J., Jr., 136, 148
Sawusch, J. R., 41, 44
Schachter, S., 144, 149
Schaffner, P., 129, 130, 150–174
Schmidt, F. L., 103, 107–108
Schönpflug, W., 169, 173
Schoon, C. G., 72, 89
Schumer, H., 155–156, 170
Scott, E. L., 257, 270
Scott, S., 154, 173
Scriven, M., 64, 90
Sears, R. R., 30, 44
Shepard, L. A., 58, 59, 60, 61–90, 91, 95, 120
Sieber, J. E., 150, 158, 173–174
Siegler, R. S., 262–263, 270
Simon, H. A., 15, 16, 27, 47, 53, 55, 56
Skakun, E. N., 62, 71, 90
Smith, A. F. M., 227, 250
Smith, C. P., 190
Smith, G. M., 154, 170
Snow, R. E., 153, 169
Solomon, H., 216, 217, 223
Spearman, C. E., 11, 46
Spence, J. T., 151, 174
Spence, K. W., 33, 44, 151, 174
Spielberger, C. D., 136, 149, 150, 151, 154, 161, 170, 172, 174
Staats, A., xii
Stern, W., 1
Sternberg, R. J., 16–17, 28, 53, 56
Stewart, L., 227, 251
Stone, M. H., 226, 234–245, 251

Stoops, R., 137–138, 141, 149
Storms, L. H., 182, 189
Stouffer, S. A., 194, 195, 197, 201, 208, 213, 223
Stuart, I. R., 154, 169
Super, D. E., 14, 28

T

Temp, G. E., 97, 108
Terman, L. M., 1
Thorndike, E. L., 32, 44
Thurstone, L. L., 11
Tobias, S., 150, 174
Toby, J., 194, 195, 197, 201, 208, 213, 223
Tolman, E. C., 33, 35, 44
Torrance, E. P., 49, 56
Trommer, P. M., 116, 127
Tryon, G. S., 136, 149
Tuddenham, R. D., 6, 8, 11, 13, 28
Tukey, J. W., 69, 90
Tulving, E., 158, 169
Tversky, A., 124, 125, 126
Twitchell, M., 142, 148

V

Vagt, G., 156, 174
Valentine, J., 21, 28
Van der Linden, W. J., 80, 83, 90
Vandeventer, M., 21, 26
van Eeden, C., 227, 250
Vroom, V. H., 35, 44, 180, 190
Vygotsky, L. S., 52, 56

W

Wachtel, P. L., 154, 174
Wainer, H., 226, 251
Wang, M., 227, 250
Ward, J., 13, 28
Webb, E. J., 82, 90
Werner, E., 95, 106
Werts, C., 97, 107
Whimbey, A., 10, 21, 22, 28
White, R. W., 143, 149
Whiteman, M., 12, 28
Wijnen, W. H. F. W., 115, 127
Wilbrink, B., 120, 127
Wilks, S. S., 248, 251
Wine, J. D., 142, 147, 149, 151, 155, 174
Wober, M., 19, 28
Wolf, T. H., 6, 28
Wolff, C., 160, 172
Wright, B. D., 226, 234–245, 251

Y

Yerkes, R. M., 35, 44, 131, 182, 190

Z

Zegers, F. E., 122, 123, 127
Zieky, M. J., xii, 73, 83, 90
Zigler, E., 21, 28

Subject Index

A

ABILITY, 233

Ability: approaches to estimation of, 225–227; efficiency related to, 35–39; as fixed parameter, 225–226; latent, Bayesian inference of, 224–251; motivation and performance related to, 32–35; prior information on, 226–227; as random variable, 226

Accreditation, and occupational standards, 101

Achievement, cumulative, and motivation, 39–40

Achievement Anxiety Test, 136

Achievement motivation: concept of, 175; and performance, 175–178, 182–183, 186–187

Achievement tests: cutoff points for, 117–124; and intelligence tests, 51–53

Action tendency, strength of, 178

Admissions: and quota free standards, 66; restricted, compromise model of, 111–117

Alverno College, competency assessment at, 99, 100

American College Test Research Institute, 39

American College Testing Program, 41, 42

American Psychological Association, 9, 23, 67, 85

Anxiety, trait and state, 151. *See also* Test anxiety

Army Alpha and Beta tests, 6

Assessment Center Research Group, 99, 106

Autoregressive model, 222

B

Balance scale, and latent trait theory, 263-269
Bayesian inference: of abilities, 224-251; and alternative approaches, 225-227; appendix for, 245-249; conditional independence in, 229-230; examples of analysis in, 234-245; as nonparametric approach, 227-229; order restriction in, 228-229, 230, 231, 234-235; plodding response pattern in, 239; posterior density in, 230-231, 232-233, 235, 237-245; prior densities in, 230-234, 235-236; reversal response pattern in, 240-241; and statistical analysis, 229-231; unusual response pattern in, 242-245
Bayes' Theorem, 226
Behavioral consistency, and assessment principles, 103-104
Binet tests, 5

C

Certification. See Placement and certification standards
Classification errors, costs of, and standard setting, 79-80
Cognitive Interference Questionnaire, 139-140,141
Cognitive psychology: and information processing, 14-17; and intelligence tests, 14-18
College Board, 10, 34, 43
Competence, performance related to, 98
Componential analysis, and cognitive psychology, 16-17
Compromise model: of admissions restrictions, 111-117; analysis of, 109-127; background on, 109-111; for combining grades, 124-126; concept of, 110-111; for cutoff points, 117-124; reservations about, 111
Consortium for Longitudinal Studies, 21, 24-25
Construct validity: and analysis of errors, 10; and correlation analysis, 10-11; for intelligence tests, 9-11; and problem solving methods, 10
Coping: performance related to, 158-161; and test anxiety, 150-174
Courts, and occupational standards, 100,101
Creativity, and intelligence heritability, 49-50
Credentials: and fair employment, 101; and occupational standards, 100-102
Criterion-referenced tests, and standard setting, 64
Cultural deprivation, concept of, 22
Cutoff points: compromise model for, 117-124; and cooperative grading systems, 123-124; decision-theoretic approach to, 120-121; and first norms, 117-119; and mastery learning, 119-120; staff and student values and, 122-123; and subsequent norms, 121-122

D

Data: raw form of, 194; by response pattern, 194-196; by score group, 195, 197
Décalage, and intelligence tests, 13
Denmark, psychic vulnerability study in, 214, 217-221
Dental auxiliaries, proficiency examination for, 98
Developmental psychology: and intelligence tests, 12-14; and motivation, 30-32
Dynamics of action theory: action

and negative action tendencies in, 178–180; and motivation, 32, 38; and test anxiety, 130

E

Educational Testing Service (ETS), 57, 71, 87, 96
Effectiveness, efficiency distinct from, 157
Efficiency: ability related to, 35–39; effectiveness distinct from, 157
Equal opportunity, conditions of, 48, 50, 51
Europe: mastery learning in, 120; occupational standards in, 91–92
Evaluation, reducing emphasis on, in schools, 147–148
Evaluational stressor, and test anxiety, 137
Executive process, concept of, 15
Experience, and occupational standards, 102–104
Experiential learning, assessment of, for credentials, 101–102

F

Factor analysis: and intelligence tests, 11–12; and learning set and transfer effect, 12
Fear of failure: and achievement motivation, 175–178; and action and negative action tendencies, 178–180; concept of, 176, 177; effects of, 183–185; and inhibitory force, 179, 181–182, 183–185; in multi-incentive condition, 185–186; and performance, 175–190; theoretical studies of, 180–188
Florida Functional Literacy Test, 84

G

Generative models. *See* Compromise models
Germany, performance-guided lottery procedure in, 113
Goddard's translation, 6
Goodness of fit, and Rasch model, 201–208
Grades: compromise model for combining, 124–126; cooperative system for setting, 123–124
Groningen University, intelligence and choice of study at, 115
Guilford's model, 11, 49

H

High school graduation tests, nature of criterion for, 68

I

Individual parameter: as ability or positiveness, 199; and observed distribution, 208–211
Information processing: and cognitive psychology, 14–17; and intelligence, 47; and test anxiety, 129, 134, 137, 157–158
Inhibitory force, and fear of failure, 179, 181–182, 183–185
Intelligence: A and B types of, 46, 47, 48, 49, 50, 53; analysis of measuring, 1–56; classical conceptions of, 46–49; concept of, 5, 52; heritability of, and creativity, 49–50; and information-processing system, 47; interest in, 1–2; modifiability of, 20–23; and motivational psychology, 29–44; new thinking and new measures for, 3; overview of measuring, 1–3; as prototype, 19; and test anxiety, 163, 165; usefulness of measuring, 45–56

Intelligence tests: and achievement
tests, 51–53; analysis of concept
of, 5–28; and cognitive psychology, 14–18; construct validity
for, 9–11; and cultural frames of
reference, 18–20; as descriptive,
8; and developmental psychology, 12–14; factor analysis of,
11–12; historical background of,
6–7; of intelligence-added,
53–55; interpretation of scores
on, 8–9; practical context of,
6–9; and present status, 8; theoretical framework for, 9–18; validation procedures for, 7–8
IQ, term of, 7
Israel: and cultural deprivation, 22;
improving academic intelligence
in, 21
Items characteristic curves (ICC):
and abilities of individuals,
224–225; as monotone increasing and nonintersecting, 227;
Rasch model as, 197–199

                      J

James-Stein approach, 226
Judgment, issue of, 104–105

                      K

Kelley true score regression analysis, 226
Knox Cube Test, 234

                      L

Latent distributions: analysis of,
with Rasch model, 208–215;
comparison of, 215–221
Latent population density, in Rasch
model, 211
Latent trait theories: analysis of,
191–270; assumptions in,

256–262; and Bayesian inference, 224–251; concerns about
applying, 252–270; conditional
item characteristic function in,
256; and educational testing,
262–269; issues of, 269; item
characteristic function in, 256,
261; and latent class analysis,
257, 260; local independence in,
256; local serial dependence in,
256; overview of, 191–192; parameter estimation in, 257; and
probability, 255; random generators in, 257, 260–261; and
Rasch model for data analysis,
193–223; and repeatability principle, 255, 256, 257, 260–261
Latent variables: correlation of,
221; in Rasch model, 211; vector-valued, 222
Law School Admission Test
(LSAT), 195, 196, 202, 203–
205, 208, 213–215
Learning, performance distinct
from, 33
Loss ratios, and classification errors,
80
Lottery, weighted, for admissions,
111–117
Louvain, University of, strength of
achievement motive study at,
186

                      M

Manifest variable, 211
Marginal probability, in Rasch
model, 211
Mastery learning, and cutoff points,
119–120
Measurement: and conditions of
equal opportunity, 48, 50, 51;
defined, 260
Mental orthopedics, concept of, 21
Minkowski model, 124–125
Modern consciousness, concept of,
19

Motivation: ability and performance related to, 32–35; analysis of, 29–44; and college aptitude test scores, 34, 41; and developmental psychology, 30–32; and dynamics of action theory, 32, 38; and efficiency, 35–39; and matching law, 38; and test scores, 39–42; and test theory, 32–33

N

National Board of Medical Examiners, 94, 107
National Teachers Examination, 60, 71
Negative action tendency, strength of, 179
Netherlands, compromise models in, 109, 112–114, 115–116
North Carolina, high school competency test in, 72

O

Occupational standards: analysis of, 91–108; assessment centers for, 99–100; background of, 92–95; and credentials, 100–102; cut score options in, 95–96; and experience, 102–104; issues in, 94–95, 104–105; job analysis issue in, 105; and performance measures, 98; purposes of, 93–94; reliability of, 96–97; research needs in, 104–106; societal risk and supply factors in, 97; validity of, 96–97; on written tests, 95–98

P

Performance: ability and motivation related to, 32–35; and achievement motivation, 175–178, 182–183, 186–187; competence related to, 98; in correlational analysis, 163, 165; and fear of failure, 175–190; learning distinct from, 33; and test anxiety, 150–174
Performance standards: analysis of, 57–127; compromise models for, 109–127; in occupational settings, 91–108; overview of, 57–60; for placement and certification, 61–90
Physicians, standards for, 94
Placement and certification standards: analysis of, 61–90; for certification, 82–83; for classroom use, 81–82; and methods for standard setting, 69–81; multiple measures for, 82; for professional licensure and competency, 85; for program evaluation, 83–85; selecting methods for, 81–85; and standard setting, 62–69
Posterior density: in Bayesian inference, 230–231, 232–233, 235, 237–245; as possible priors, 233
Prior density: in Bayesian inference, 230–234, 235–236; properties of, 231–234; as subjective choice, 233–234
Probability, concepts of, 255
Program evaluation: placement and certification standards for, 83–85; tests for, 67–68
Psychic vulnerability, Rasch model analysis of, 214, 217–221

R

Rasch model: and analysis of latent distributions, 208–215; for analyzing data, 193–223; basic elements in, 197–208; and Bayesian inference, 226, 227, 228–229, 234, 242, 244; and comparison of latent distribu-

tions, 215–221; comparison of
subjects in, 262, 266; and data
forms, 194–197; extensions of,
221–222; and goodness of fit,
201–208; individual parameter
in, 197–199; as item characteristic curve, 197–199; and item parameter, 199–200, 205–207;
longitudinal model of, 222; observed distribution in, 208–211,
212; score group estimates in,
202–203, 206–207; sufficient
statistics in, 200–201
Raven Progressive Matrices, 16
Reliability, of occupational standards, 96–97
Repeatability principle, 255, 256,
257, 260–261
Repression-Sensitization   Scale
(RSS), 161, 162

S

Scholastic Aptitude Test (SAT), 10,
197, 198, 200, 201, 205–207,
208
Self-monitoring, and intelligence
modification, 22
Simulation models, in cognitive psychology, 16
Social support, and test anxiety,
144–146
Standard, concept of, 91
Standard   setting: compromise
models for, 109–127; contrasting-groups method for, 73–75;
and criterion nature, 68–69; dichotomy required in, 62; educational consequences model of,
76–78; and empirical validation,
72–78; issues in, 62–69; as judgmental, 62–63; known-groups
validation in, 73; methods for,
69–81; normative and absolute
values in, 64–65; properties of,
58–60; quotas free or fixed in,

65–66; and test content judgments, 69–72; and test uses,
67–68; and utility functions,
78–81
Stanford-Binet test, 7, 11, 49
State-Trait Anxiety Inventory for
Children (STAIC), 161
Sufficient, in statistical theory, 196,
201
Superordinate models. *See* Compromise models

T

Task analysis, of a culture, 20
Tendency to succeed, concept of,
176
Test anxiety: analysis of, 133–146;
assessment and correlates of,
134–137; attention hypothesis
of, 147, 151, 154–155; and autonomic arousal, 151, 153–154,
160; background on, 133–134;
and cognitive appraisal, 137,
151–152, 153–154; concept of,
143; coping strategies and performance related to, 150–174;
correlational analysis of, 163–
165; effects of, 137–141; and
emotionality, 151, 153–154;
empirical studies of, 152–153,
161–169; experimental study of,
137–148; and fear of failure,
175–190; and information processing, 129, 134, 137, 157–
158; and intelligence, 163, 165;
interest in, 134–135; measures
of, 136; moderators of, 143–
148; multiple-regression analysis
of, 165–166; overview of, 129–
131; path analysis of, 166–169;
performance related to, 151–
158; and preparation, 155–161,
166; reducing effects of, 141–
143; and repression-sensitization, 159–161, 162–163, 165,

166, 168; and social support, 144–146; stimulus-response approach to, 151; and structure of learning, 155–156, 157, 160; and test performance, 129–190; and waiting time, 138–139, 141

Test Anxiety Inventory (TAI), 136, 154, 161

Test Anxiety Questionnaire, 136, 154, 176

Test Anxiety Scale (TAS), 136, 137–142, 144, 146

Test Anxiety Scale for Children, 136

Testing: applying latent trait models in, 252–270; for certification, 67; diagnostic, 67; error of measurement in, 253; goal of, 8; and motivation, 32–33; for program evaluation, 67–68; psychologically unfounded assumptions in, 253–254; reformulation of theory in, 254–255

Thematic Apperception Test (TAT), 176

Threshold, nonparametric definition of, 227–228

U

Uganda, concept of intelligence in, 19

United States, improving academic intelligence in, 21

V

Validation: concurrent and predictive, 7; criterion-related, 7; empirical, and standard setting, 72–78; for intelligence tests, 7–8

Validity: construct, 9–11; convergent and divergent, 10–11; of occupational standards, 96–97

Vermaat model, 112

W

Wechsler test, 6

Weighted lottery model: for admission, 111–117; arguments for, 114–116; student opinion on, 116

Worry-Emotionality Questionnaire, 136

Z

Zone of Proximal development, and intelligence, 52–53, 54